I0803116

IMAGES
of America

CASTINE

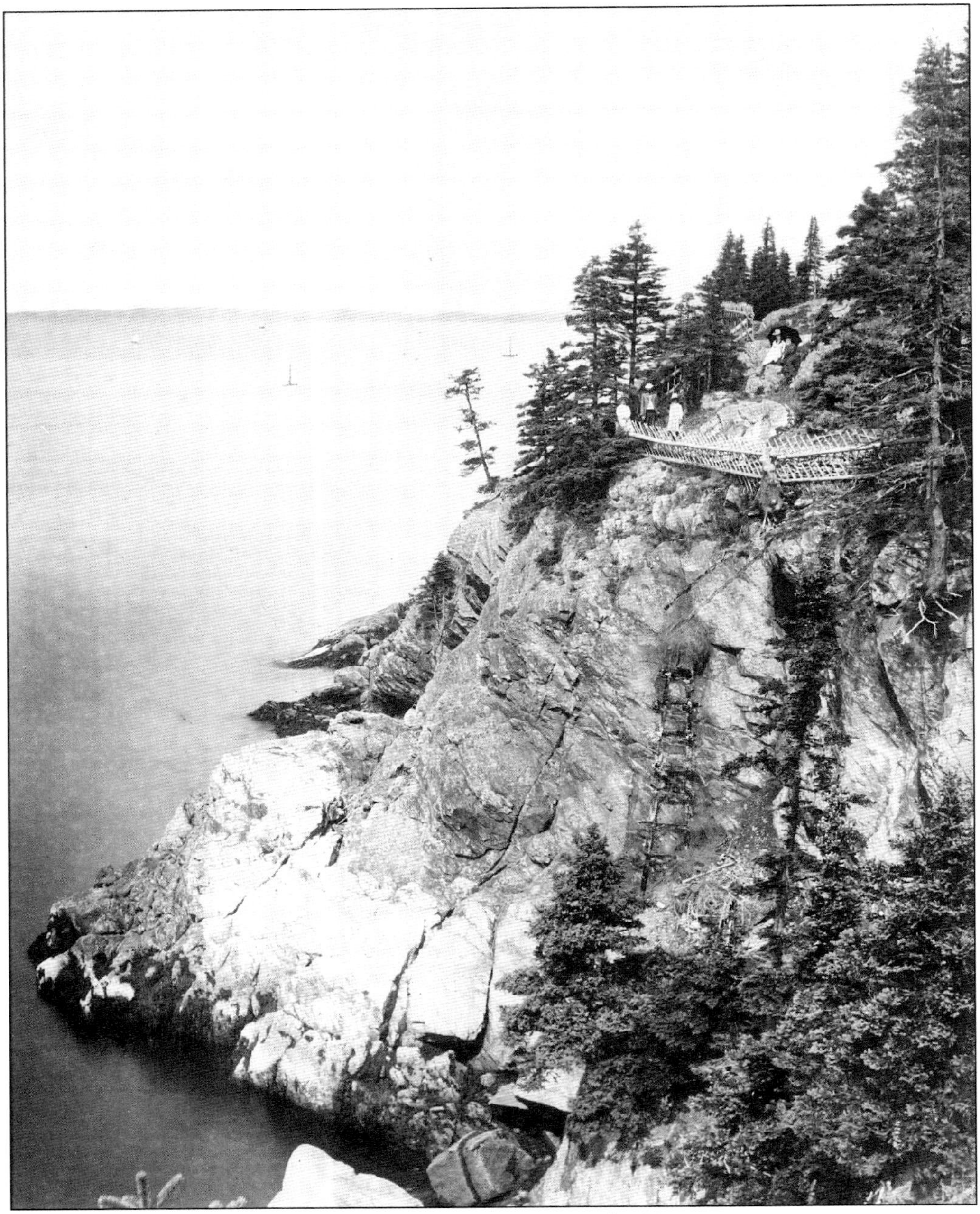

Winonah Cliff at Dyce's Head, 1894.

IMAGES
of America

CASTINE

The Castine Historical Society

ARCADIA
PUBLISHING

ISBN 978-0-7385-8956-5

Published by Arcadia Publishing
Charleston, South Carolina

Printed in the United States of America

For all general information contact Arcadia Publishing at:
Telephone 843-853-2070
Fax 843-853-0044
E-mail sales@arcadiapublishing.com
For customer service and orders:
Toll-Free 1-888-313-2665

Visit us on the Internet at www.arcadiapublishing.com

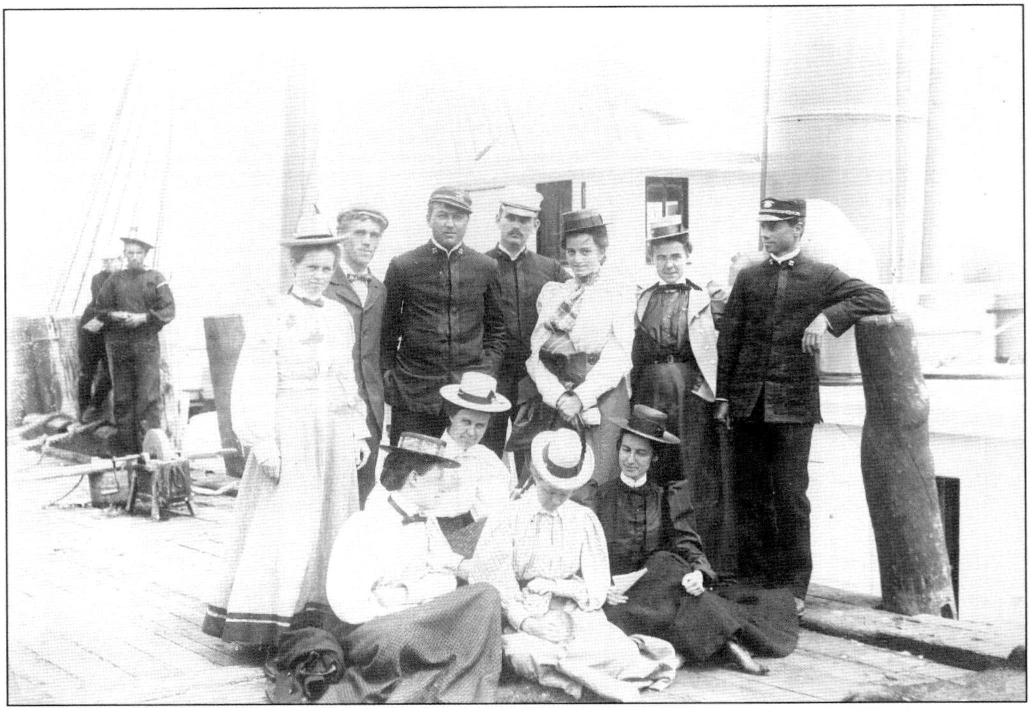

Cover Photograph: On the event of Castine's Centennial in 1896, Mary Elizabeth Bates (pictured with the kitten) wrote in her journal about the officers visiting on the USS *Columbia*: "Great joy! Brass buttons prove irresistible, and Mr. Robinson and Mr. Washington disturb the equilibrium of more than one fair maid. Question...Could the girls write an essay on 'Variations in Temperature on Board an American Warship' or would they prefer as a subject 'Brass Buttons, Brown Eyes and a Smile' or, 'How I Lost My Heart'?"

Contents

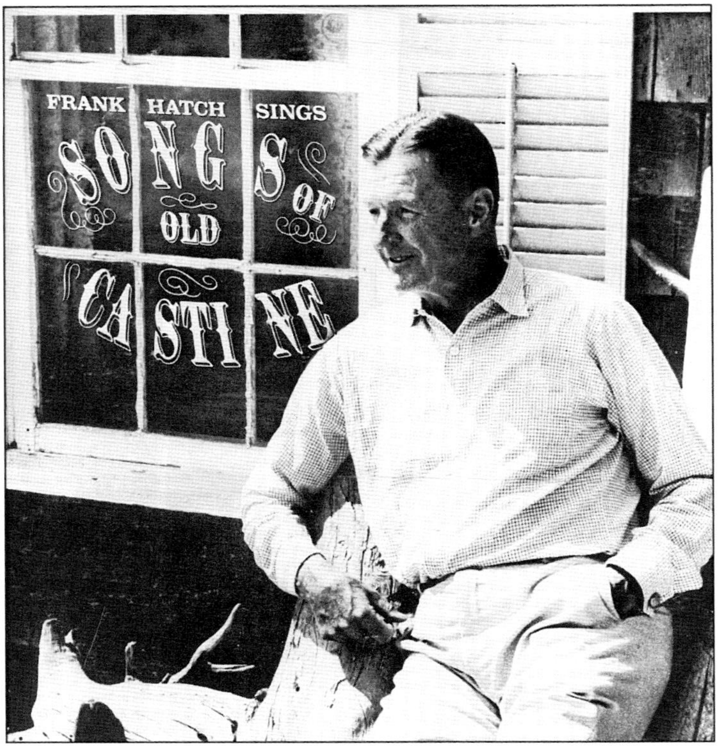

Windmill Hill

"Many a long, long day
Since I went away.
What's so fresh and green?
My mem'ry of Castine.

When I climb up the road to Windmill Hill
And I look down on the town,
I've come back home again,
Back home where I belong.

Once more I'll feast my eyes and take my fill
Of islands and shore I adore,
And then my heart picks up
The chorus of my song.

Smoke from chimneys rises in a peaceful sky,
Seagulls float aloft on a graceful wing.
When I climb up that winding road I'll find
Contentment and peace of mind,

For I'm back home again,
Back home where I belong."

Frank Hatch

Introduction

Castine, Maine, has long been cherished by families who have placed deep roots in the town over the years. The family of Francis W. Hatch has strong ties dating from the eighteenth century, and continuing with his great-grandchildren today. Born in Medford, Massachusetts, Frank graduated from Harvard in 1919 and spent his working life in Boston, returning to Castine whenever he could. Musically talented, he wrote and acted in many amateur musicals during the 1930s and '40s and wrote songs about places and people in Castine which are still remembered today. Many people fondly recall the Sunday night dinners at the Castine Golf Club when Frank would sit down at the piano and play and sing his songs. He even made a record in 1961 called *Frank Hatch Sings Songs of Old Castine*. For the cover of the record, he wrote the following:

"It has been said that Castine packs more varied history per square yard than any early American outpost. Its harbor, deep and island-studded, was well known to French traders fifty years before the Pilgrims' arrival at Plymouth. On early maps it was identified as "Pentagoet", a rocky peninsula knifing into Penobscot Bay between the Penobscot and Bagaduce rivers. Its accessibility by water made it a natural trading base where Indians swapped furs and salt fish for European trade goods. John Smith paid a visit here in 1614 and reported that it was the most important settlement in the north east. Paul Revere arrived in 1779 as a chief of artillery in a singularly unsuccessful attempt by the Yankees to dislodge the British. Longfellow and Whittier chose the romantic theme of the Baron Castin's marriage to the daughter of the local sachem Madockawando in 1666, which resulted in the town adopting his name.

The French were the first to fortify the place. But when they yielded to the British, Fort George, whose ramparts still tower above the town, was spaded up by the King's soldiery to the same scale as Fort Ticonderoga. The redcoats returned to occupy the town during the War of 1812, and upon their departure, the community, throughout the 19th century, became a thriving center of ship building and maritime trade with as many as five hundred vessels lying at anchor in the harbor on many a day.

The day of shipping passed, and with it the prosperous days buttressed by local commerce. The town remains today a modest vacation resort blessed by the same natural beauty which Europeans noted with delight in their journals four centuries ago."

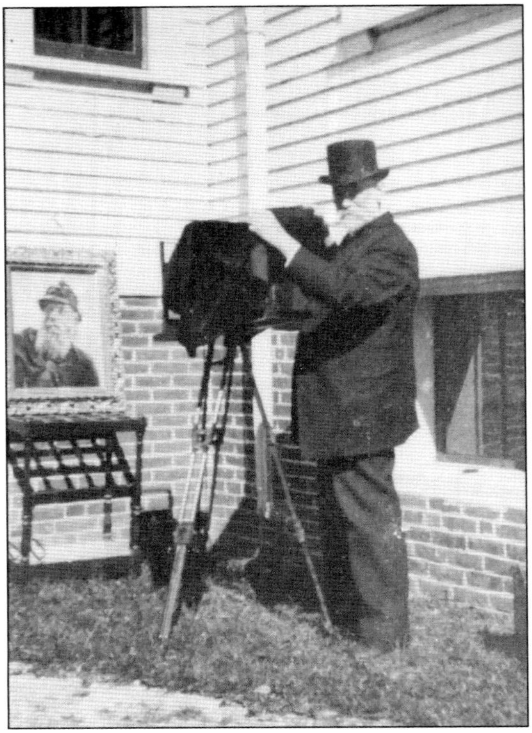

Making a photograph of the Baron de St. Castin portrait. It was created as an ideal likeness in 1881, and was reproduced by lithography first and later by photography. The likeness has been reproduced countless times on calendars, sheet music, china, flags, postcards, and other memorabilia, and remains the unofficial logo of Castine. Included in this book are the images of many photographers, some as well known as A.H. Folsom of Boston, and some who were just making a record for their family albums. All the pictures succeed in capturing the spirit of a small town in Maine, from the 1850s, with the introduction of the first daguerreotypes, to the 1940s, when the relative sophistication of film made taking photographs easy.

References

Aldrich, James. *Fair Winds–Stormy Seas*. Stonington: Penobscot Bay Press, 1991.
Bourne, Miriam Anne. *The Ladies of Castine*. New York: Arbor House, 1986.
Editions of the *Castine Patriot*.
The Castine Visitor, the newsletter of The Castine Historical Society.
Doudiet, Ellenore W. *Majabigwaduce*. Castine: Castine Scientific Society, 1978.
Gregory, Gardiner. *Battleground of Four Nations: Outline History of Castine*, 1994.
Paper Talks, 1982.
Penobscot Bicentennial: 1787–1987.
Penobscot Historical Society Newsletter.
Wasso, George, and Colcord, Lincoln. *Sailing Days on the Penobscot*. Salem: Marine Research Society, 1932.
Wheeler, George. *Castine Past and Present*. Boston: Rockwell and Churchill Press, 1896.
———. *History of Castine*. Cornwall: Cornwall Press, 1923.
Wilson Museum Bulletin.
The Witherle Memorial Library collections.

One

Around the Town

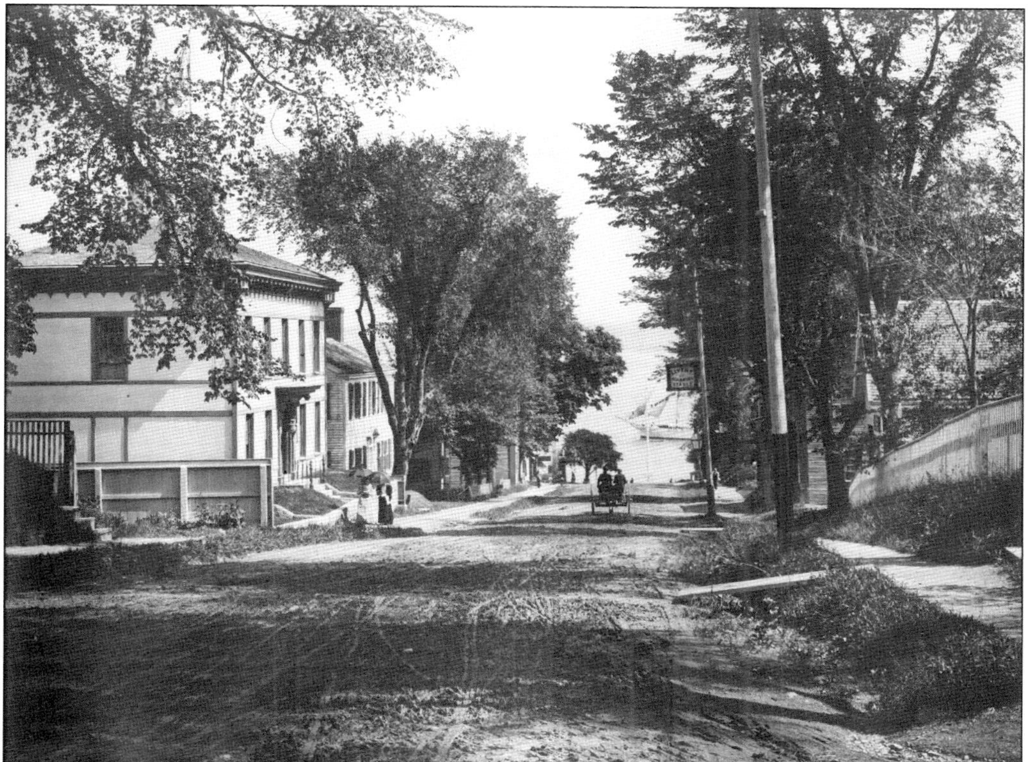

Lower Main Street is shown here in the 1880s, with the post office on the left and the sign for Hooper's Livery on the right. Castine was already a popular summer destination.

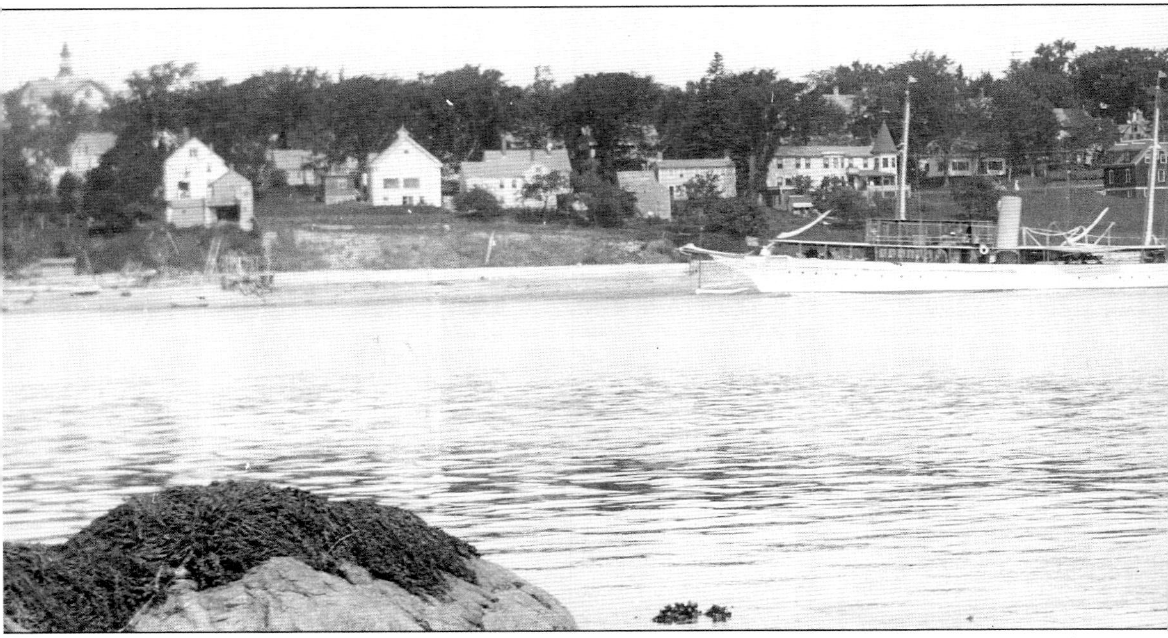

This photograph of the harbor was taken in 1904 from Nautilus Island. Although only one yacht and a steamer are evident here, the harbor was often filled with a variety of ships,

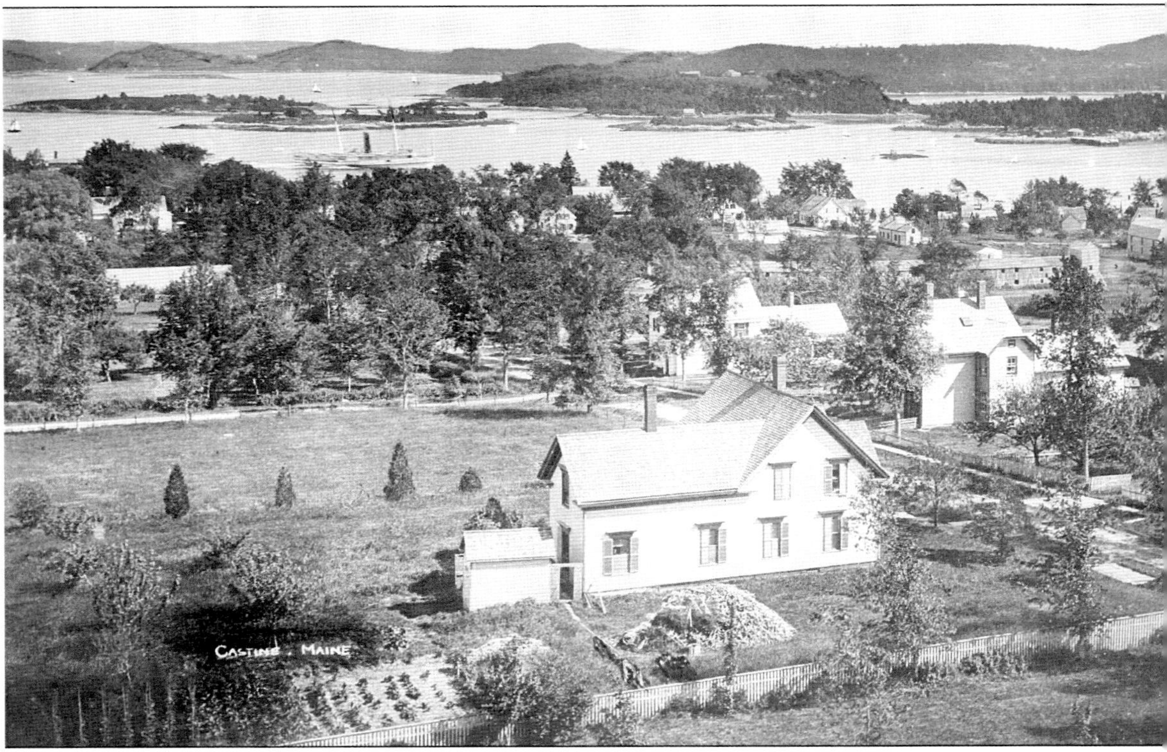

This scene of the Bagaduce River was taken from the roof of the Eastern State Normal School about 1904. The land had been cleared by the British in 1779 and again in 1814, and it wasn't

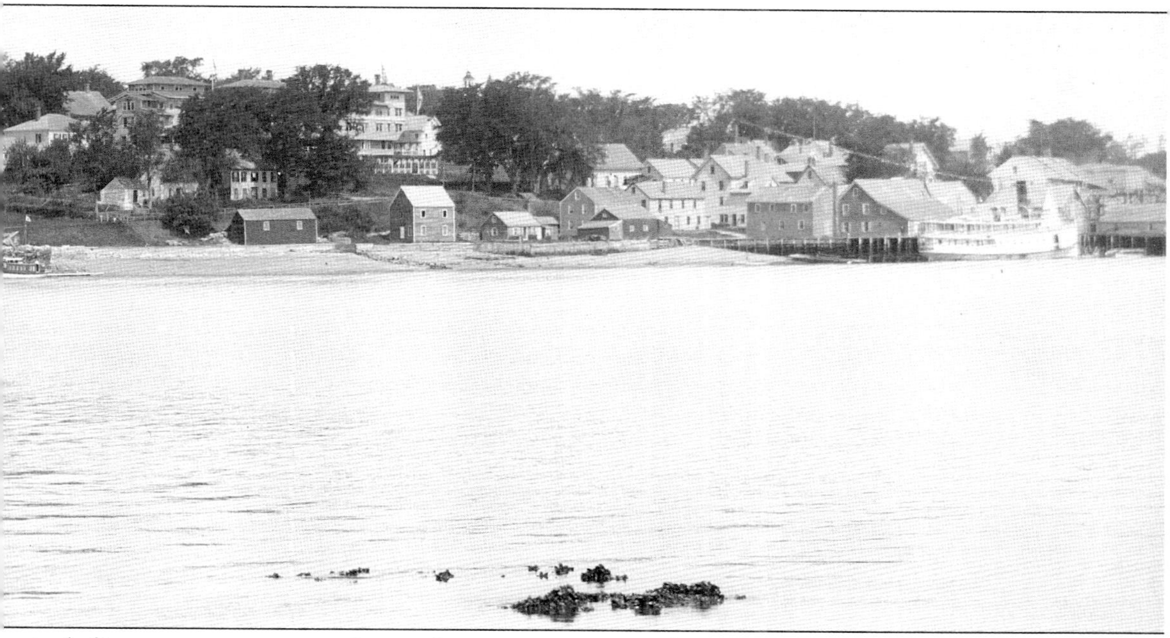

including revenue cutters, yachts, and sometimes even warships.

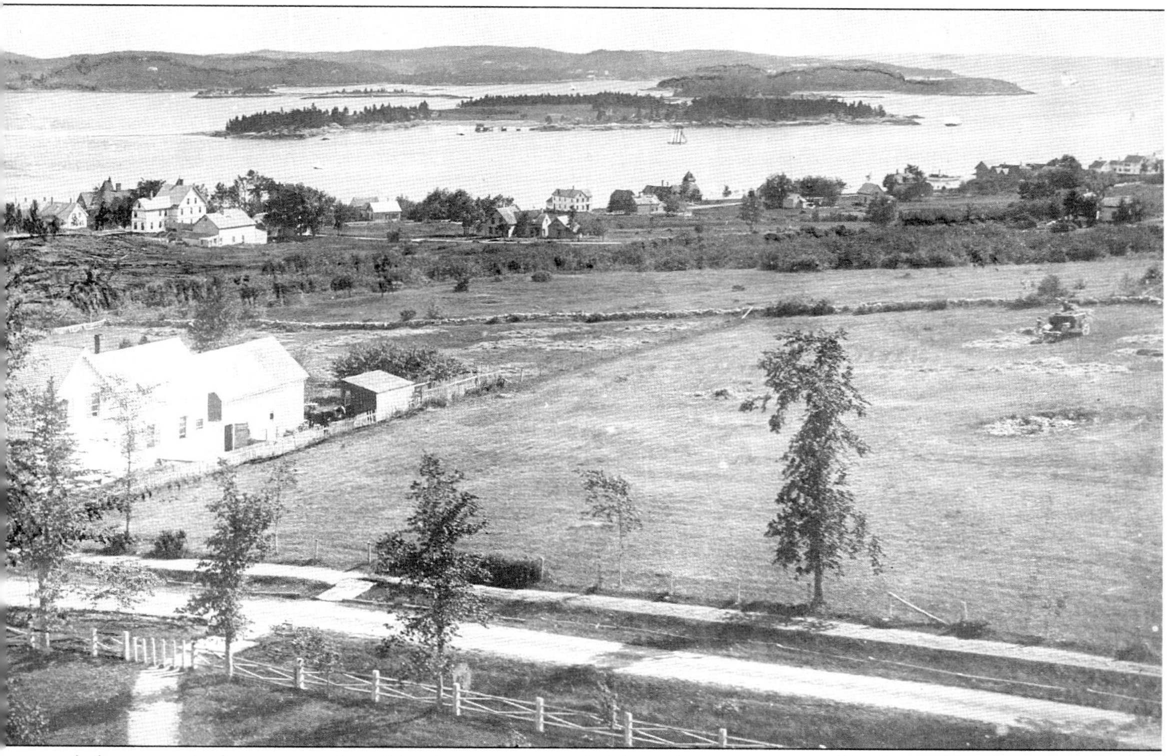

until the twentieth century that Castine was again thick with trees, especially the giant elms.

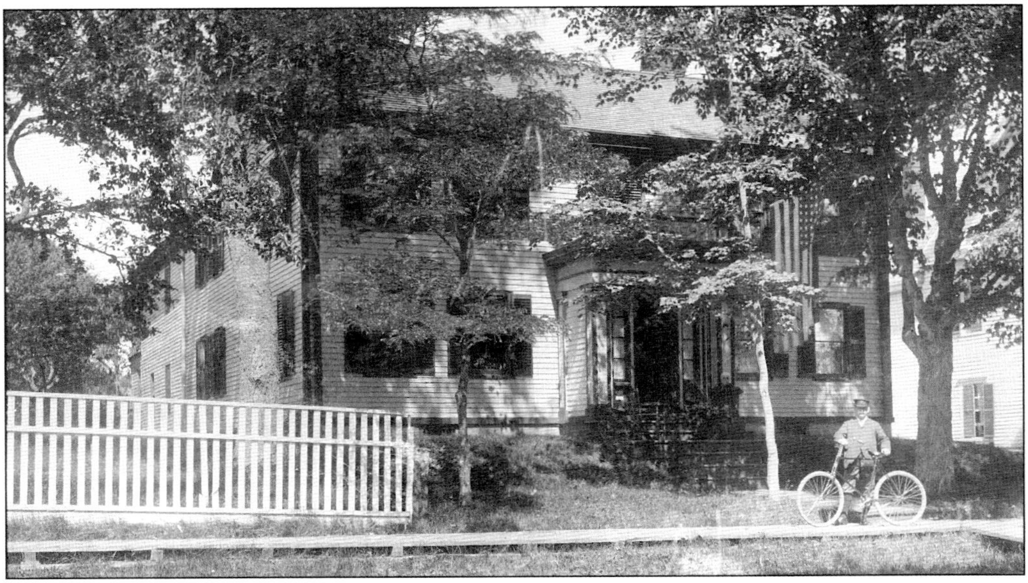

C.W. Noyes lived in this house on Pleasant Street. Prior to 1912, Noyes and the Village Improvement Society marked all the important historical places around town with signs, noting the sites of battles and the location of important colonial buildings, forts, and Indian encampments. At one time there were one hundred and fifty signs. About forty still stand today; however, their accuracy is questionable (see p. 35).

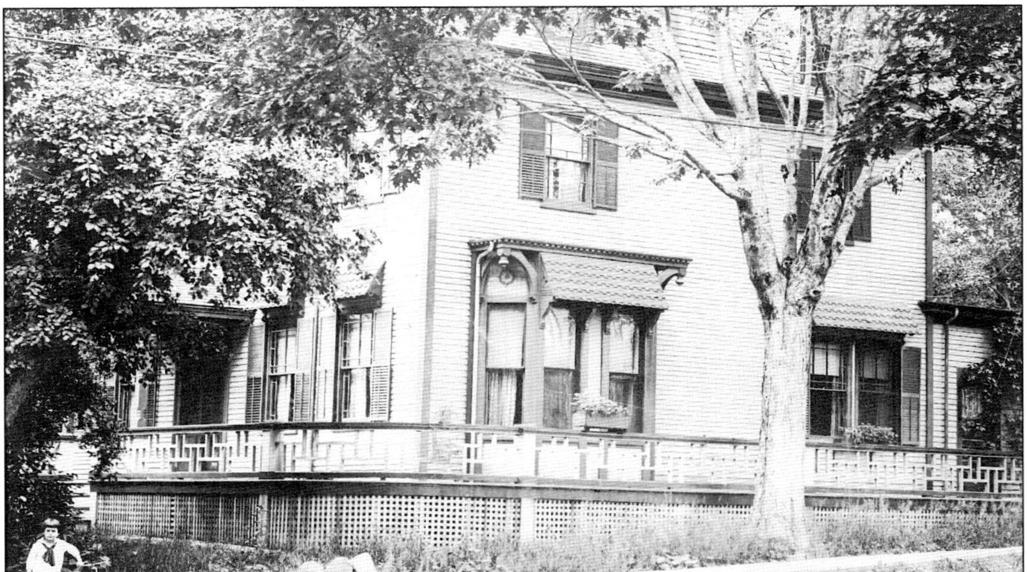

Artist Fitz Hugh Lane was a frequent guest of Joseph Stevens Jr. at his father's house on upper Main Street. It was built c. 1805, in the then-popular Federal style. Dr. Stevens and his bride moved into it in 1821, and for fifty-five years Stevens "doctored" the town. The house was later owned by F.P. Wood, who modernized it in the Victorian fashion of the 1870s, including the addition of a mansard roof to create dormitory rooms for students at the new Eastern State Normal School.

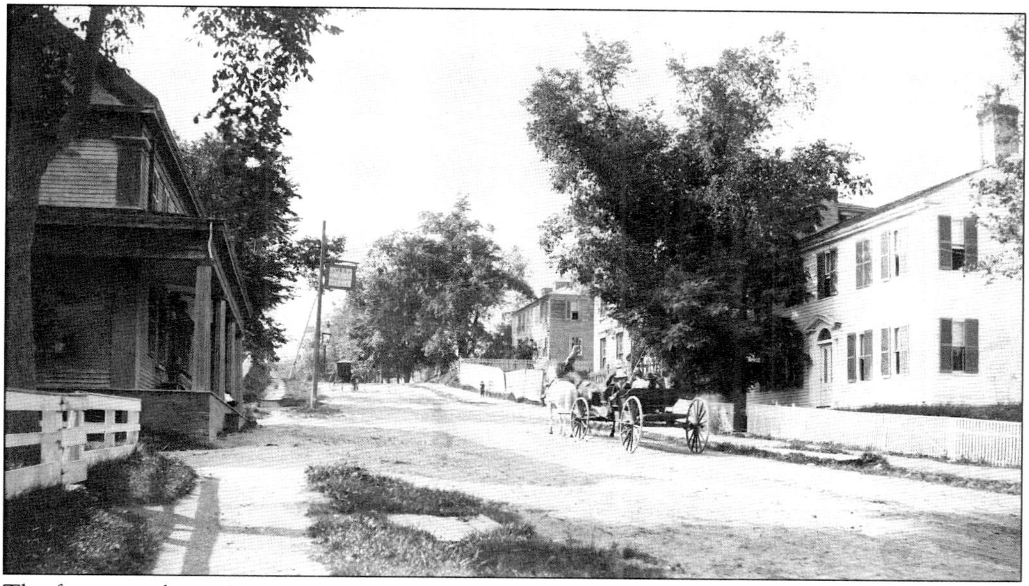

The fences on lower Main Street served to keep out errant cattle.

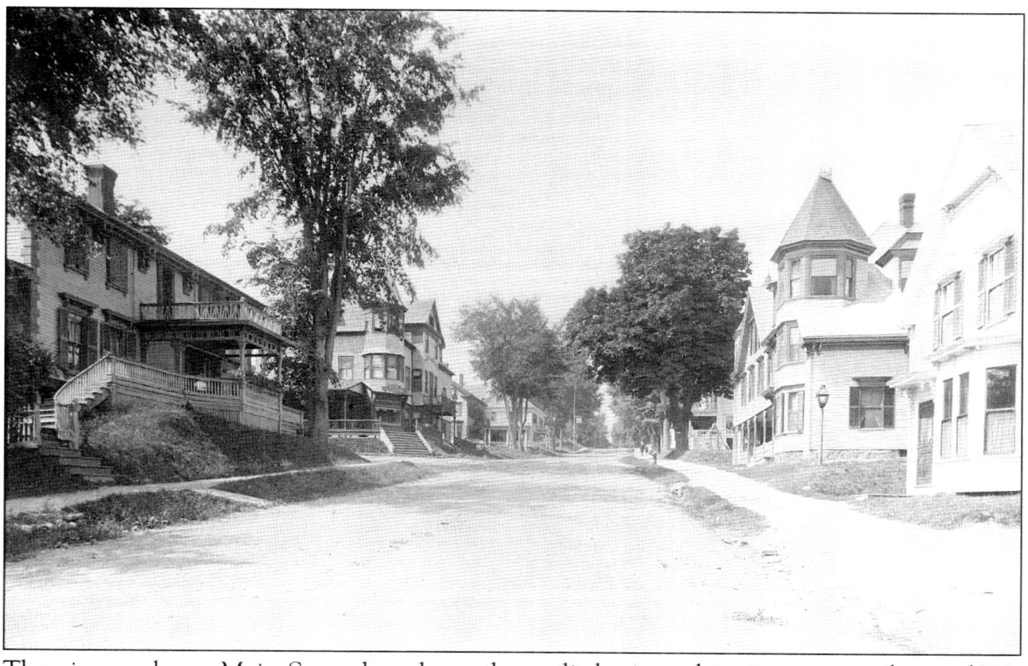

The view up lower Main Street has changed very little since this picture was taken *c*. 1880, except for the John Lee House on the left, which has had all its Victorian gingerbread trim removed. The house has an upper-floor theatre which was used for entertainments during the British occupation of 1814.

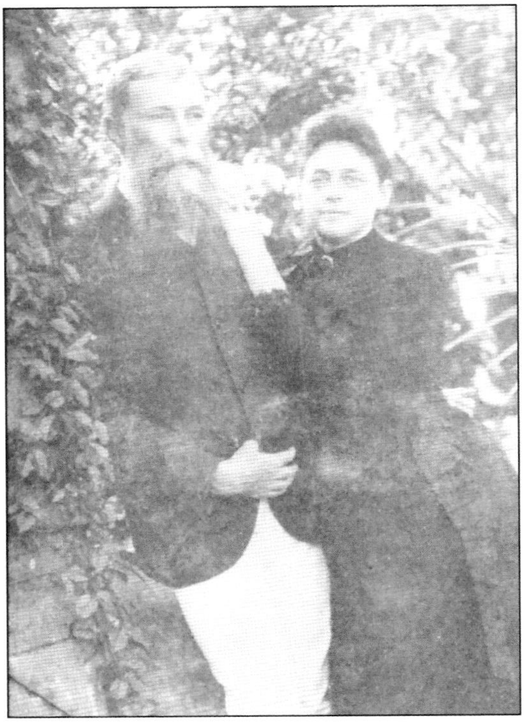

Anna Cate, whose grandfather built the Adams-Cate House on Court Street in 1803, married Sanford B. Dole in 1873 and moved with him to Hawaii. Dole made his fortune there and was appointed the only president and first governor.

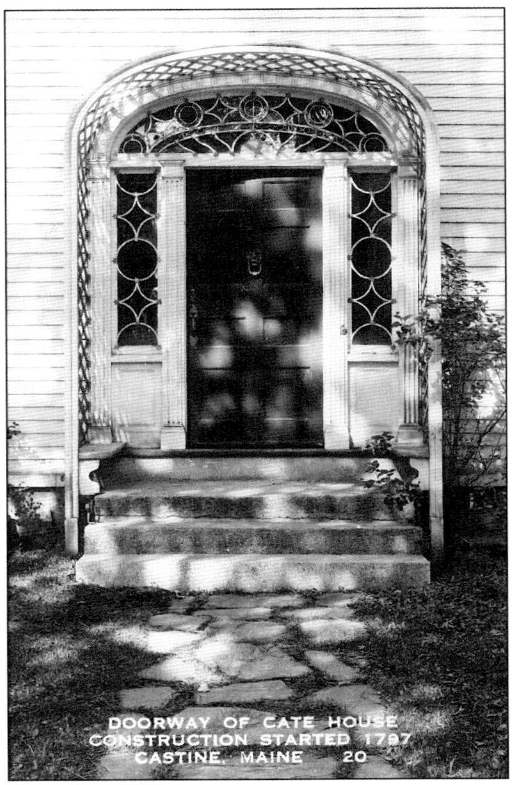

Harriet Beecher Stowe was a visitor at the Adams-Cate House in the 1870s.

Possibly the oldest image presented here is this daguerreotype of Mrs. William Abbott (Rebecca Atherton), who moved as a new bride into the Abbott House on Battle Avenue, after her marriage in 1802.

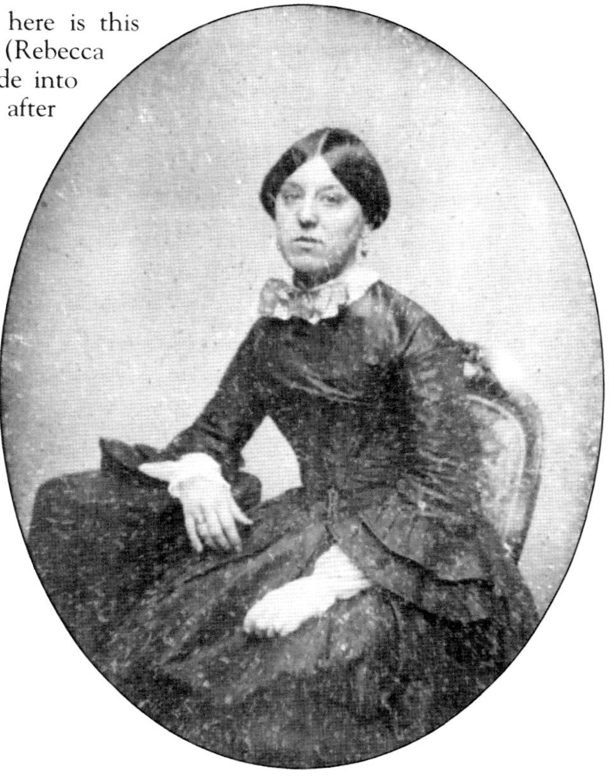

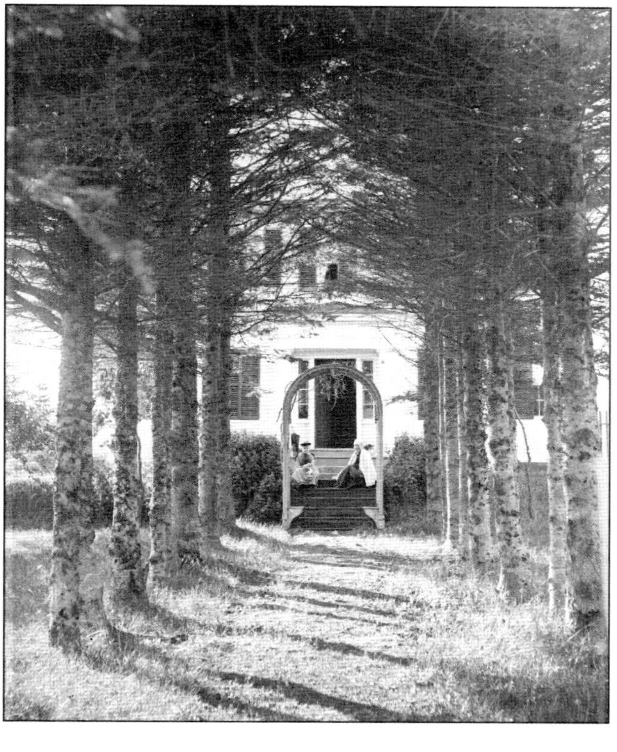

The doorway of the Abbott House is beautifully-framed in this image. According to legend, Judge William Abbott didn't want to clutter the front hall of his house with a staircase, so he had a flight of narrow, very steep stairs which led to the second floor built behind the parlor. Mrs. Abbott wanted a home with a grand staircase like the ones on Main Street, and she was never happy here.

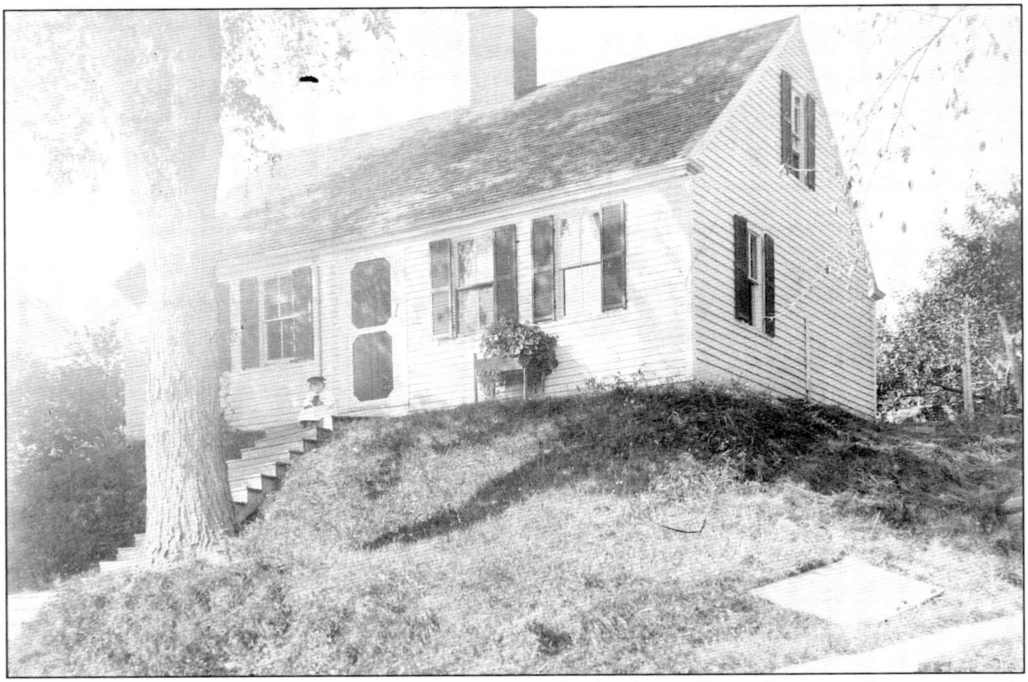

Fishing shacks and small houses like this one were built along Water Street in the nineteenth century. There are many Cape-style houses in Castine. This one has had its front windows replaced and a window added on the side.

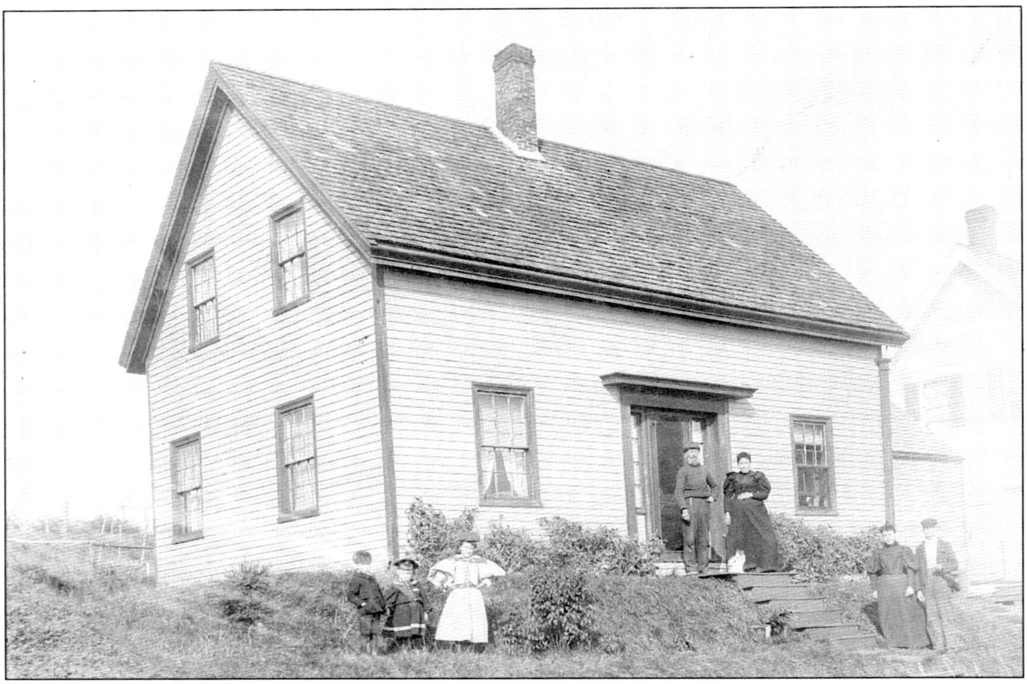

Otis and Mary Morey lived on Water Street in another Cape-style building.

Noah Brooks and George Witherle are shown here on the steps of Witherle's house on upper Main Street. This was one of the first homes with a tennis court. George Witherle and his brother William were wealthy merchants who, with their families, were generous benefactors to the town. George Witherle was an early conservationist who bought up Fort George and Witherle Woods in the 1860s and 1870s and preserved the land for the enjoyment of all. Noah Brooks was a journalist and author (see p. 29).

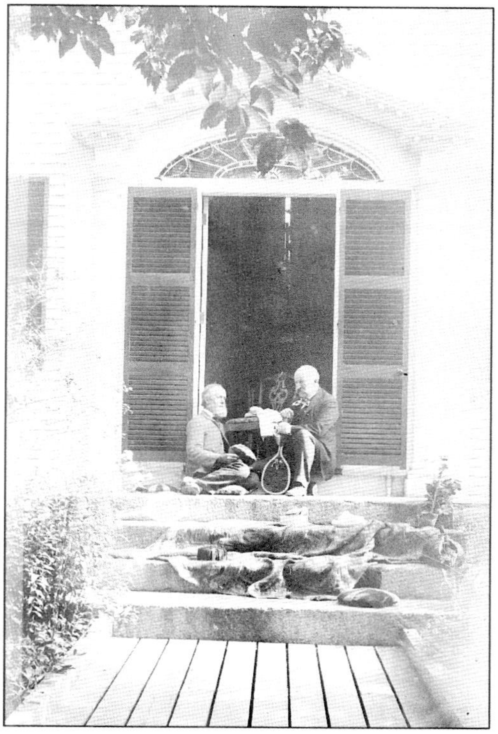

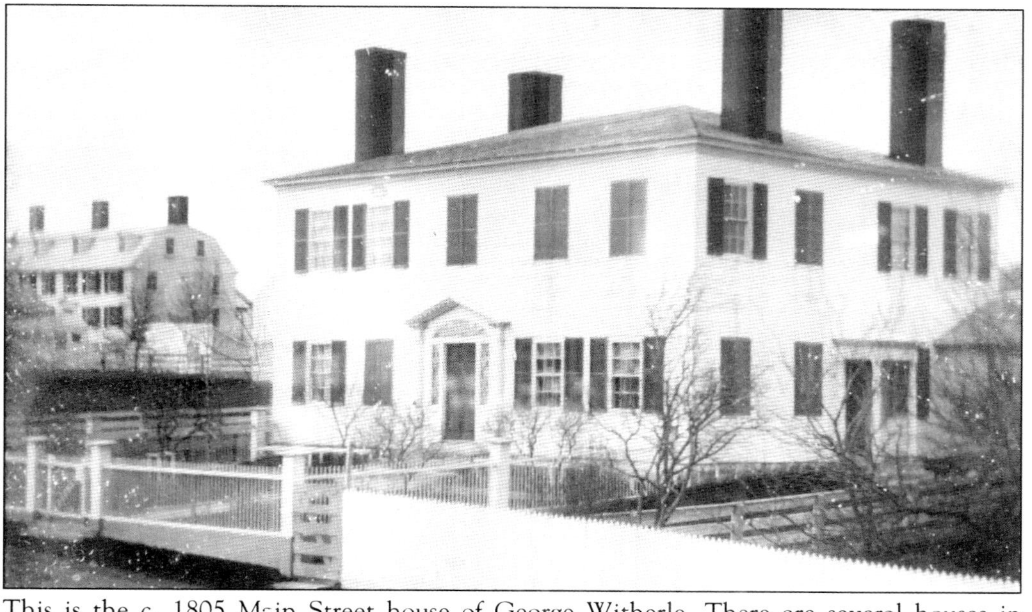

This is the c. 1805 Main Street house of George Witherle. There are several houses in present-day Castine built in the 1700s, and many more built by sea captains in the 1800s. Different styles of architecture are evident throughout the town: Early American, Georgian, Federal, Greek Revival, and Victorian. Some houses have been altered from one style to another. The house on the left was built by Joseph Perkins in the late 1700s and torn down in the late 1800s.

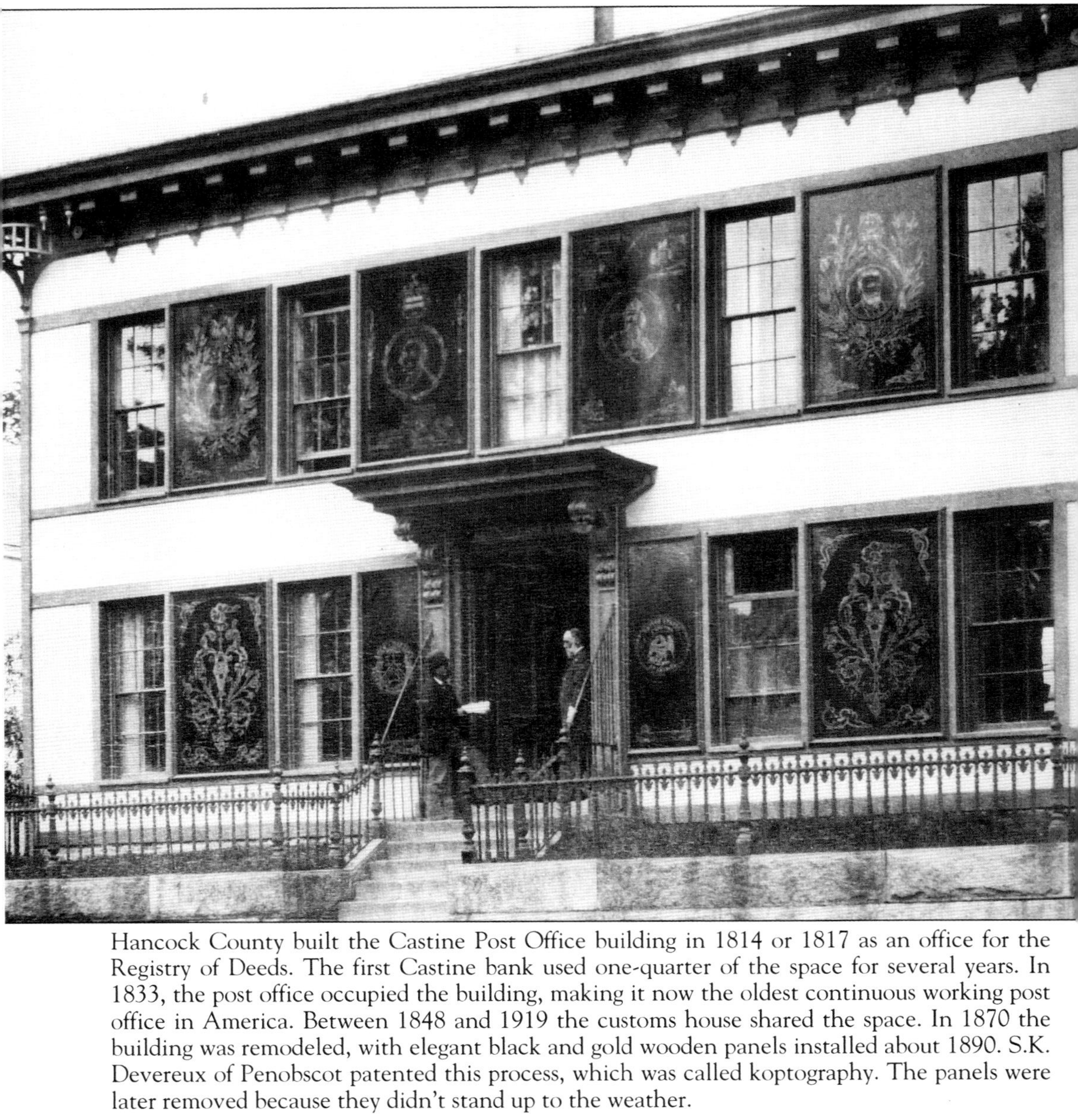

Hancock County built the Castine Post Office building in 1814 or 1817 as an office for the Registry of Deeds. The first Castine bank used one-quarter of the space for several years. In 1833, the post office occupied the building, making it now the oldest continuous working post office in America. Between 1848 and 1919 the customs house shared the space. In 1870 the building was remodeled, with elegant black and gold wooden panels installed about 1890. S.K. Devereux of Penobscot patented this process, which was called koptography. The panels were later removed because they didn't stand up to the weather.

The Johnston House doorway on Main Street, with its fan-light above the front door, is particularly beautiful because of the Palladian window on the second floor. The house is known for its flying staircase, which could be lifted for dances and parties.

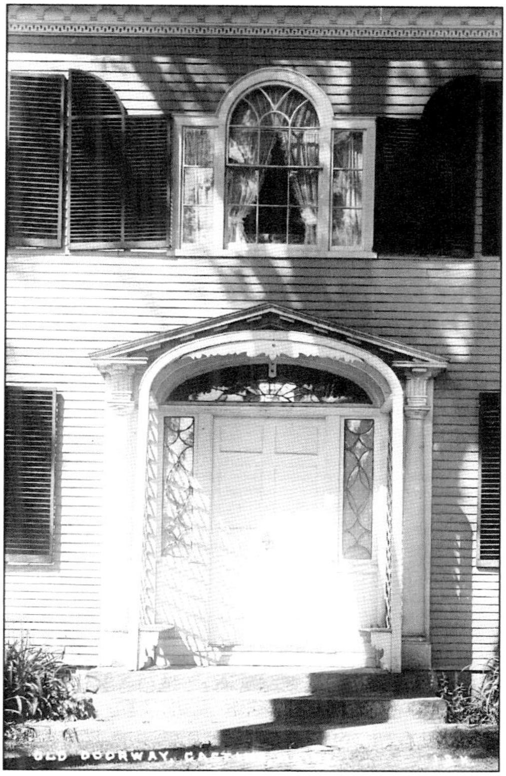

The Parson William Mason House, on the corner of Court and Main Streets, was built in 1797. The Parson represented the town during the War of 1812, rowing out to the British warships anchored in the harbor to surrender the town on September 1, 1814, waving one of his wife's white damask tablecloths as a flag of truce. The British occupation lasted less than a year.

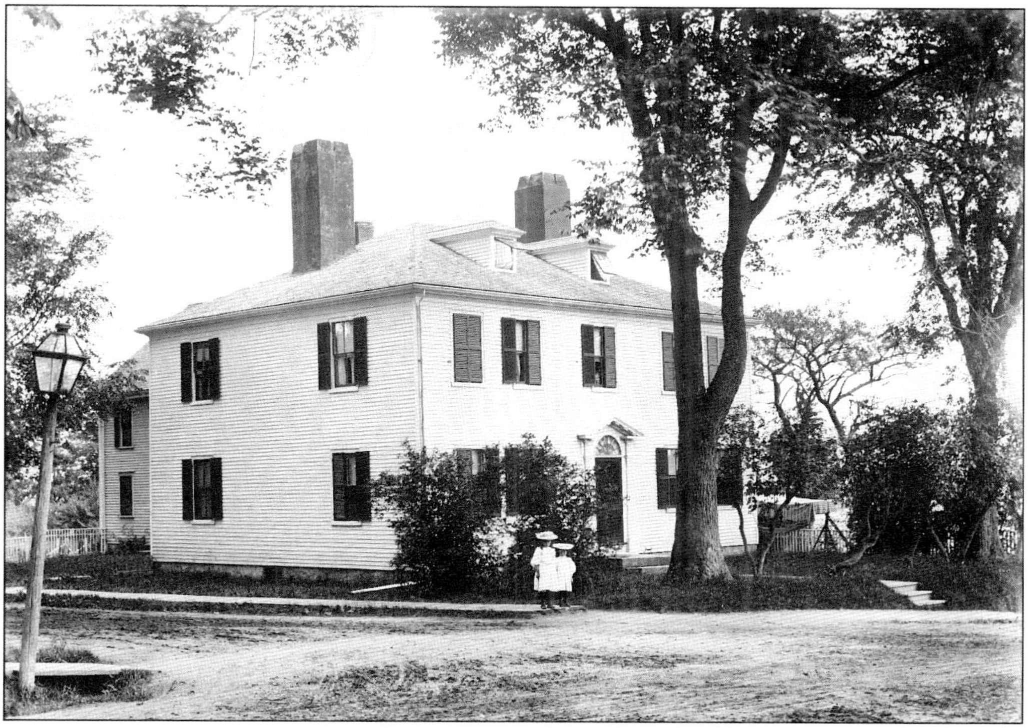

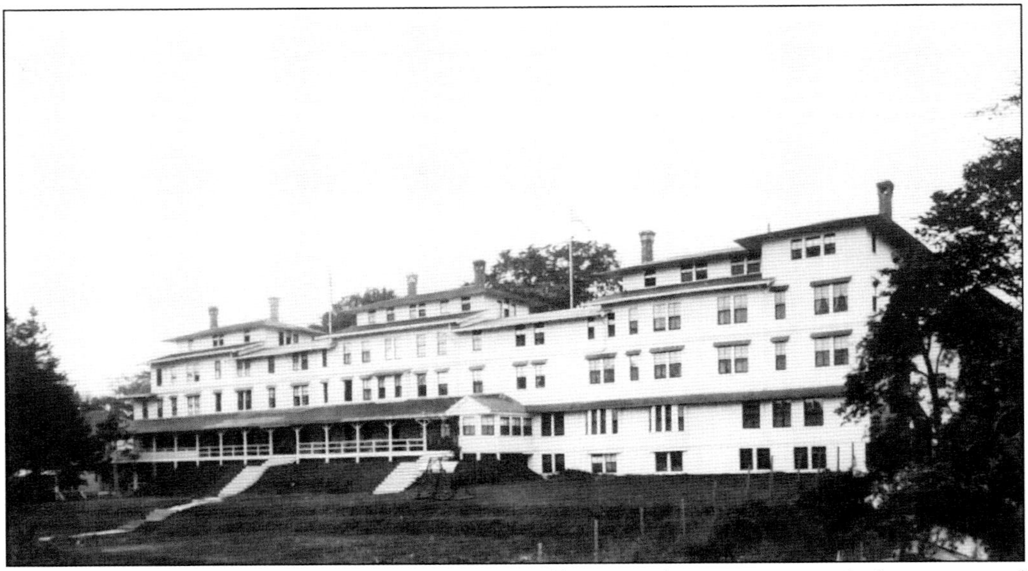

The Acadian Hotel expanded from a small colonial house with spacious grounds sloping toward the harbor, to a huge hotel, covering almost the whole lot on the corner of Perkins and Pleasant Streets. Guests disembarked at Steamer Wharf and carried their bags up the steps. The Acadian was finally torn down in 1943, after providing wonderful memories of Castine summers for many hundreds of people for more than half a century.

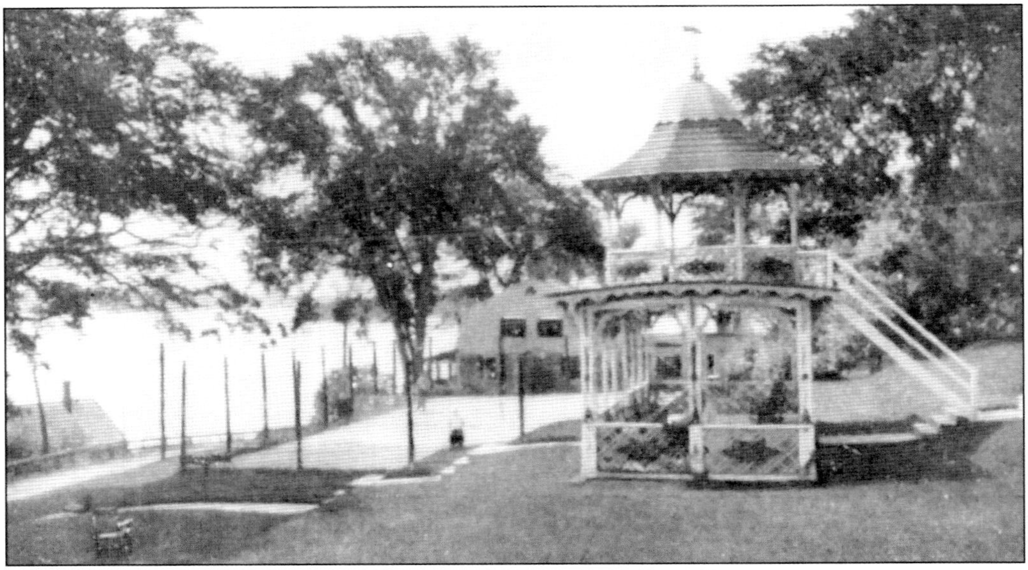

The bandstand in front of the Acadian was the site of many popular concerts on warm summer evenings attended by guests and townspeople. There was always a band in Castine in those years. There was also a tennis court on the front lawn.

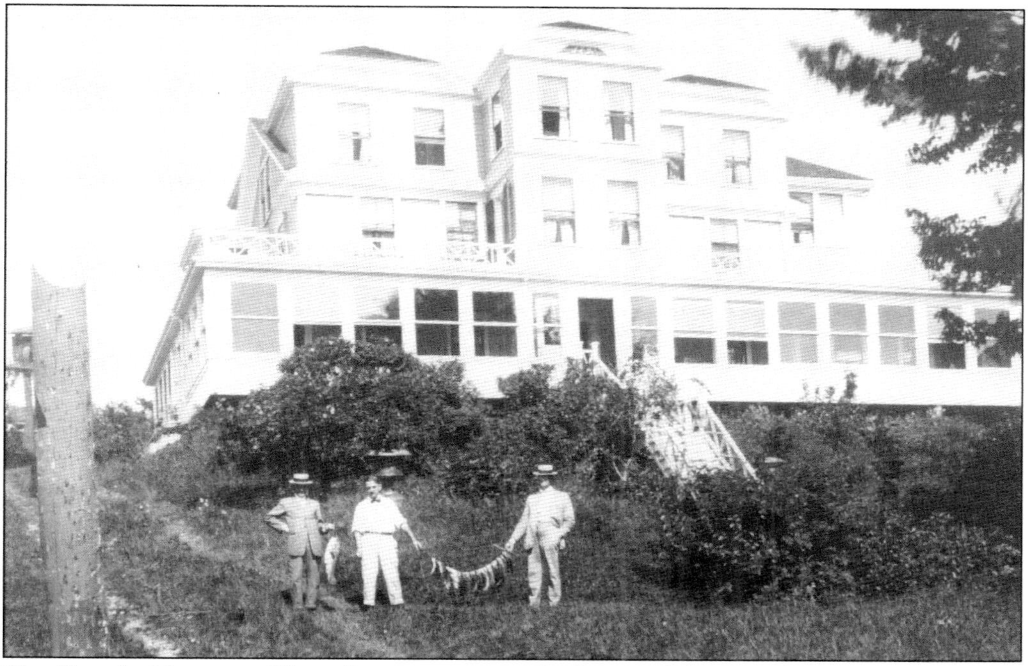

The Shetola House on Water Street was once the home of the Gay family, sea captains of Castine, and was later converted to a hotel. When A.W. Clark bought it, he greatly enlarged it. Guests paid $13.50 a week, including meals. Saltwater baths were provided by pumping salt water from the bay to storage tanks. Today it has been returned to its former glory as a gracious Federal house situated on a high bluff overlooking Oakum Bay.

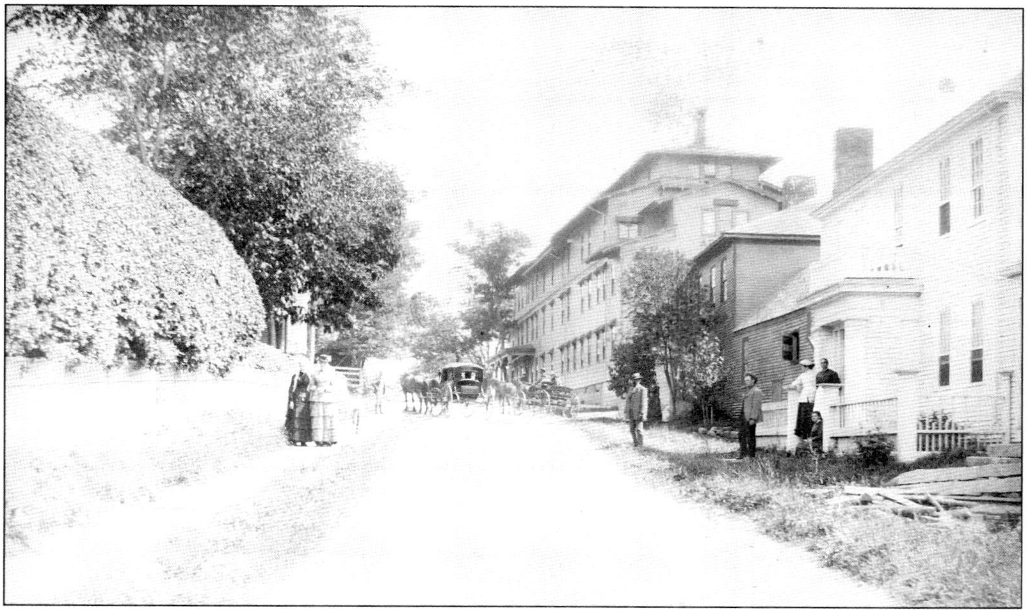

The Acadian Hotel extended out to the edge of the sidewalk on Perkins Street. The kitchen was on the corner in the foreground of this image, and the noise of cleaning up after dinner kept many residents awake late into the night.

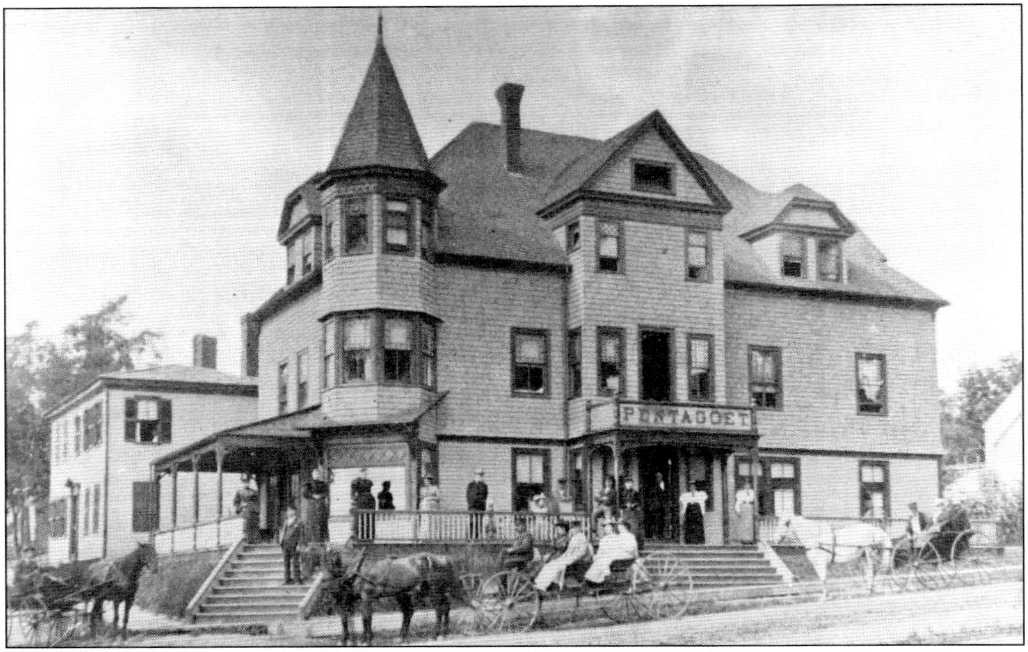

The Pentagoet Inn was built in 1894 and has been a popular hotel ever since. Maine Maritime Academy had its origins at the Pentagoet, where it started out as the Maine Nautical Training School in 1941.

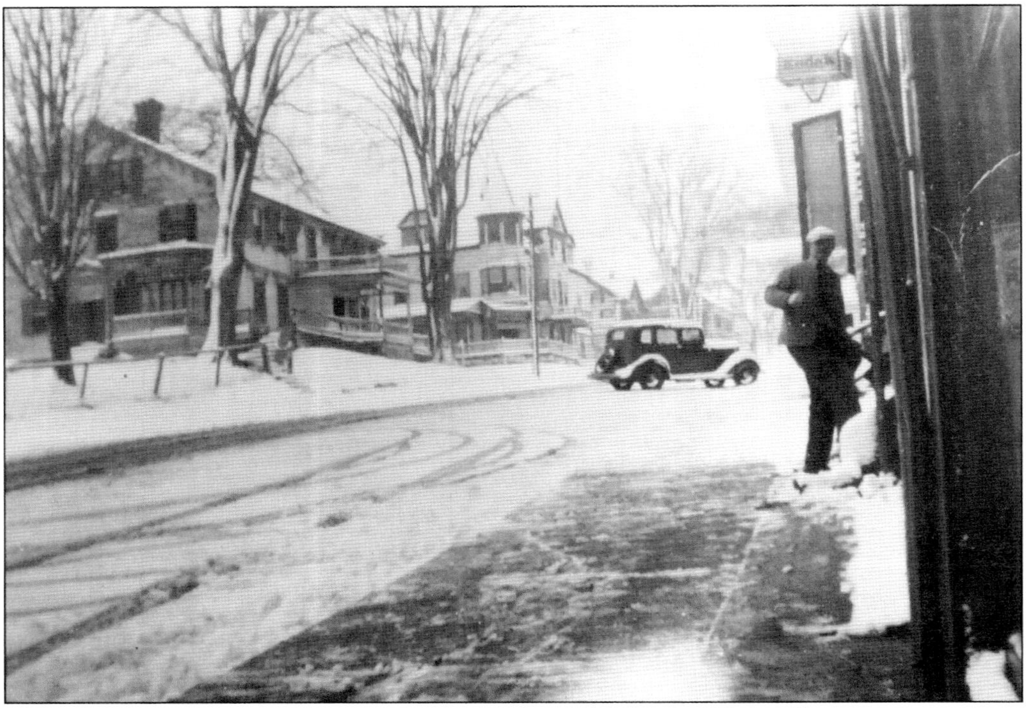

Lower Main Street is shown here, *c.* 1930, on a beautiful (but treacherous) winter day.

In the early 1900s, these smiling young women worked long hours for little pay as chambermaids and waitresses at the Castine House.

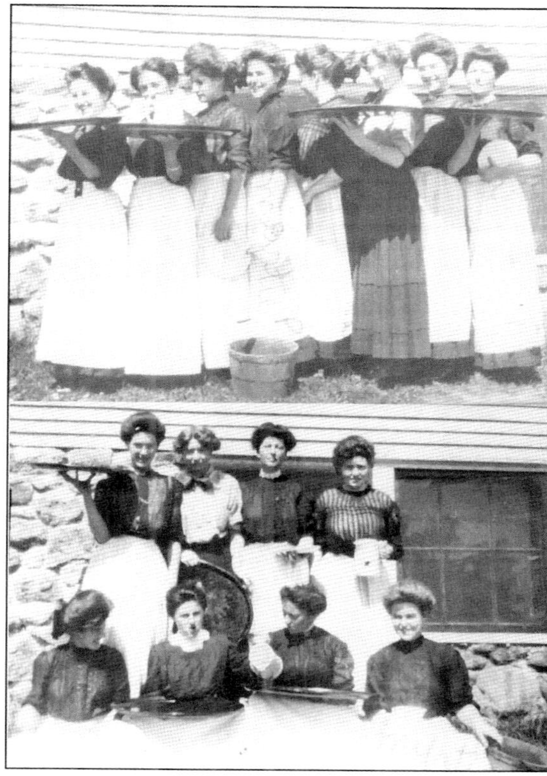

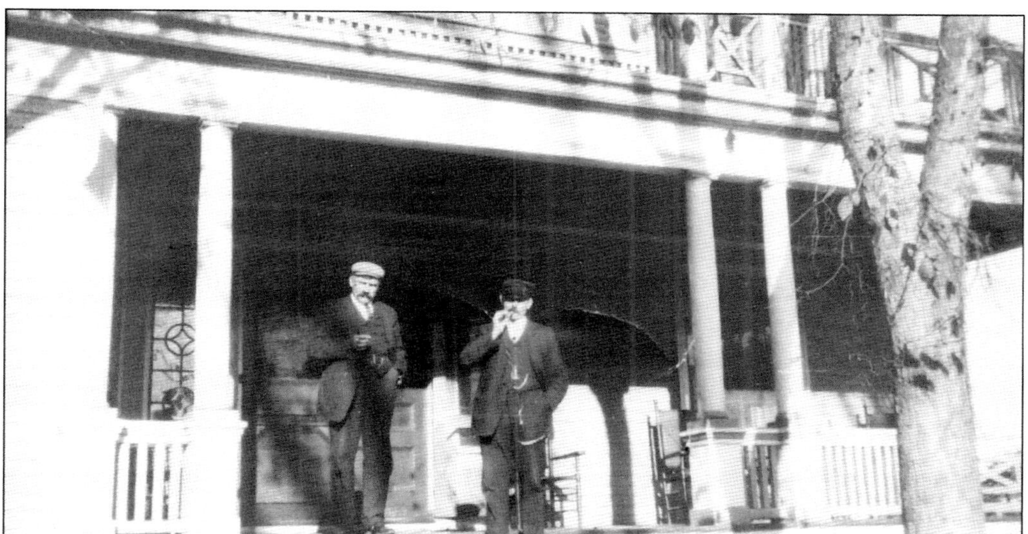

The Castine House was built by John M. Vogell in 1897. The name was later changed to the Castine Inn. Shown on the porch are Vogell (left) and "Fats" Bowden. In the early 1900s Castine had five hotels, a number of boarding houses and cottages for rent, and two livery stables.

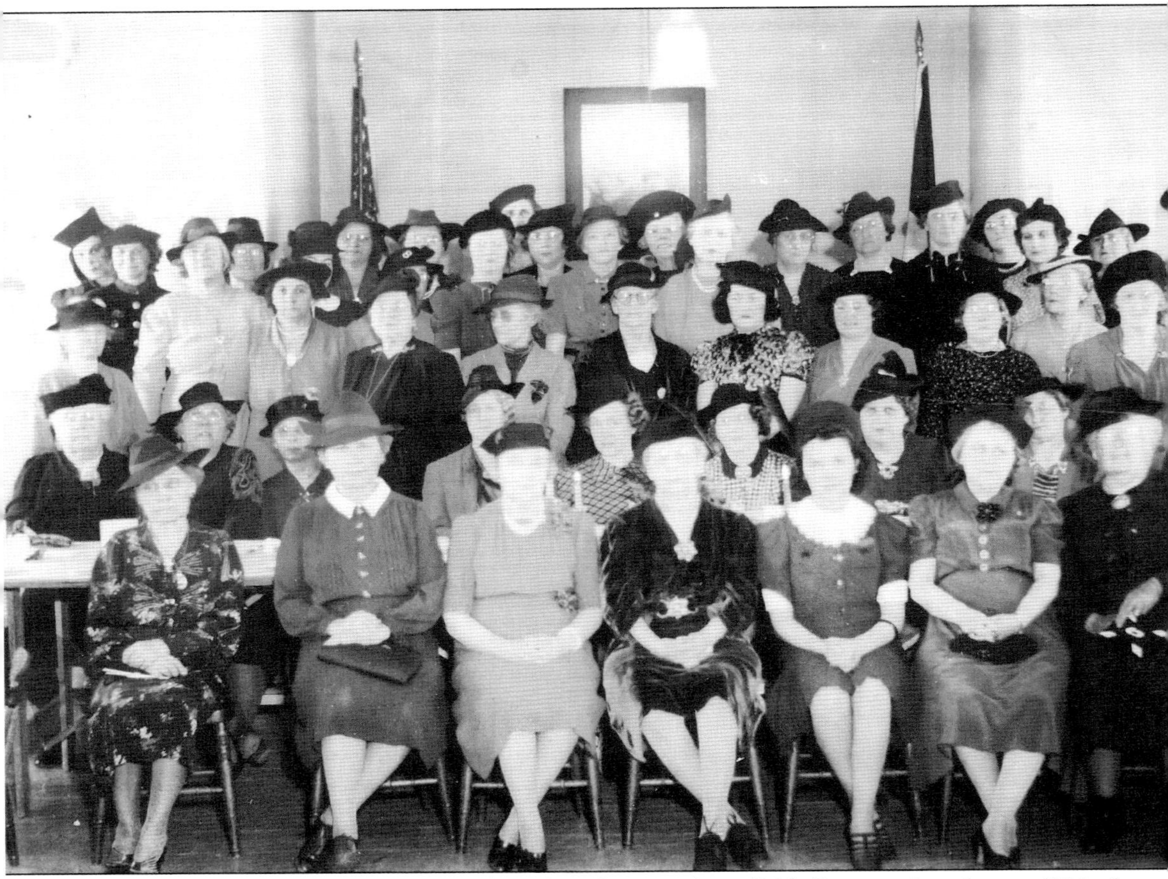

The Castine Woman's Club posed for this photograph, c. 1935. From its founding in 1913, the club was determined to "voice the spirit of modern sociology" (minutes of December 27, 1918). Founder Lizabeth Maxcy Hooke, grandmother of poet Philip Booth, is seated at the far left behind the table. Others are: (second row) Alice Vogel (second from the left), Bea Spurling (fourth from the right), and Anna Witherle (first on the right); (third row) Amy Witherle (fourth from the left).

The following lines are from the historical sign located at the top of Windmill Hill, now known as State Street (see p. 6):

"On Hatch's Hill there stands a mill,
Old Higgins he doth tend it,
And every time he grinds a grist,
He has to stop to mend it."

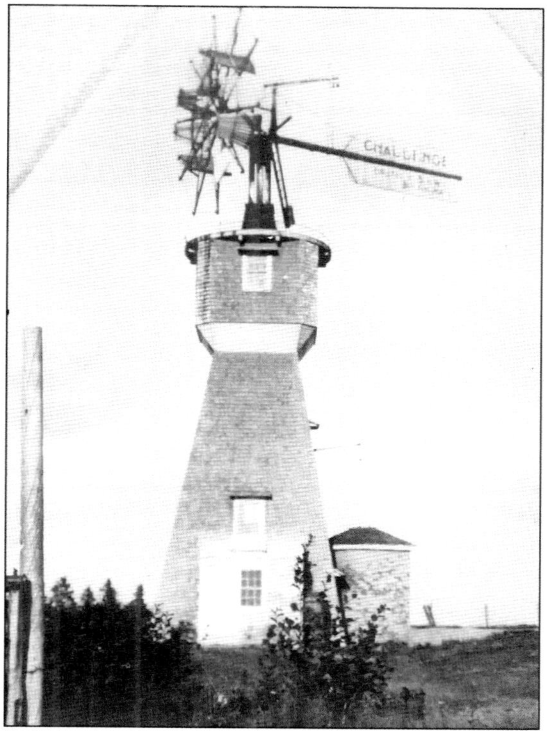

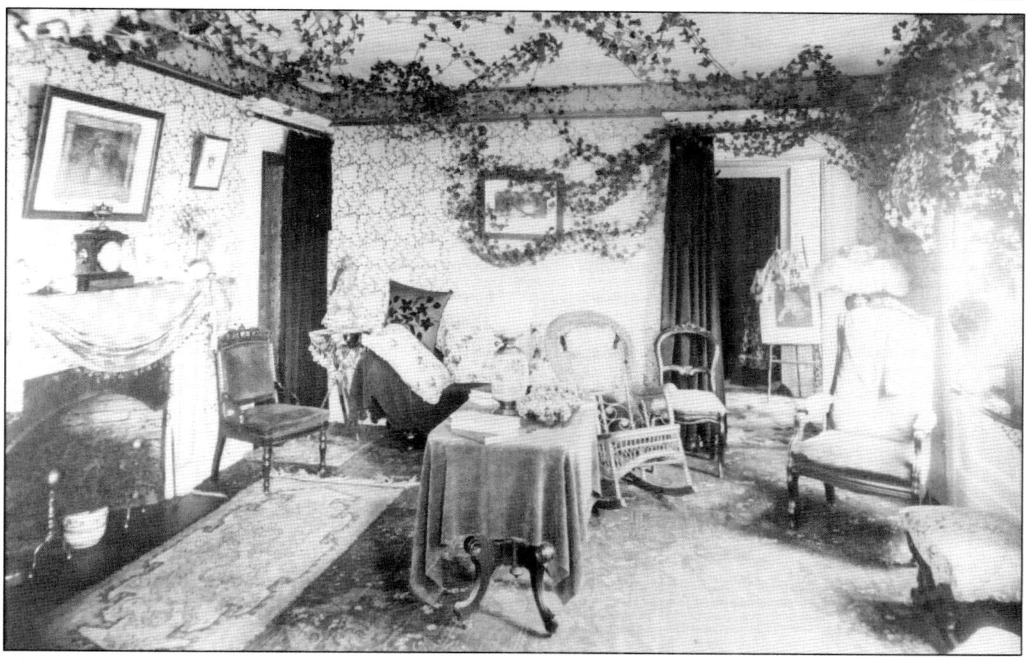

The parlor of the George A. Wheeler House shows a proper Victorian decor, with ivy trailing up the walls and along the ceiling. The stuffed crane in the right background was one of two pets which were stuffed and presented as wedding gifts to Dr. Wheeler's two daughters (see pp. 27 and 56).

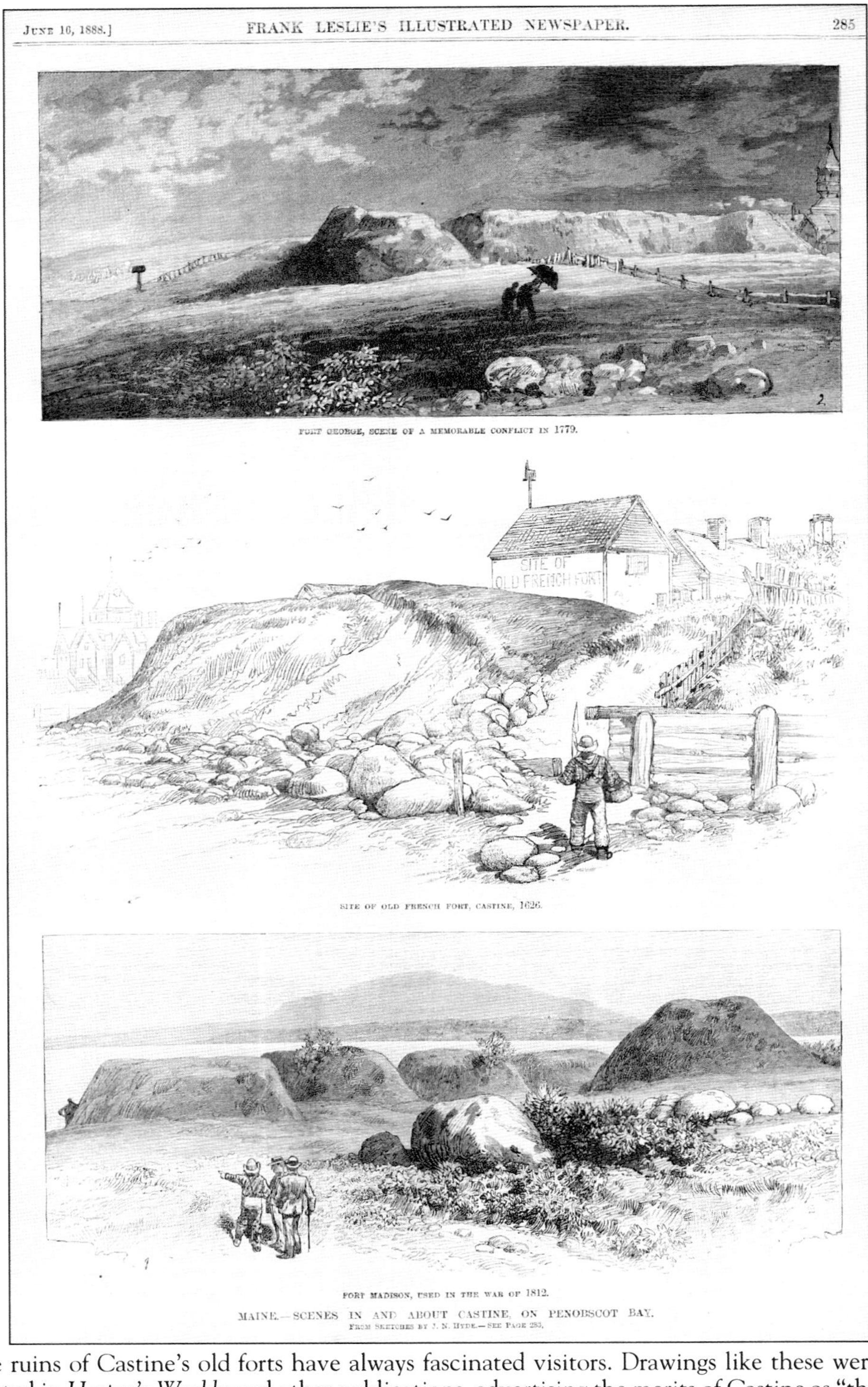

JUNE 16, 1888.] FRANK LESLIE'S ILLUSTRATED NEWSPAPER. 285

FORT GEORGE, SCENE OF A MEMORABLE CONFLICT IN 1779.

SITE OF OLD FRENCH FORT, CASTINE, 1626.

FORT MADISON, USED IN THE WAR OF 1812.

MAINE.—SCENES IN AND ABOUT CASTINE, ON PENOBSCOT BAY.
FROM SKETCHES BY J. N. HYDE.—SEE PAGE 283.

The ruins of Castine's old forts have always fascinated visitors. Drawings like these were also printed in *Harper's Weekly* and other publications, advertising the merits of Castine as "the new watering hole."

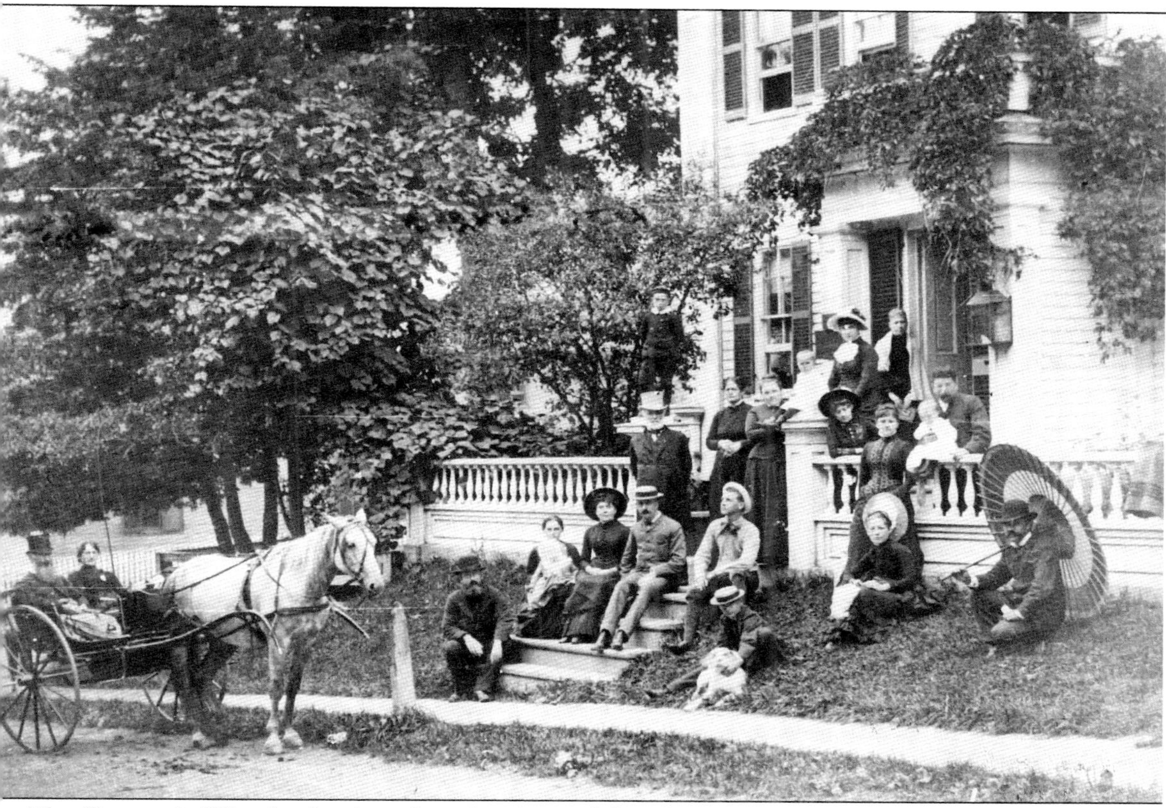

The George A. Wheeler family gathered in front of their home on the corner of Perkins and Pleasant Streets in the late 1800s. Dr. George A. Wheeler is pictured in the buggy with his daughter, Louise Wheeler Bartlett. Daughter Elizabeth is seated on the steps with her husband, Frederick Smith. Among the boys are sons George Dean Wheeler and Clarence Albion Wheeler. Mrs. George Wheeler is standing in the doorway. The porch is gone now, but the house retains many of its Federal features (see pp. 25 and 56).

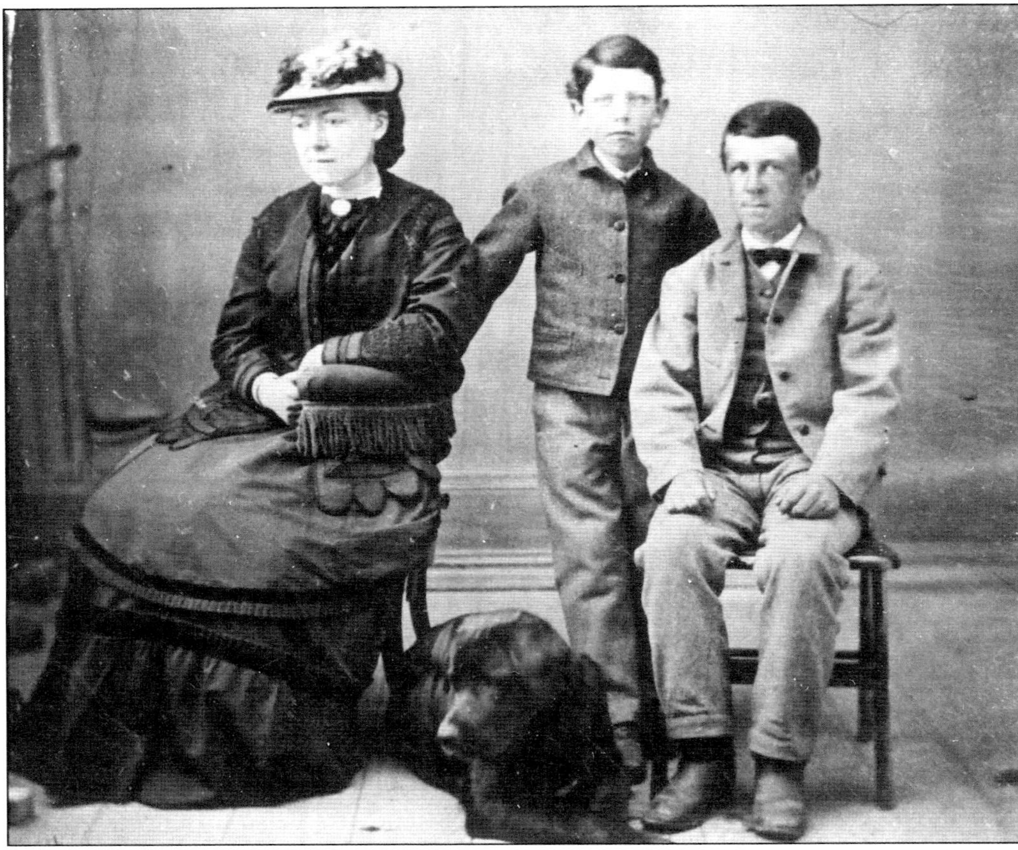

This is an early tintype of Mary Witherle Hooke (1849–1915), who taught primary school in Castine for almost forty years. The Castine Woman's Club furnished a "Children's Corner" in the Witherle Memorial Library in her memory. Pictured also are her brothers, Charles and George, and their dog.

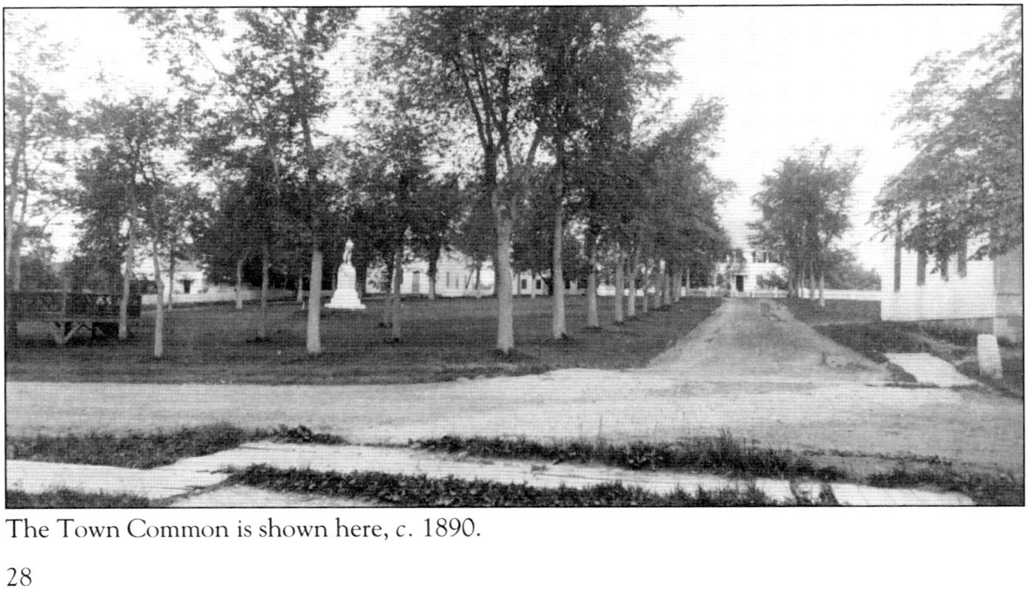

The Town Common is shown here, *c.* 1890.

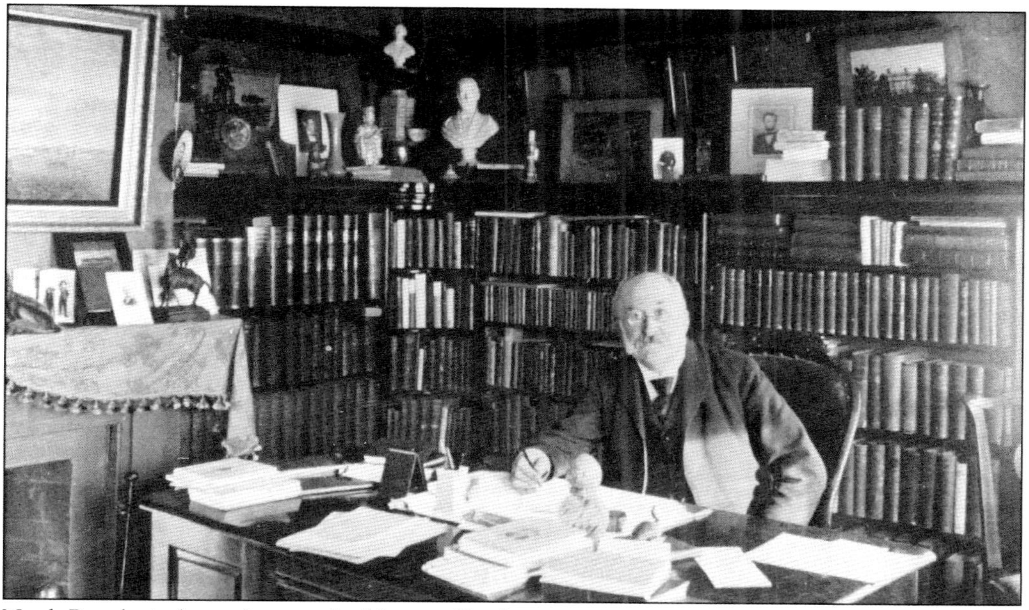

Noah Brooks is shown here in the library of his house on Main Street. He was a native of Castine who became a journalist and a well-known author of boys' books. Brooks was a confidant of President Lincoln, whom he visited the night before Lincoln's assassination. After a career in California and New York, where he was on the staff of the *Herald Tribune* and *New York Times*, he retired to Castine. He wrote more than fifteen books on Lincoln and other statesmen.

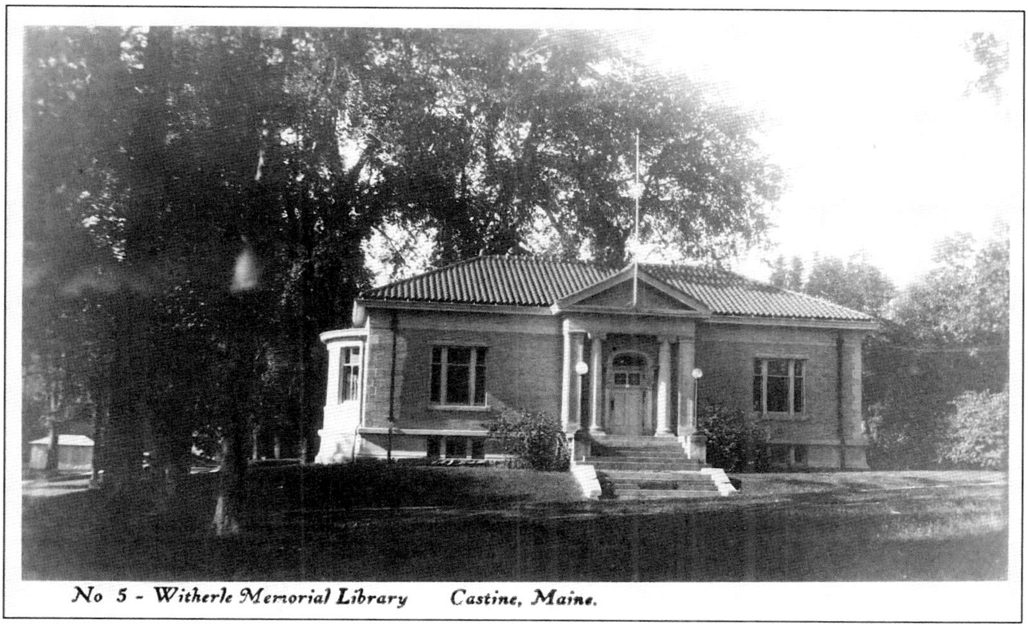

The Witherle Memorial Library was built on the site of the old courthouse in 1912, on land given by George Witherle, with funds left by his wife in her will. Noah Brooks bequeathed a painting by Fitz Hugh Lane to the library, along with a collection of his books.

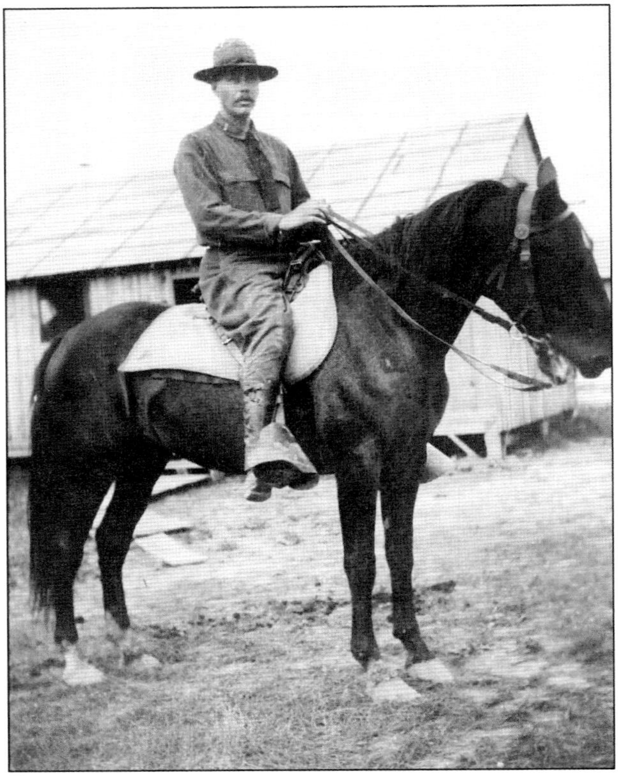

Dr. Harrison B. "Bunny" Webster started the first hospital in Castine in the J.W. Dresser House on Main Street in 1914, adding a sun porch and operating room to the house. A dedicated doctor, and a strong, athletic man, he once swam across the Bagaduce River to reach a patient, when he couldn't get a boat. He volunteered for service in World War I and was killed in 1918 while carrying a wounded soldier from the battlefield. He was awarded the Distinguished Service Cross.

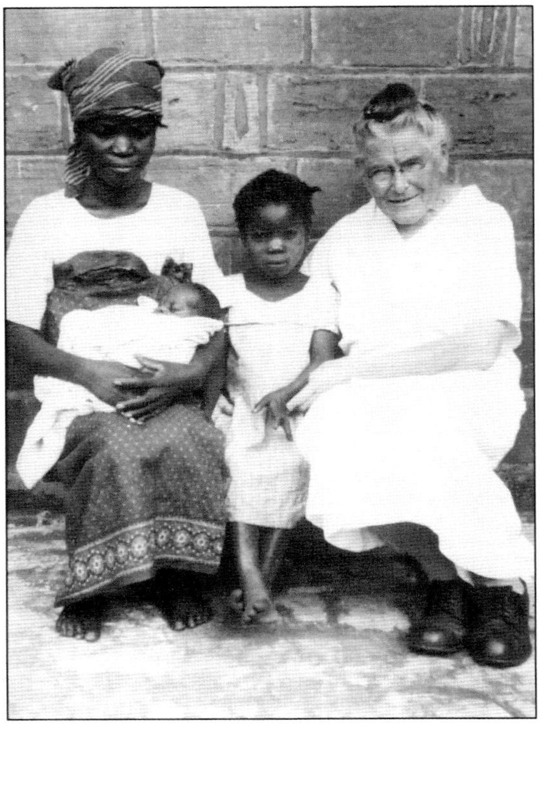

Dr. Mary F. Cushman, born in 1870, graduated from the Boston University School of Medicine in 1892, and established a hospital in Angola, West Africa, in 1922. Her father was the minister of the Trinitarian Church from 1884 to 1901. The Mary Cushman Circle, a women's group named in her honor at the Trinitarian Church, is still active today.

Dr. Harold Babcock was photographed with one of his prize hunting dogs, c. 1940s. Dr. Babcock took over Dr. Webster's hospital and practice in 1917, practicing for more than forty years. He traveled all over the peninsula, leaving a car in Brooksville at the ferry landing, ready to be picked up when needed. On one memorable visit, he arrived at a home for the delivery of a baby on a Friday during a snowstorm, but wasn't able to leave until the following Tuesday, cooking and taking care of the family until the husband was able to get home.

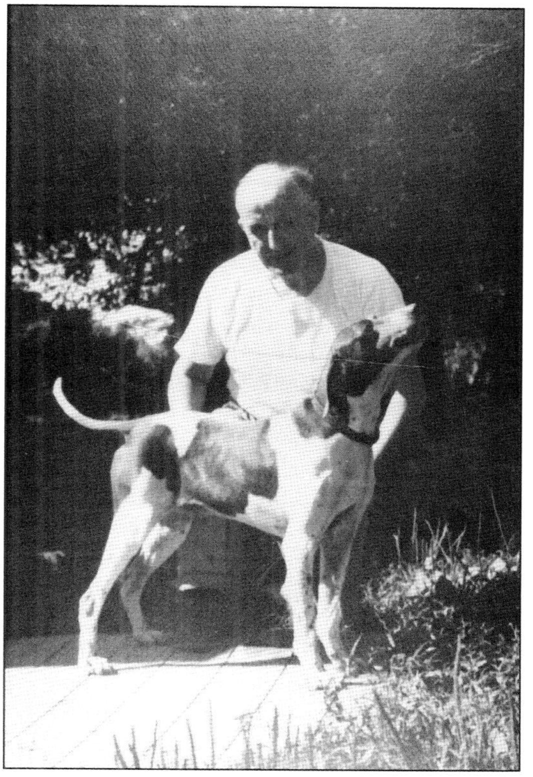

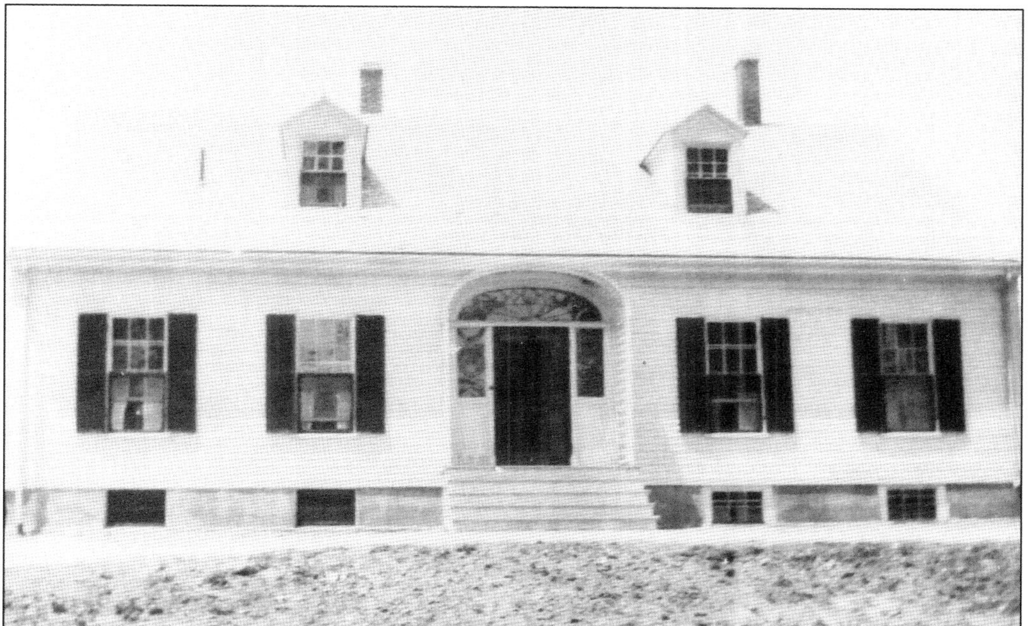

The Castine Hospital on Court Street, founded by Dr. Harold Babcock, was built in 1928. It was expanded in 1948 and 1954, before being closed in 1990. Hundreds of babies were delivered here, not only from Castine, but from the neighboring towns as well.

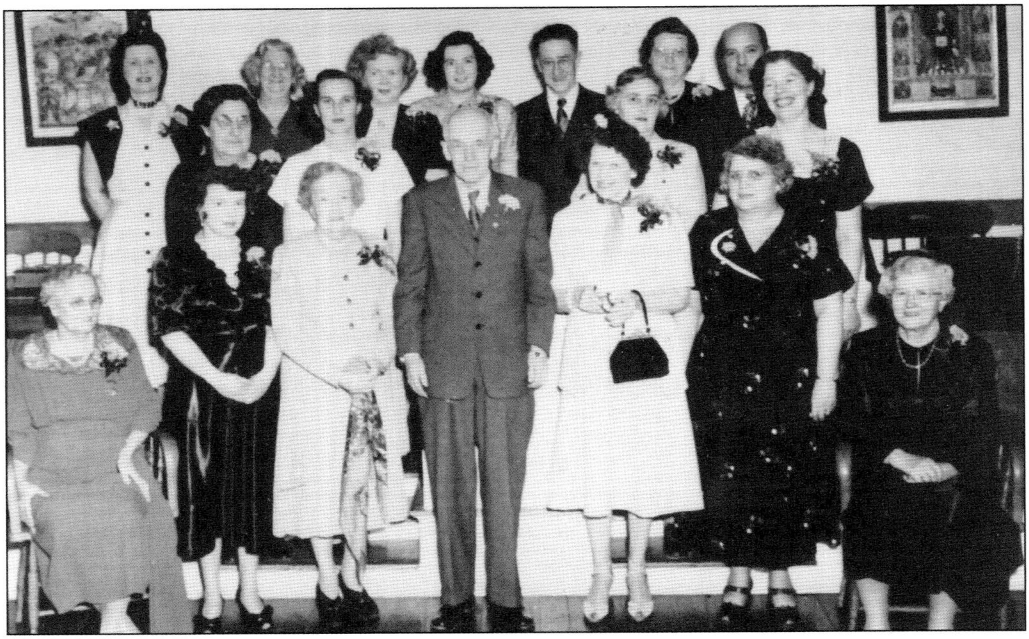

These Eastern Star members were photographed in the 1940s with Willis Arthur Ricker. Identified are: (front row) Laura Hatch (second from the left); (second row) Marjorie Babcock (second from the left) and Irene Bowden (second from the right); (third row) Bea Spurling (third from the left) and Jeannette Kennaday (fourth from the left). They met in the Masonic Hall on Main Street, a large building with a turret, containing meeting rooms, a dining room, a billiard room, and a store.

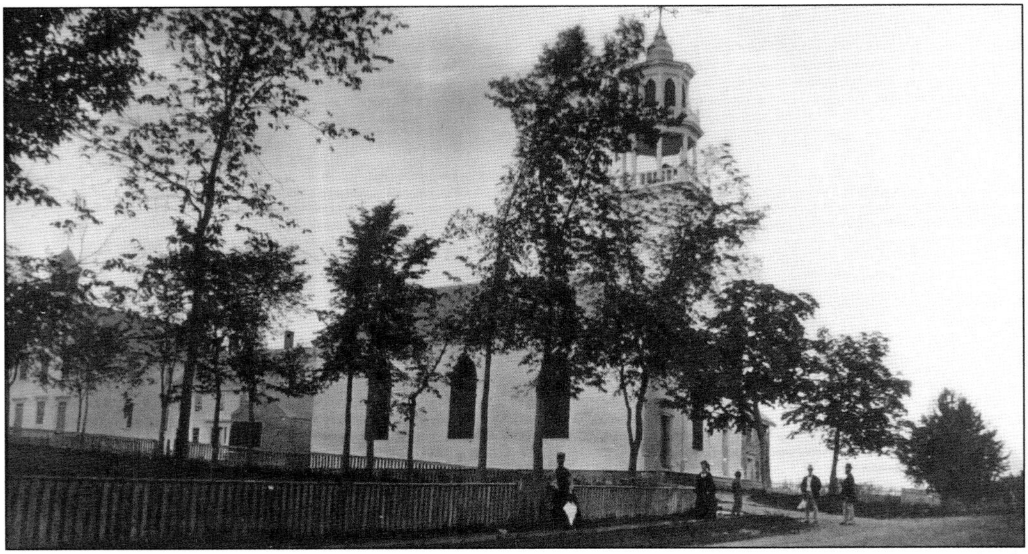

The Unitarian Church on the edge of the Town Common was the first church in Castine, built as a meetinghouse in 1790. It is the oldest church in eastern Maine and originally contained a Paul Revere bell. When it was rebuilt in 1832, a new belfry was added, based on a design by Charles Bulfinch. The original bell was returned to the Revere Copper Company and replaced by the present one, bought from Joseph Revere, son of Paul Revere.

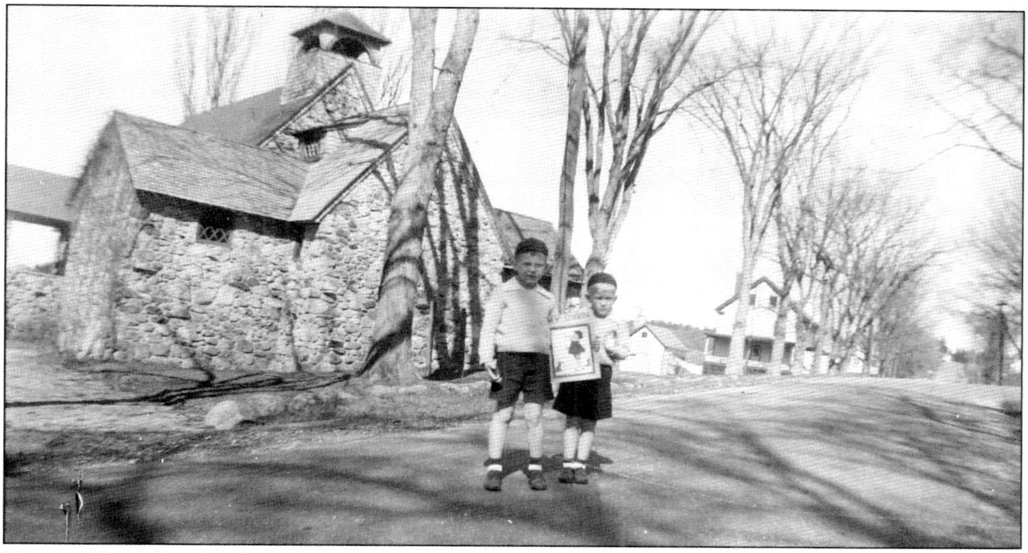

Trinity Chapel on Perkins Street was erected in 1897–98 as a summer chapel for Episcopalians. At that time there was only one Episcopalian among the Castine inhabitants, so the building was entirely financed by summer residents. Colonel A.K. Bolan donated the land across the street from his own "Agoncy" cottage as the site (see p. 94).

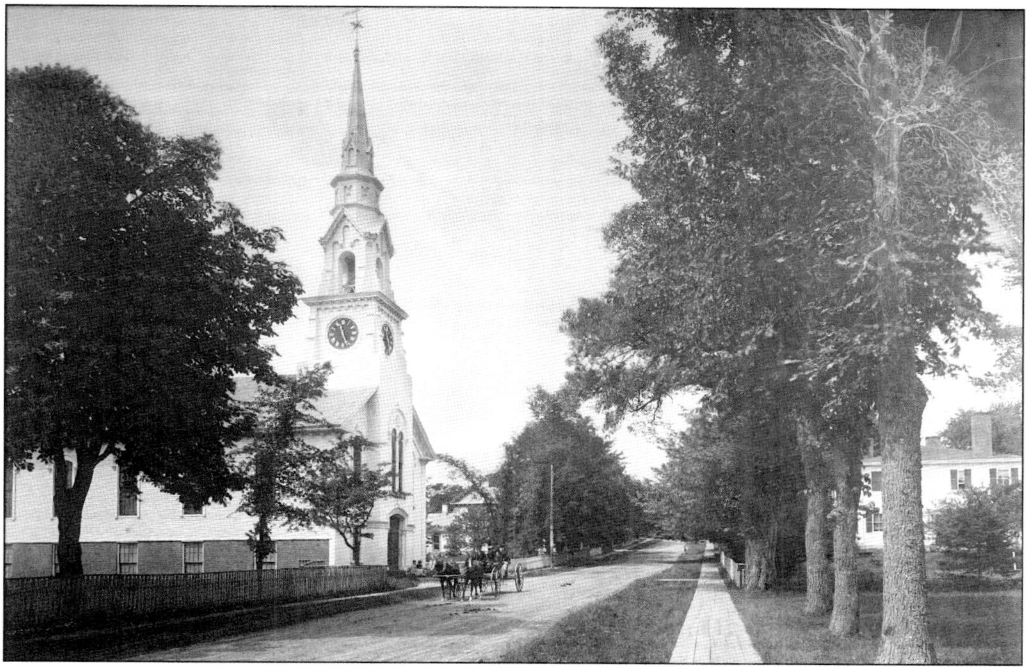

The Trinitarian Church was organized in 1820. In 1829 a church building was erected on Main Street for its thirty members. In 1848 it was enlarged, and in 1867 it was almost completely reconstructed. A new spire about 120 feet tall was added, with a bell weighing about 1,600 pounds. Stained-glass windows were installed, and the building was raised to its present foundation. The clock in the bell tower was bequeathed to the town by Mrs. Daniel Johnston Jr. in 1889.

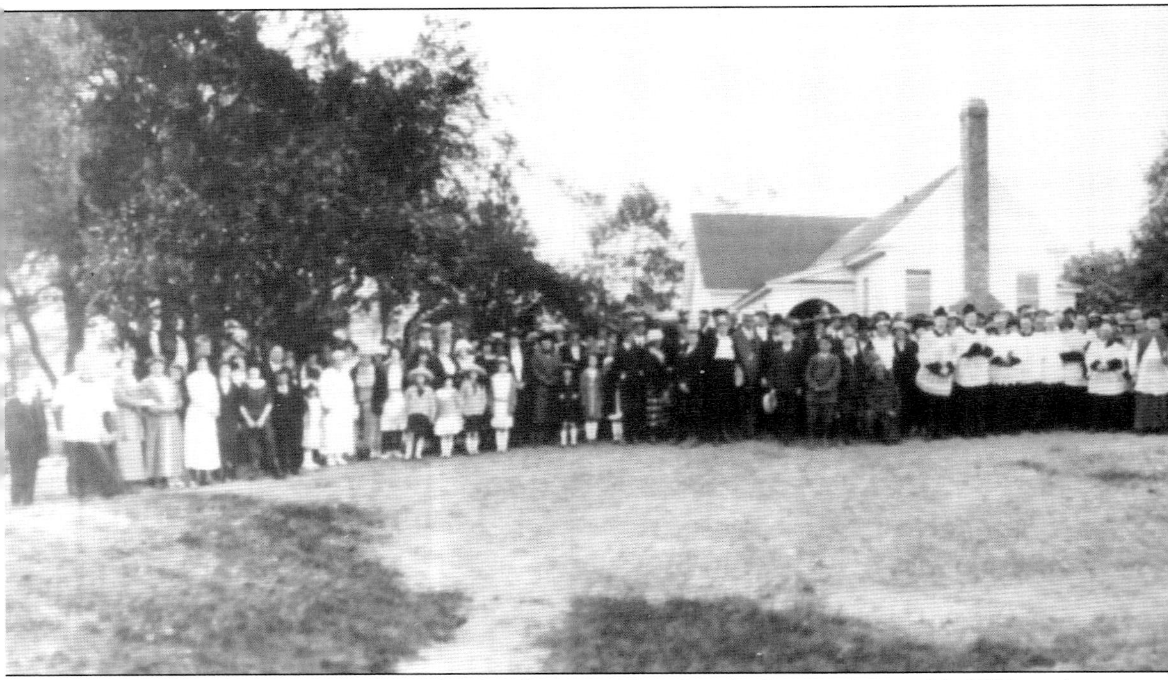

The dedication of the Our Lady of Holy Hope Chapel took place on August 28, 1921, with more than 1,000 people present, including clergy from all parts of Maine, New York, Baltimore,

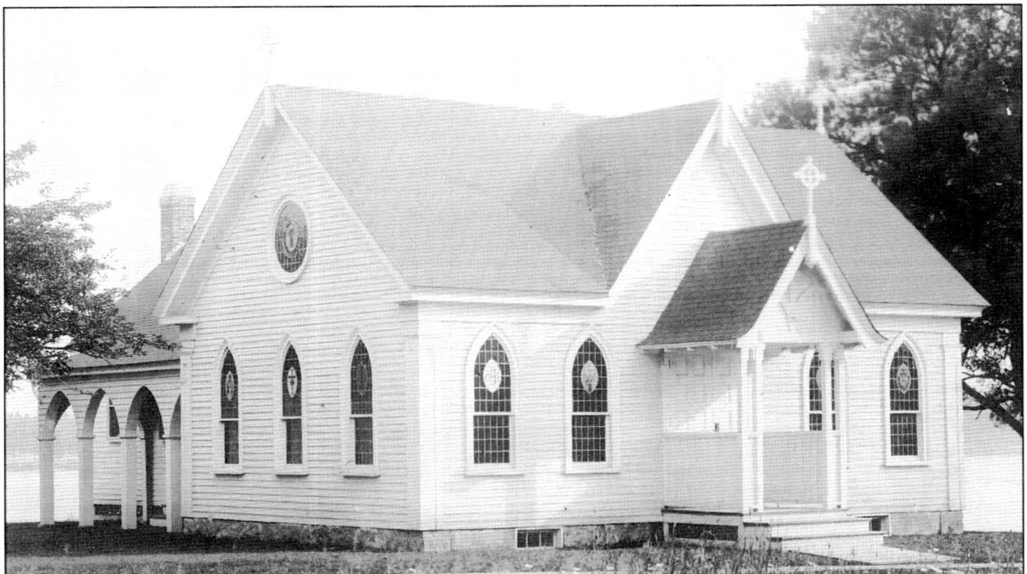

The Our Lady of Holy Hope Roman Catholic Chapel was converted from the George Webb House on Perkins Street in 1921. It is on the site of Fort Pentagoet, which contained the original Chapel of Our Lady of Holy Hope. In 1865 a copper plate was found on the beach in front of the ruins of the old fort, which, when cleaned and translated from Latin, was found to read: "11 June 1648. I, Father Leo Capuchin, of Paris, France dedicate this land to our Lady of Holy Hope."

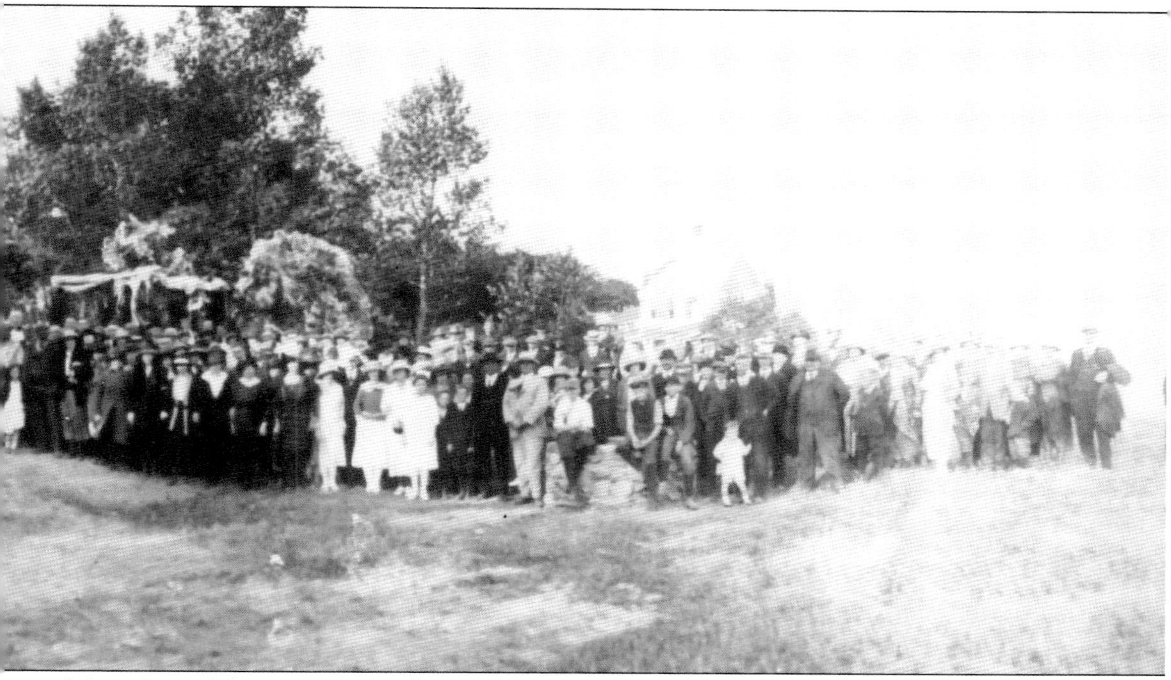

and Canada, and thirty members of the Penobscot tribe, in full tribal regalia.

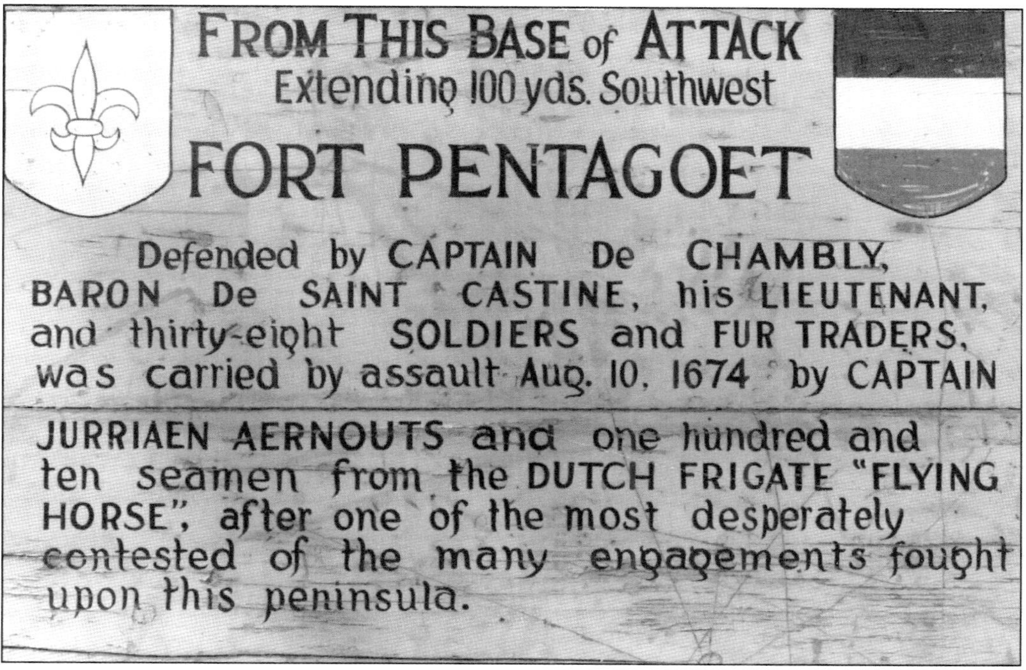

The historic sign at the site of Fort Pentagoet on Perkins Street recounts the story of the French occupation. The Baron de St. Castin, after whom Castine is named, came to this peninsula in 1666, and occupied the area in the name of France until 1693. He sailed for France in 1701, never to return.

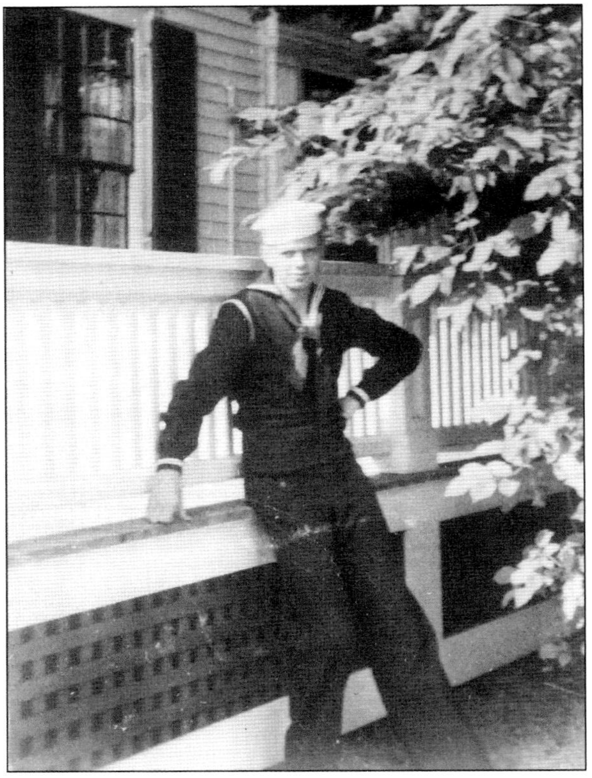

Willis Leach was one of the local boys who went off to serve his country in World War II, along with seventy-five other men and women from Castine.

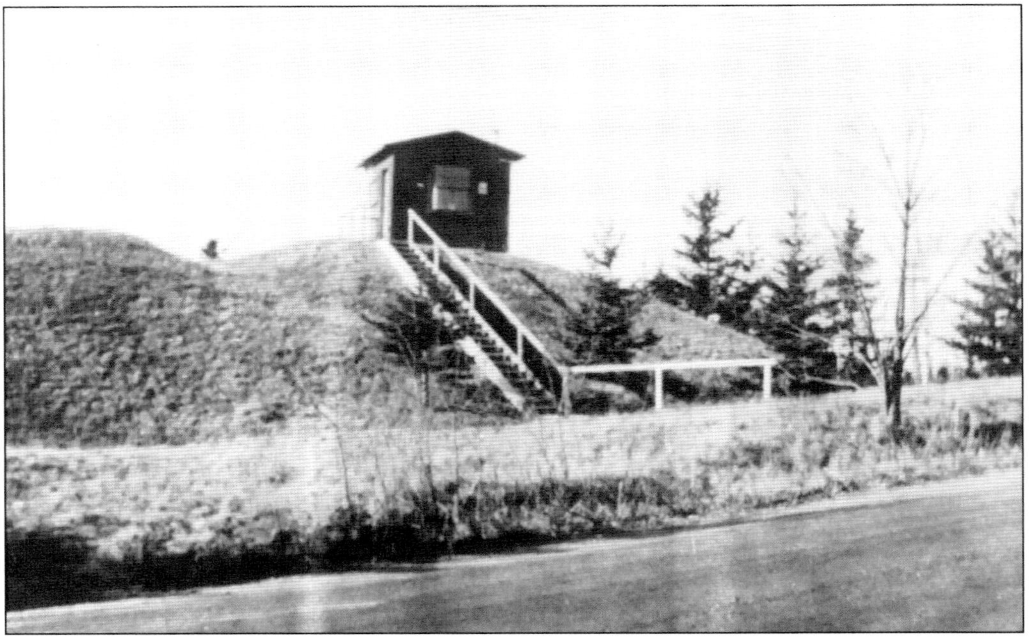

During World War II, high on the banks of the old Fort George, Castine volunteers anxiously scanned the skies from this "air-raid command headquarters," the last war effort to ever take place on the peninsula.

Two

School Days

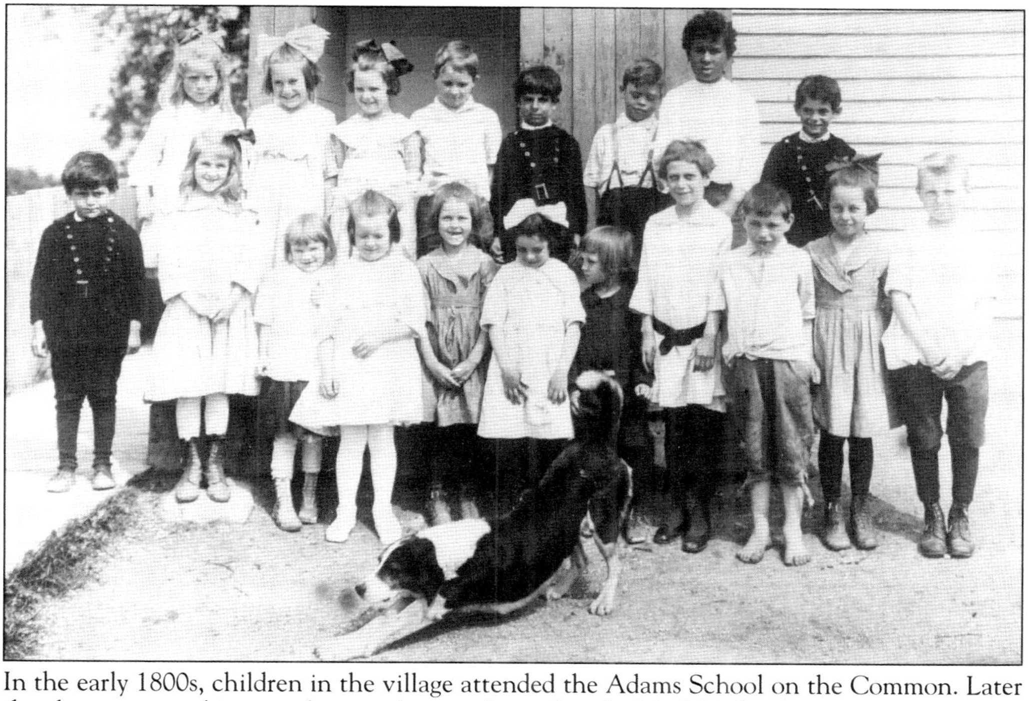

In the early 1800s, children in the village attended the Adams School on the Common. Later the elementary and intermediate grades were housed in the Model School section of the Eastern State Normal School before returning to the Common in 1942.

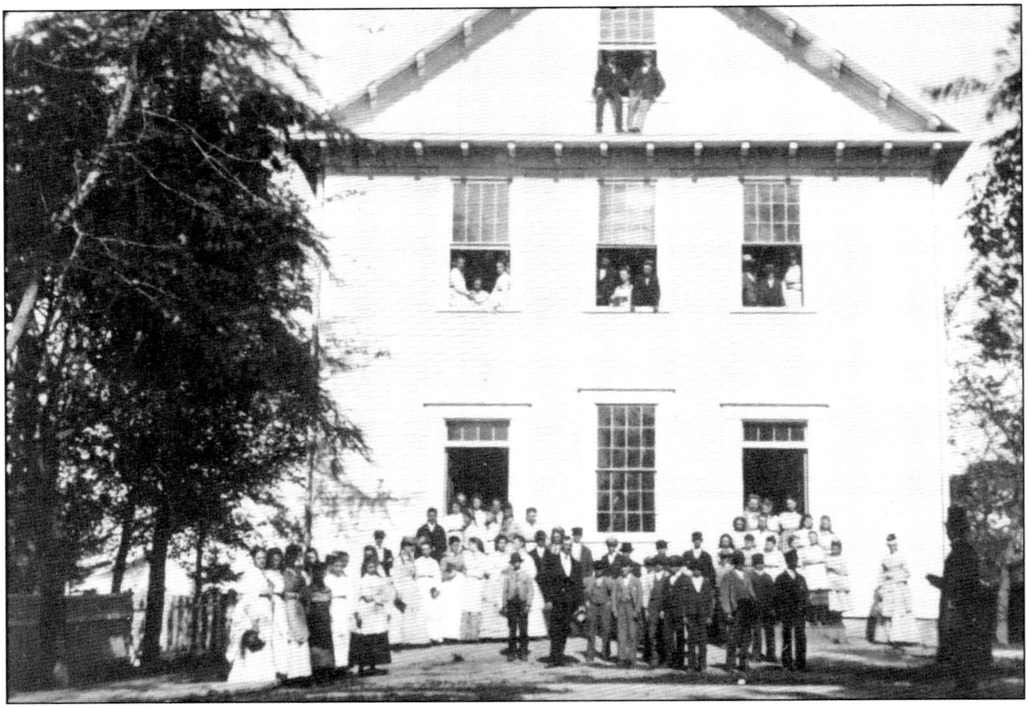

Students at the Adams School are shown here, *c.* 1870s.

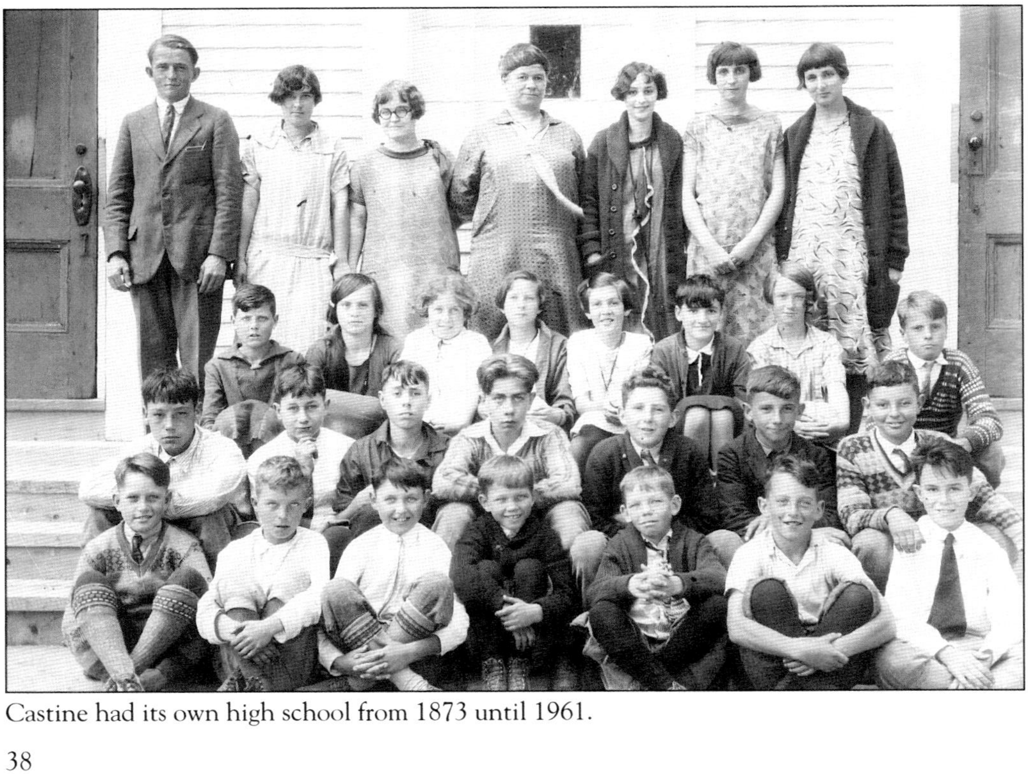

Castine had its own high school from 1873 until 1961.

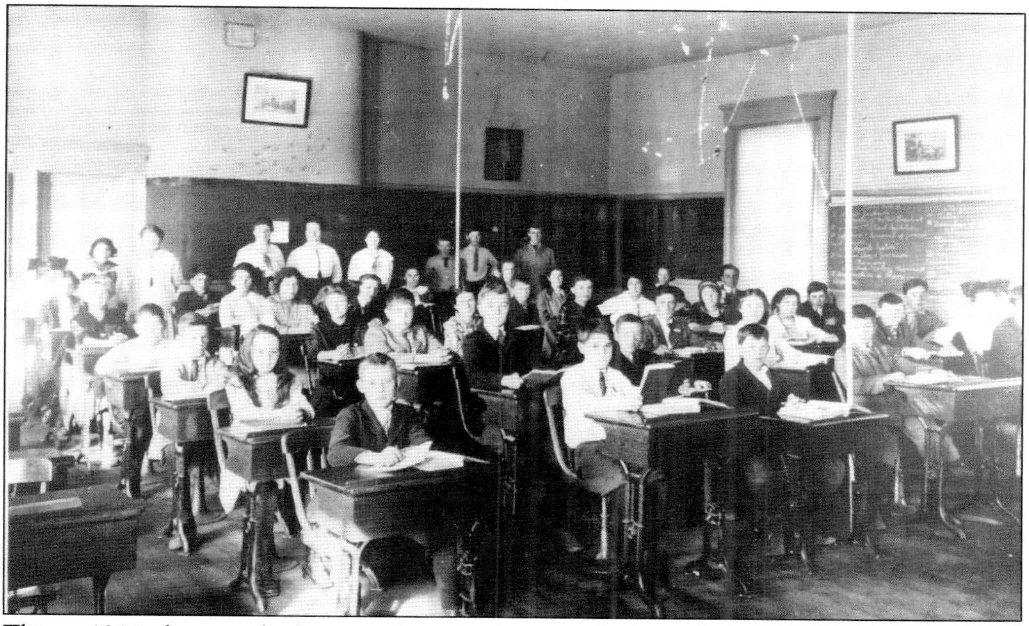

This c. 1914 photograph shows students in the seventh through ninth grades at the Castine Primary School.

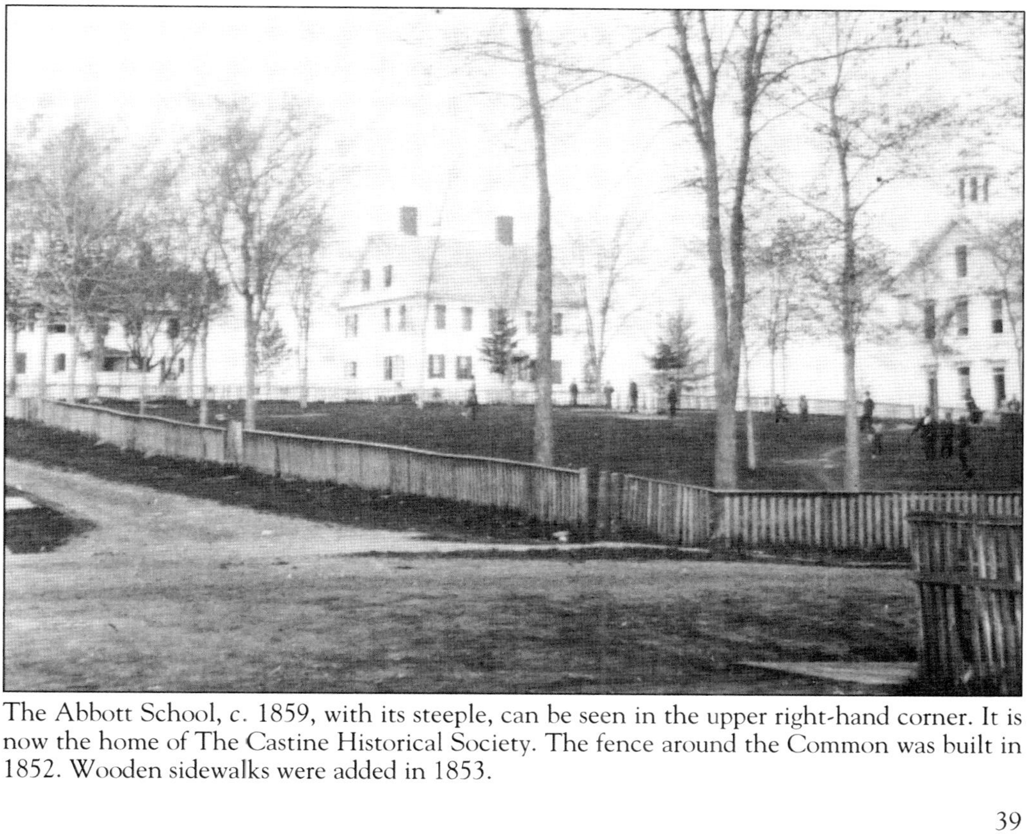

The Abbott School, c. 1859, with its steeple, can be seen in the upper right-hand corner. It is now the home of The Castine Historical Society. The fence around the Common was built in 1852. Wooden sidewalks were added in 1853.

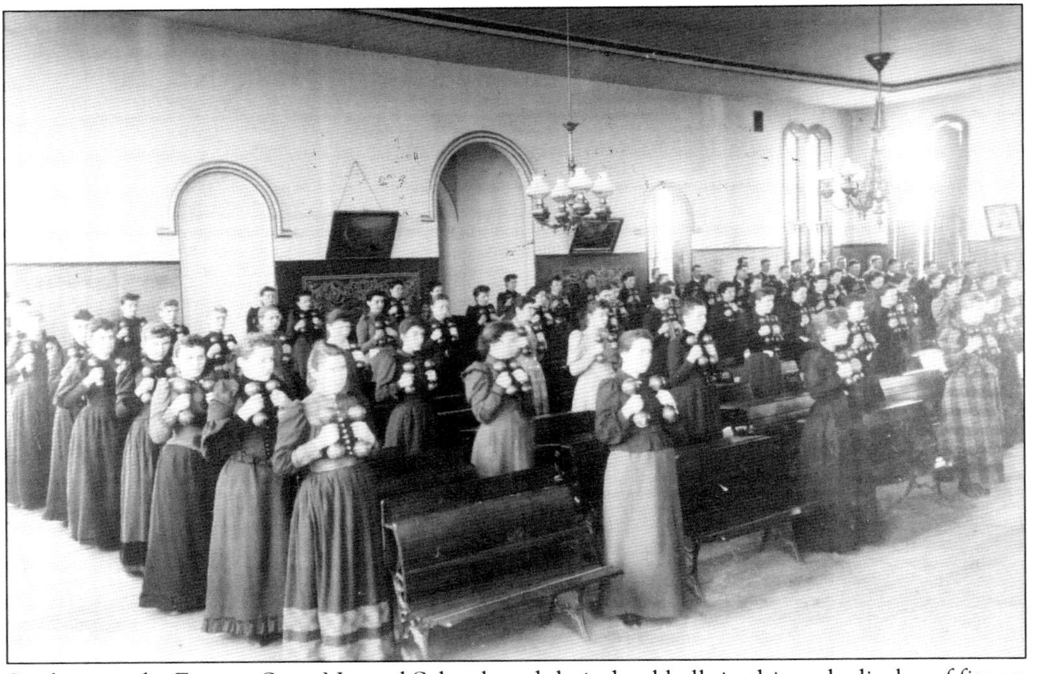

Students at the Eastern State Normal School used their dumbbells in this early display of fitness training at a gym class in the late 1800s. The school prepared young men and women from down east Maine for teaching careers from 1867 to 1942.

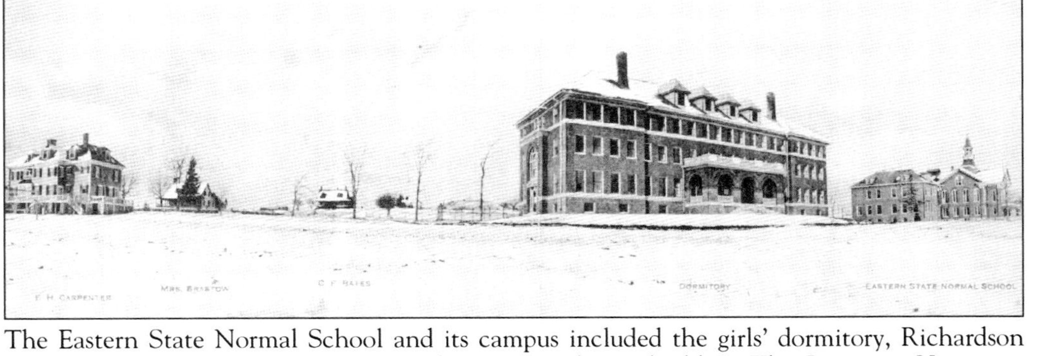

The Eastern State Normal School and its campus included the girls' dormitory, Richardson Hall (now known as Leavitt Hall), plus the annex and main building. The Carpenter House, on the far left, became the house of the president of Maine Maritime Academy.

Letitia Alma Hatch is shown here on the day of her graduation from the Eastern State Normal School in May 1901.

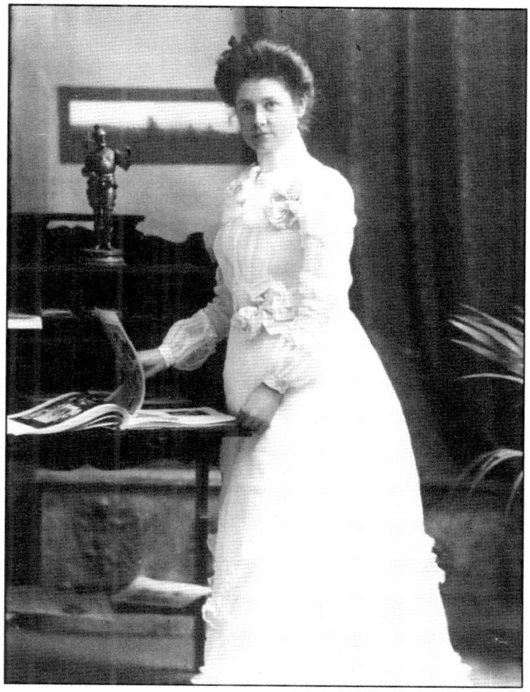

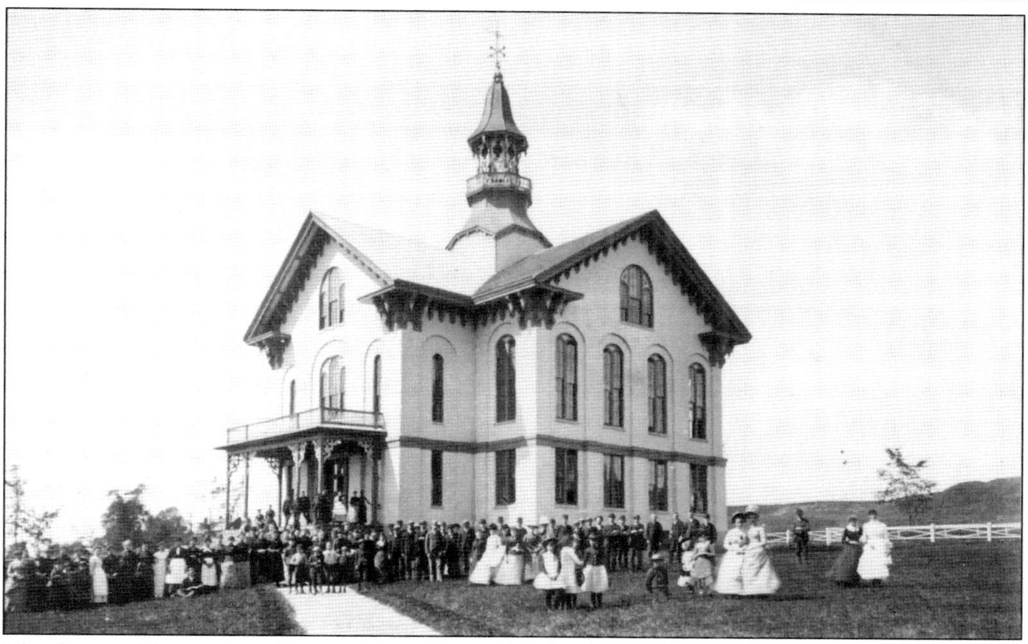

The first building of the Eastern State Normal School was dedicated on May 22, 1873. Prior to that time, classes were held in the Abbott School on the Common. An annex was added for the Model School, laboratory, gymnasium, and domestic science departments in 1909. The dormitory was added in 1910. In the early years, the young students boarded at homes in Castine. This building was renamed for Rear Admiral Douglas Dismukes, the first superintendent of Maine Maritime Academy after the Academy took over the campus in 1942.

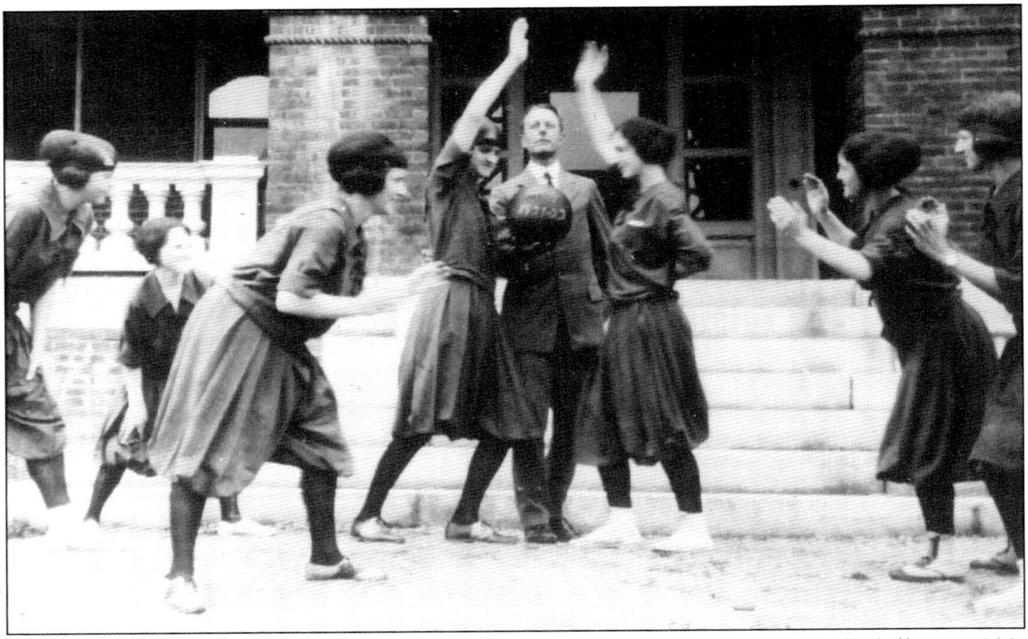

Young Women at the Eastern State Normal School practice their basketball skills, c. 1922, with coach W.D. Hall.

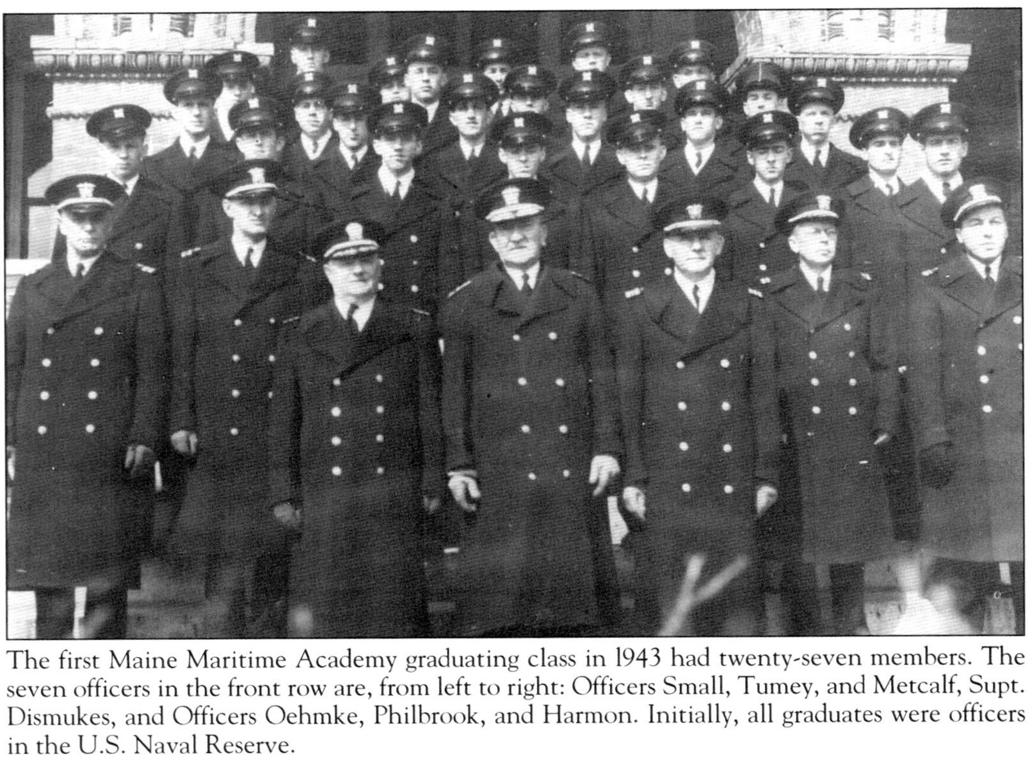

The first Maine Maritime Academy graduating class in 1943 had twenty-seven members. The seven officers in the front row are, from left to right: Officers Small, Tumey, and Metcalf, Supt. Dismukes, and Officers Oehmke, Philbrook, and Harmon. Initially, all graduates were officers in the U.S. Naval Reserve.

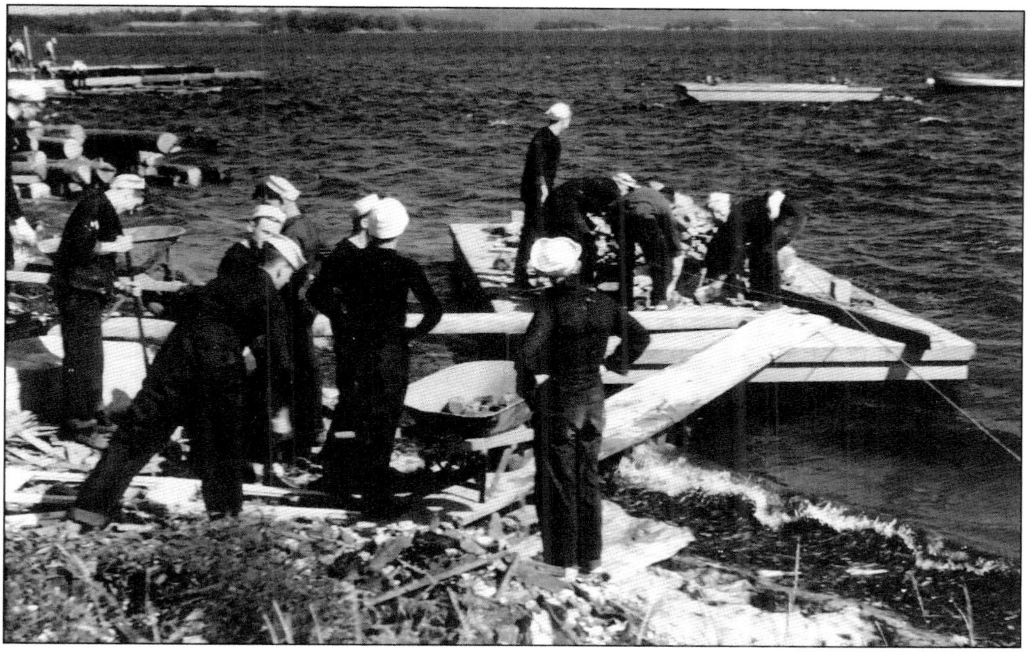

Students from Maine Maritime Academy were required to be in uniform at all times. These midshipmen built the first wharf for the Academy in the early 1940s.

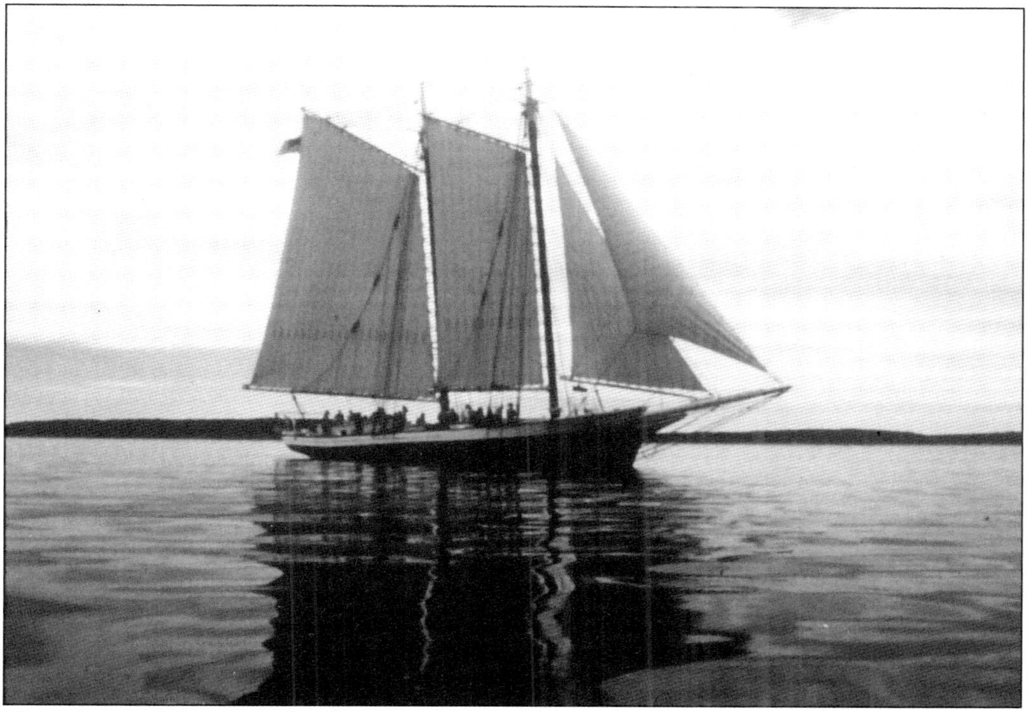

The schooner *Mattie* was the first training ship of Maine Maritime Academy. It left on its first training cruise on Penobscot Bay on May 30, 1942, with twenty-eight members of the Class of 1943. The threat of enemy submarines precluded more extensive trips until after World War II.

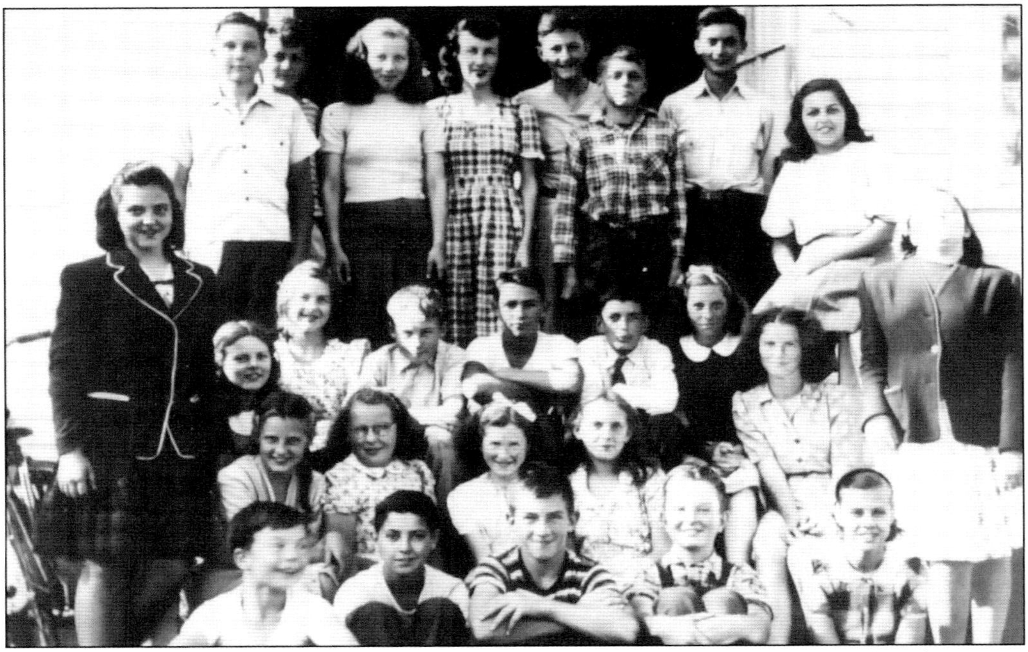

This is a group of sixth, seventh, and eighth-grade students at the Adams School in the 1940s. From left to right are: (front row) Dyke Dennet, Chandler Apt, William McLaughlin, Frank Richardson, and Barbara Little; (second row) Ruth Bowden, Janet Leach, Peggy Bowden, Jean Witham, Connie Gray, Lena Bakeman, and Mary Macomber; (third row) Joan Fernald, Hope Guild, Robert Witham, Wilbert Ordway, Leeland Leach, and Ivey Witham; (back row) Peter Marchoon, Philip Sawyer, Arlene Wood (teacher), Billy Macomber, Lee Perkins, Mark Sawyer, and Marie Kaden.

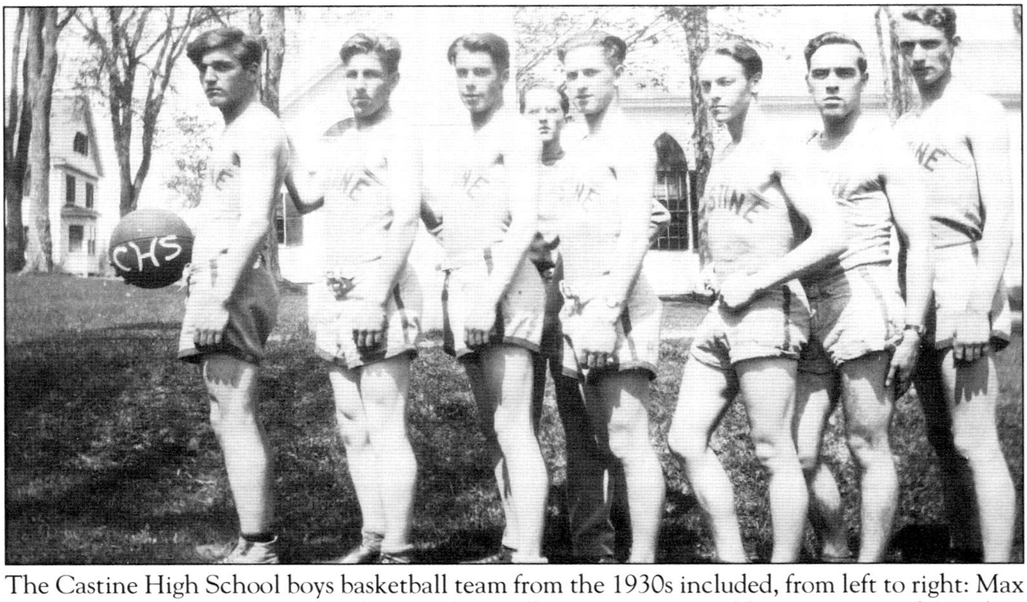

The Castine High School boys basketball team from the 1930s included, from left to right: Max McKinnon, Edward Howard, Eddie Douglass, Billy Patterson, Arnold Veague, Lionel Bowden, "Baylo" Connor, and Durwood McIntyre.

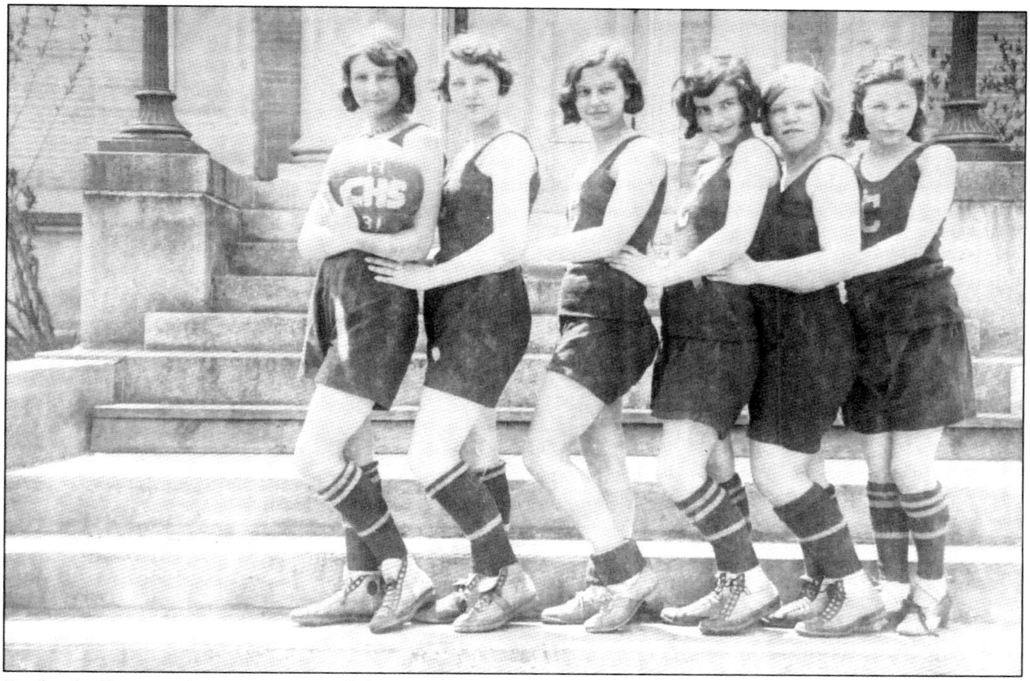

Basketball was a favorite sport of the girls of Castine. In the 1920s and '30s there was an average of only forty students in the high school, so every able-bodied student was needed to fill out the roster of the teams.

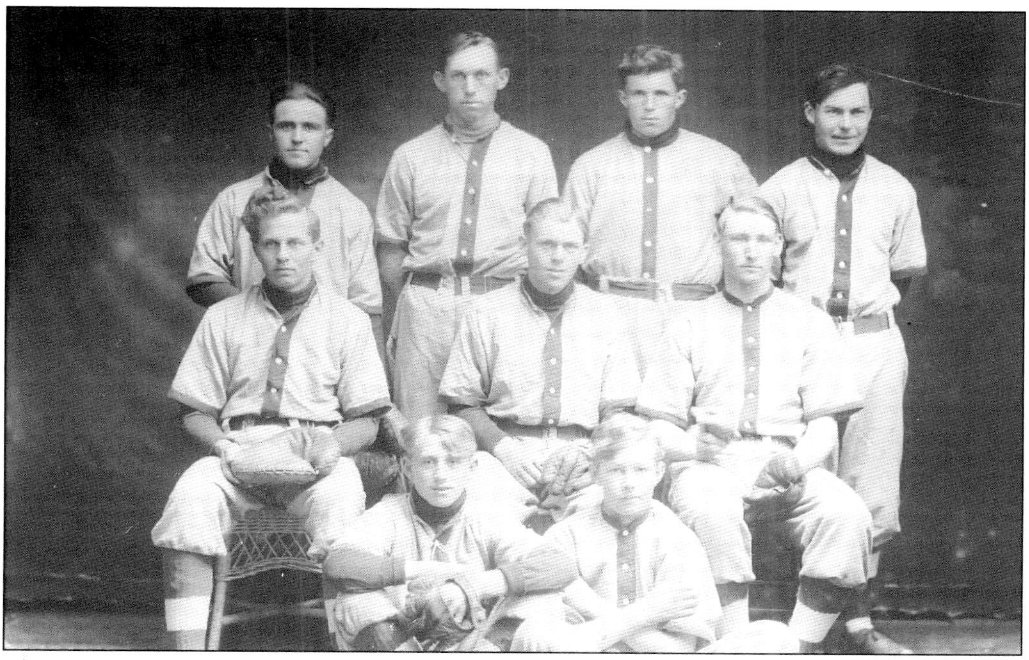

The Castine High School baseball team is shown here, c. 1910.

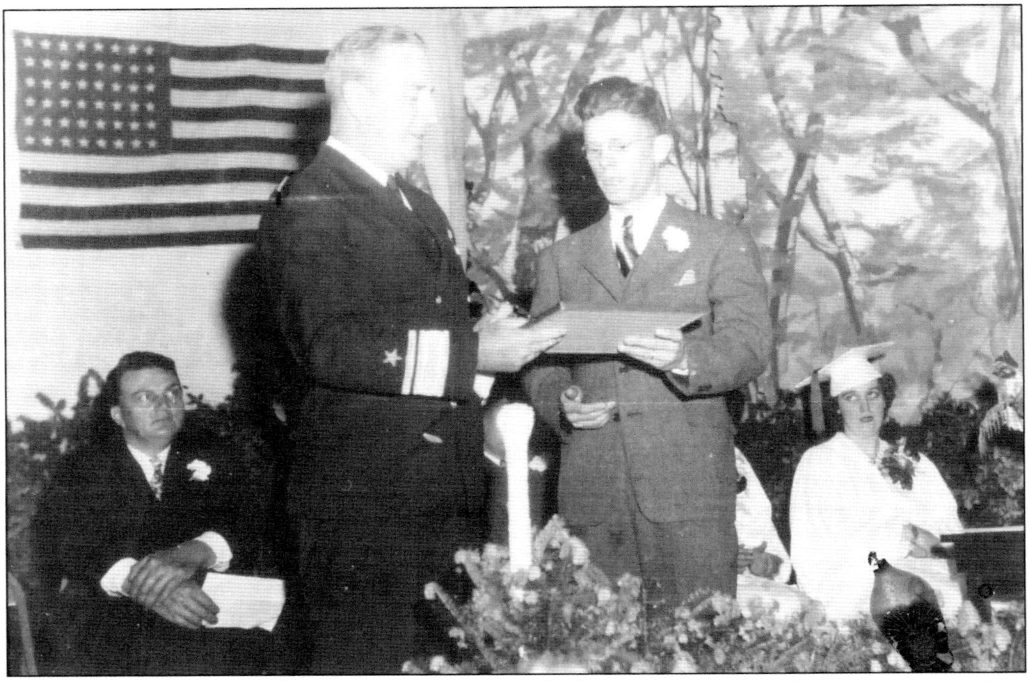

At the Castine High School graduation in 1945, Principal Gardiner Gregory presented an award to Admiral McCall, superintendent of Maine Maritime Academy. Gregory's father had also served as principal of the Castine High School.

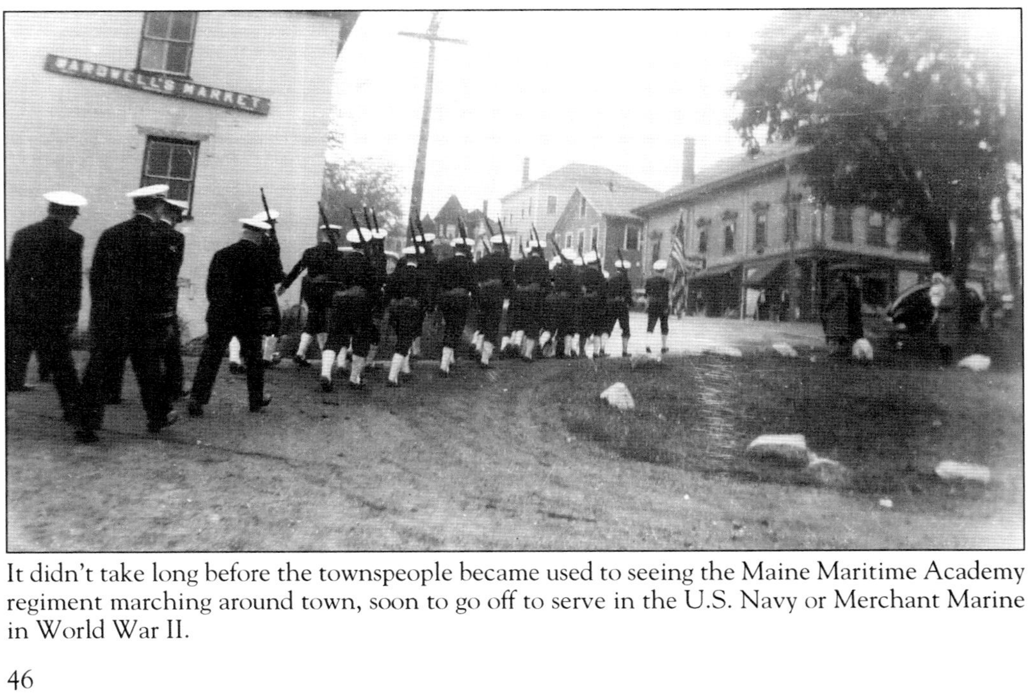

It didn't take long before the townspeople became used to seeing the Maine Maritime Academy regiment marching around town, soon to go off to serve in the U.S. Navy or Merchant Marine in World War II.

Three

Celebrations

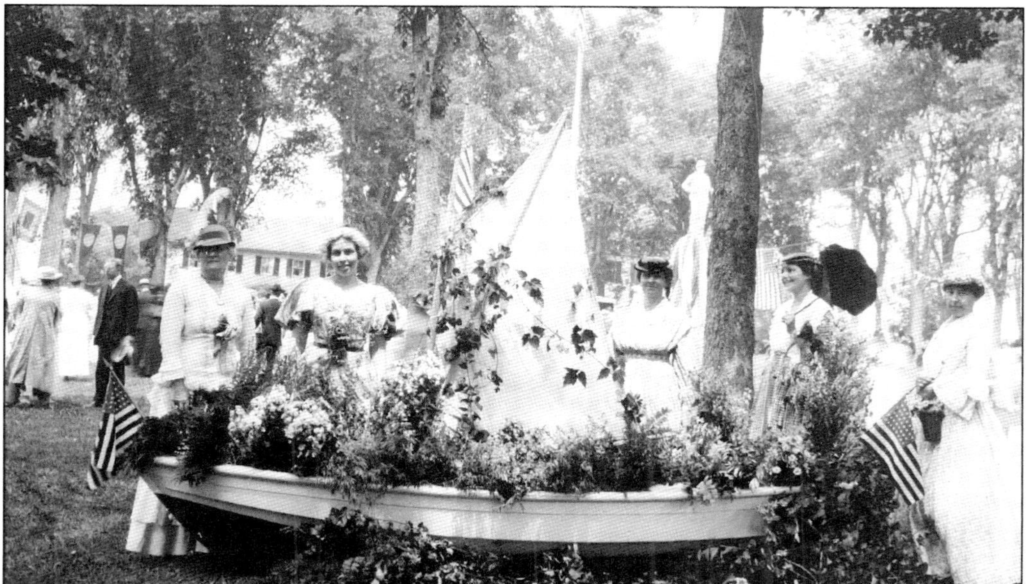

This photograph was taken on the Town Common during the celebration of the centennial of Maine's admission to statehood on August 5, 1920. From left to right are: Louise Wheeler Bartlett, Nan Hooke, Lillian Carpenter, Jean Hooke, and Maud Wheeler, all participants in the Woman's Club pageant.

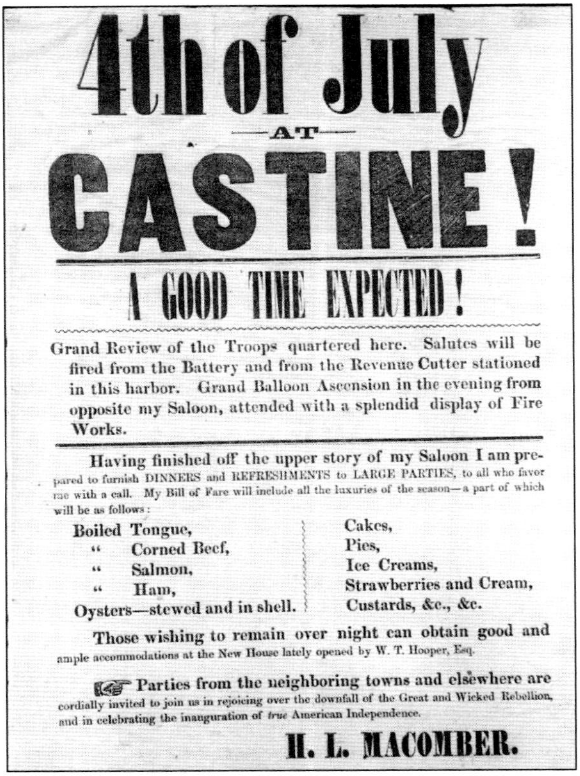

4th of July

—AT—

CASTINE!

A GOOD TIME EXPECTED!

Grand Review of the Troops quartered here. Salutes will be fired from the Battery and from the Revenue Cutter stationed in this harbor. Grand Balloon Ascension in the evening from opposite my Saloon, attended with a splendid display of Fire Works.

Having finished off the upper story of my Saloon I am prepared to furnish DINNERS and REFRESHMENTS to LARGE PARTIES, to all who favor me with a call. My Bill of Fare will include all the luxuries of the season—a part of which will be as follows:

Boiled Tongue,	Cakes,
" Corned Beef,	Pies,
" Salmon,	Ice Creams,
" Ham,	Strawberries and Cream,
Oysters—stewed and in shell.	Custards, &c., &c.

Those wishing to remain over night can obtain good and ample accommodations at the New House lately opened by W. T. Hooper, Esq.

☞ **Parties from the neighboring towns and elsewhere are** cordially invited to join us in rejoicing over the downfall of the Great and Wicked Rebellion, and in celebrating the inauguration of *true* American Independence.

H. L. MACOMBER.

This poster promoted the 1865 Fourth of July Celebration in Castine.

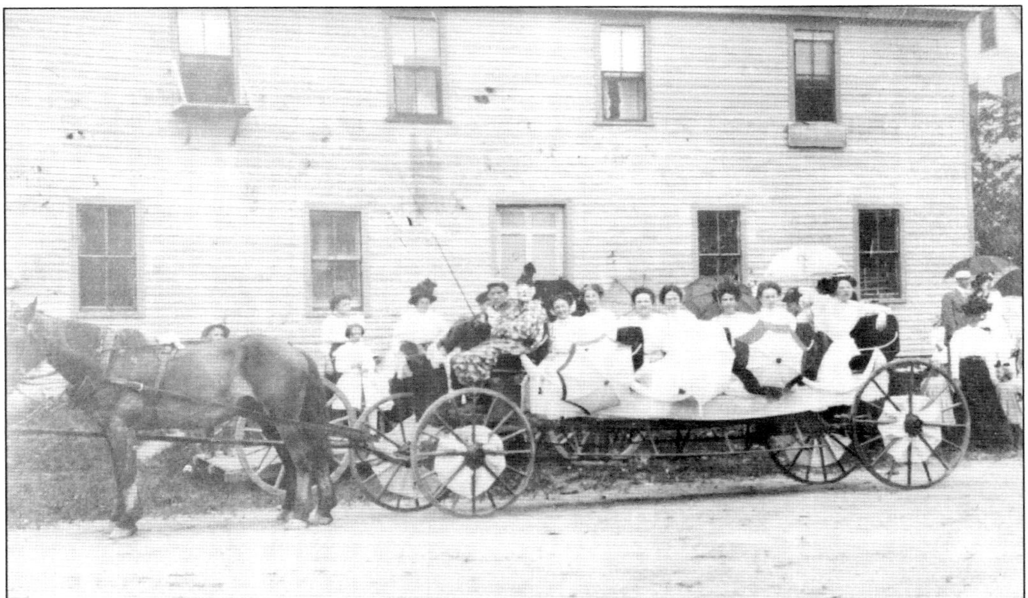

A lively-looking group of young ladies with parasols, escorted by a clown driving the buckboard, was photographed at a Fourth of July parade in the 1880s.

At a Castine Woman's Club house tour in 1920, Miriam and Caroline Walker display their period costumes in front of the Adams-Cate House. Caroline Perkins Walker, the great-granddaughter of John Perkins, who helped settle the town in the 1700s, was one of the founders of the Castine Woman's Club in 1913, and is featured in the book *The Ladies of Castine* by Miriam Anne Bourne (see p. 24).

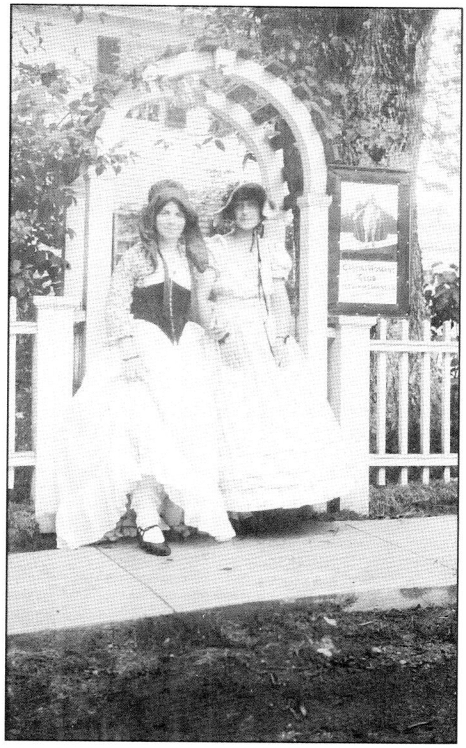

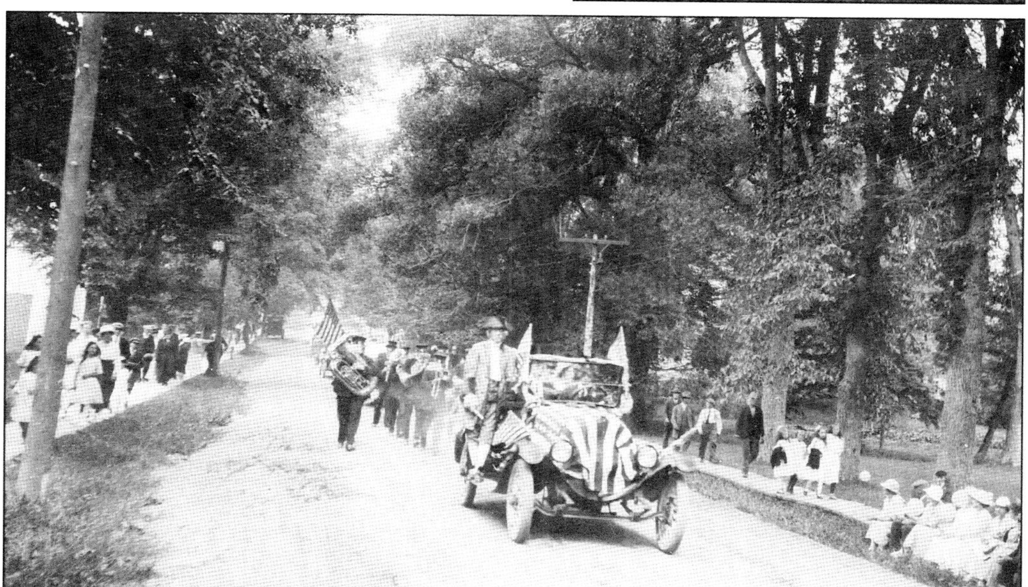

A parade along upper Main Street on August 4, 1919, was a highlight of the Woman's Club carnival. Events of the day included booths on the Common with all kinds of food for sale, while in the parish hall of the Unitarian Church there was an art exhibit. An agricultural fair was held in Emerson Hall, with vegetables, canned goods, jellies, fancy work, and manual training exhibits.

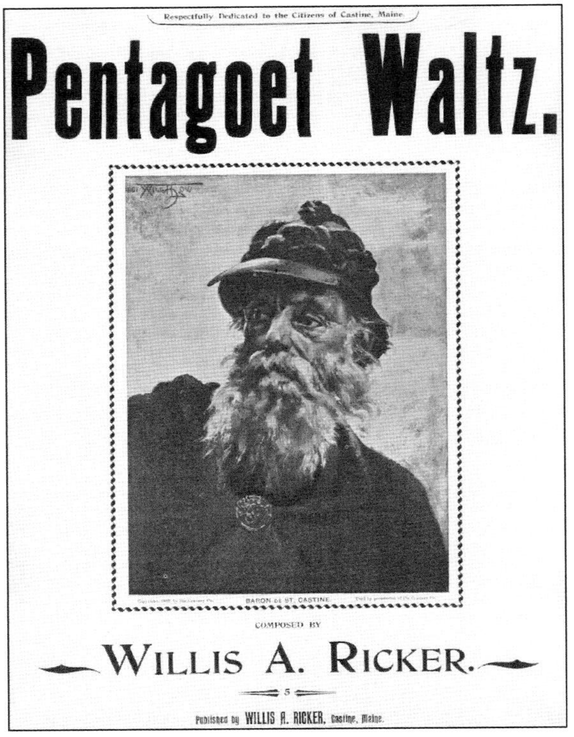

Willis Avon Ricker wrote music, organized and played in a cornet band, and operated a music store on Water Street, which also sold souvenir postcards and other sundries. He also wrote music in the 1890s celebrating the virtues of Castine. The ideal likeness of the Baron de St. Castin is reproduced on the cover of his sheet music (see p. 4).

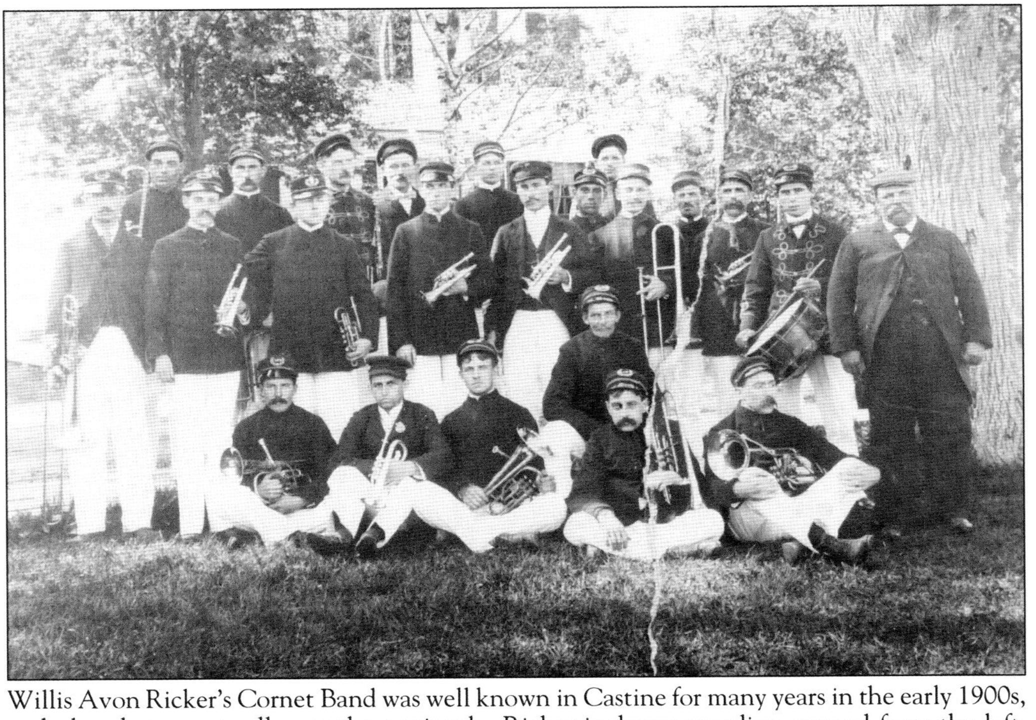

Willis Avon Ricker's Cornet Band was well known in Castine for many years in the early 1900s, and played at events all over the peninsula. Ricker is shown standing, second from the left, holding his cornet.

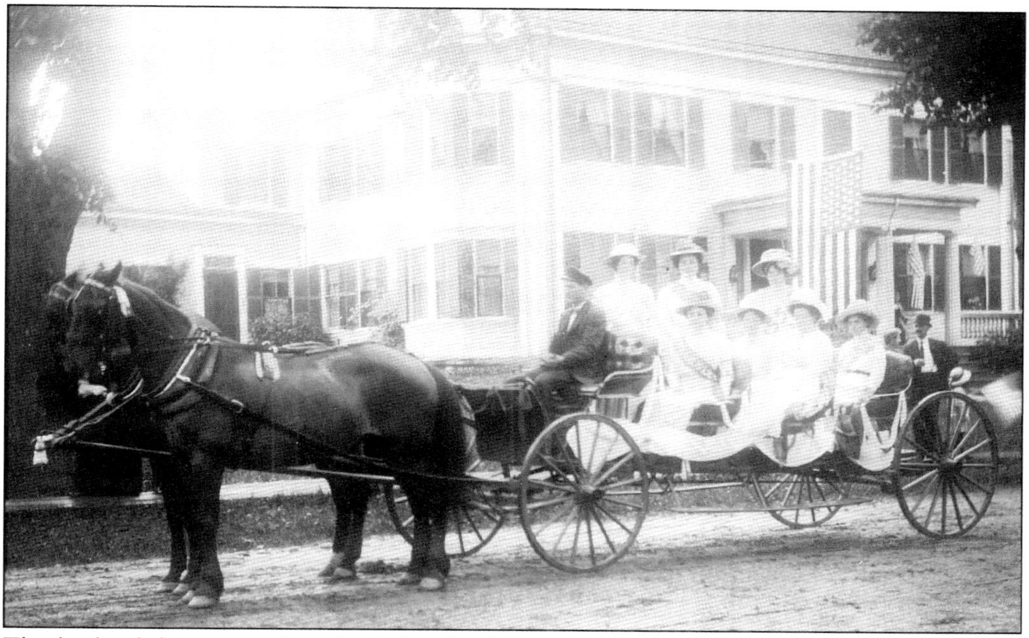

The back of this postcard reads: "This (buck)board took the first prize in the parade today of $5.00 which was divided among eight girls. You will probably see your daughter. We were 'college girls'. I am in the middle of the standing. EJW." The message dates from July 4, 1910.

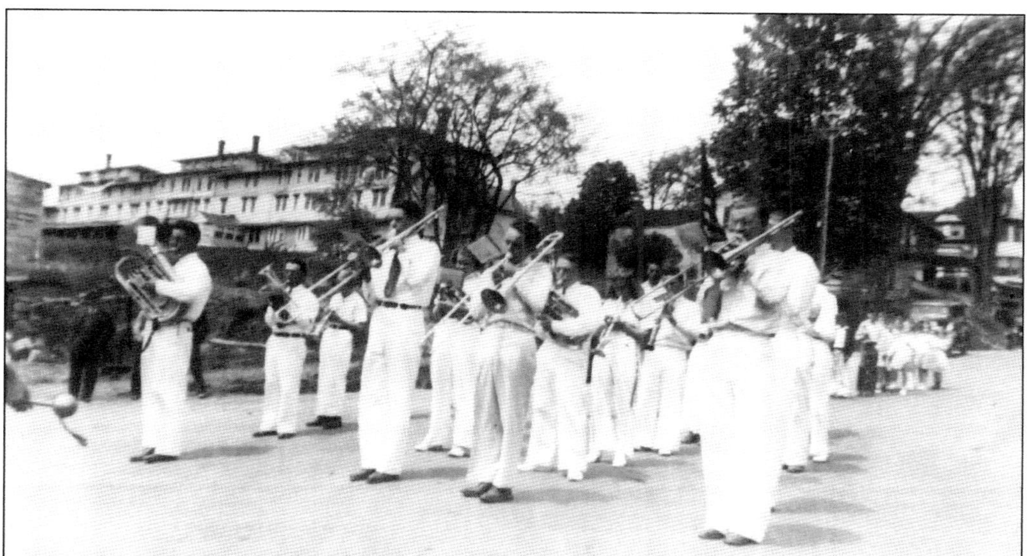

The Castine Band was photographed on the move on July 4, 1939. Castine has a long tradition of Fourth of July parades, dating back to the 1880s. At that time townspeople often paraded in costume. Today the town's children continue that tradition.

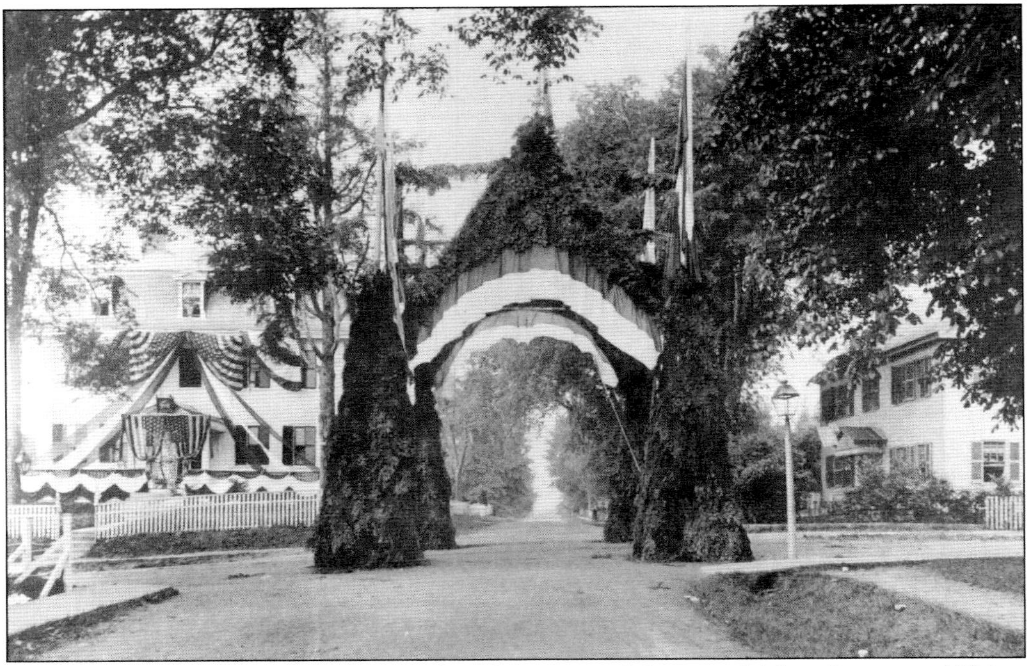

A huge four-sided arch was constructed at the corner of Court and Main Streets in 1896 to mark the centennial of the incorporation of Castine. The arch was covered with fresh evergreen boughs and was large enough for carriages to pass through.

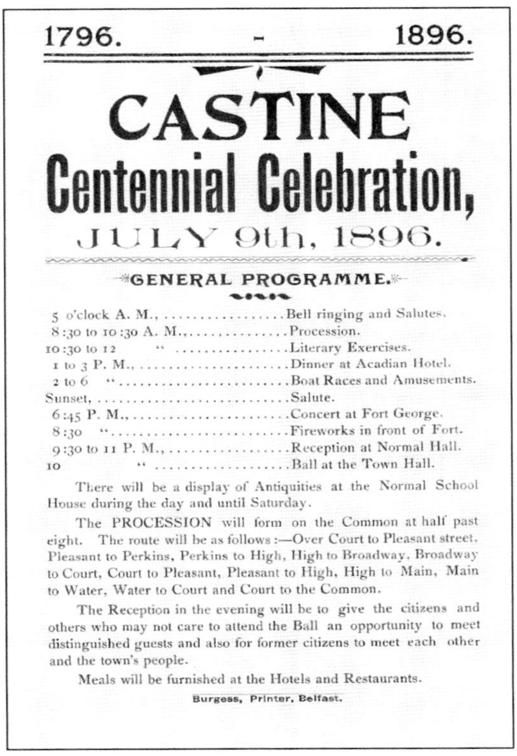

1796. - 1896.

CASTINE
Centennial Celebration,
JULY 9th, 1896.

GENERAL PROGRAMME.

5 o'clock A. M., ...Bell ringing and Salutes.
8:30 to 10:30 A. M., ...Procession.
10:30 to 12 " ....Literary Exercises.
1 to 3 P. M., ...Dinner at Acadian Hotel.
2 to 6 " ....Boat Races and Amusements.
Sunset, ...Salute.
6:45 P. M., ...Concert at Fort George.
8:30 " ....Fireworks in front of Fort.
9:30 to 11 P. M., ...Reception at Normal Hall.
10 " ....Ball at the Town Hall.

There will be a display of Antiquities at the Normal School House during the day and until Saturday.

The PROCESSION will form on the Common at half past eight. The route will be as follows:—Over Court to Pleasant street, Pleasant to Perkins, Perkins to High, High to Broadway, Broadway to Court, Court to Pleasant, Pleasant to High, High to Main, Main to Water, Water to Court and Court to the Common.

The Reception in the evening will be to give the citizens and others who may not care to attend the Ball an opportunity to meet distinguished guests and also for former citizens to meet each other and the town's people.

Meals will be furnished at the Hotels and Restaurants.

Burgess, Printer, Belfast.

Events at the Castine Centennial Celebration on July 9, 1896, included a parade through decorated streets, literary exercises at the Trinitarian Church, boat races, and a concert at sunset at Fort George, followed by fireworks in front of the fort, culminating in a grand ball at thetown hall.

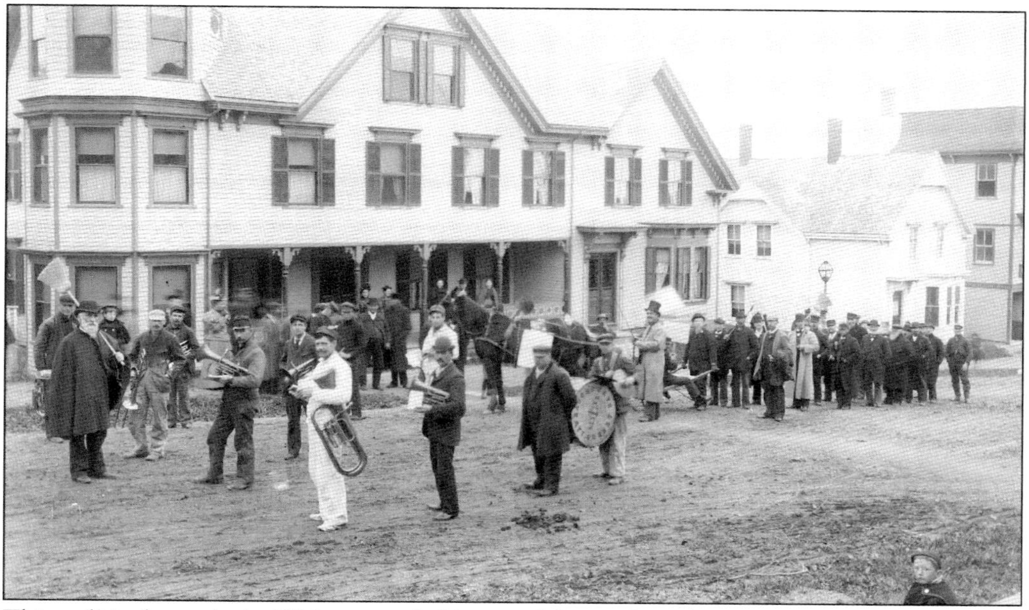

This political parade in 1896 was probably to celebrate the "clean sweep" of the election of President McKinley and the Republicans. Some of the participants have been identified as: Edward Davies (with the broom), Ed and Roll Brown (with the drum), Frank Rea (driving the horse), and John Gardner (with a large instrument). John Vogell is in a wheelbarrow behind the horse, being pushed up Main Street after winning a bet.

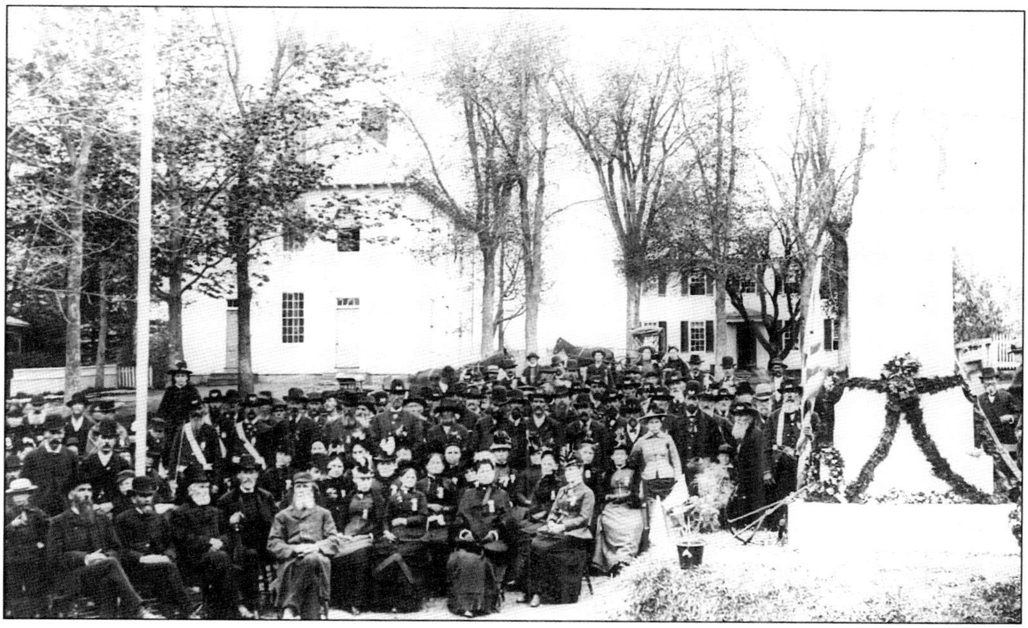

The dedication of the Civil War monument on the Town Common was held on May 30, 1887, with Dr. George A. Wheeler as the key speaker. Castine sent 157 of its men to fight in Company B, 1st Regiment, 17th Division of the State Militia.

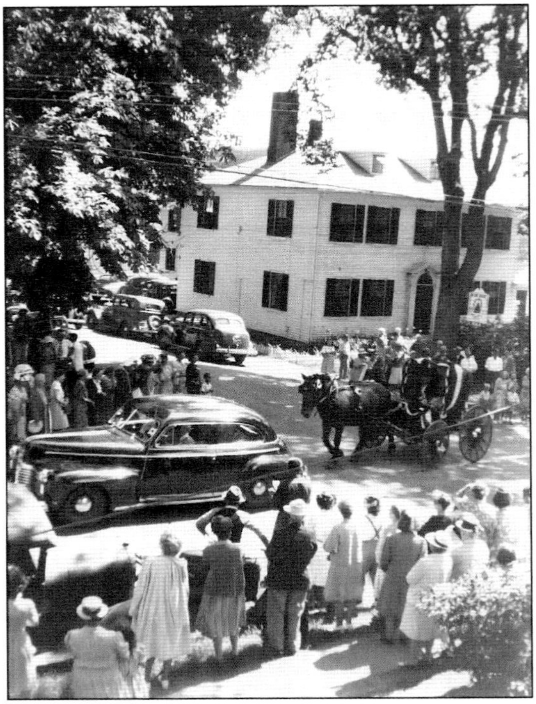

In this 1940s photograph of a Memorial Day parade at the corner of Court and Main Streets, the sign in front of the house in the background reads "Blake House." It was one of many small hotels in Castine at that time.

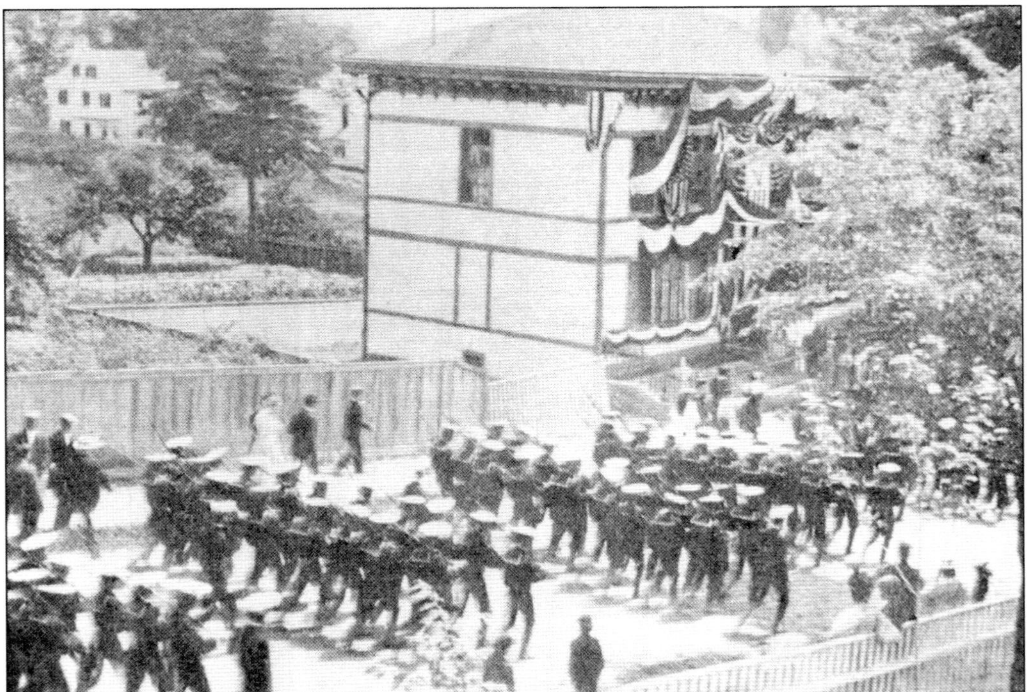

The crews of the United States cruiser *Columbia* and the revenue cutter *Levi Woodbury*, anchored in the harbor along with many visiting yachts, joined in a parade down Main Street at the Castine Centennial Celebration on July 9, 1896.

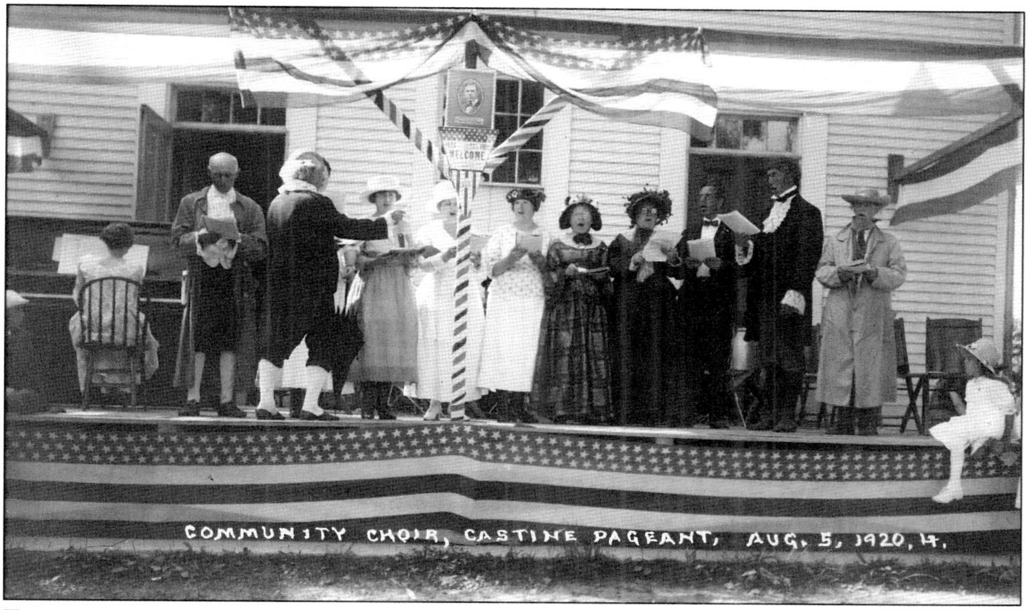

Town committees and the Woman's Club worked together to hold a carnival on August 5, 1920, commemorating Maine's centennial. A performance by a community choir was just one of the many events which took place.

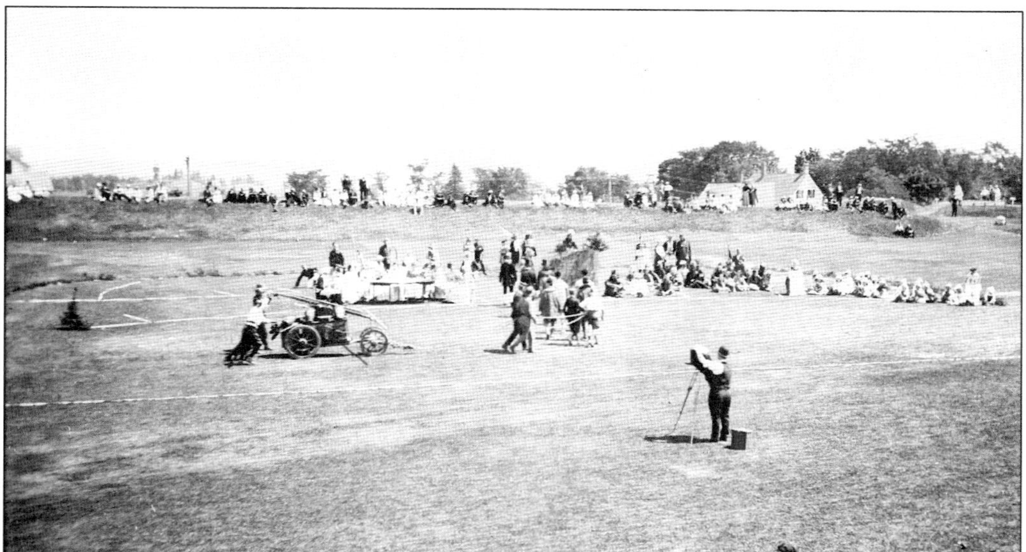

There was also a historical pageant in Fort George as part of the festivities. The pageant presented a review of Castine history from the time of the first Indian tribes, ending with the march of the World War I veterans.

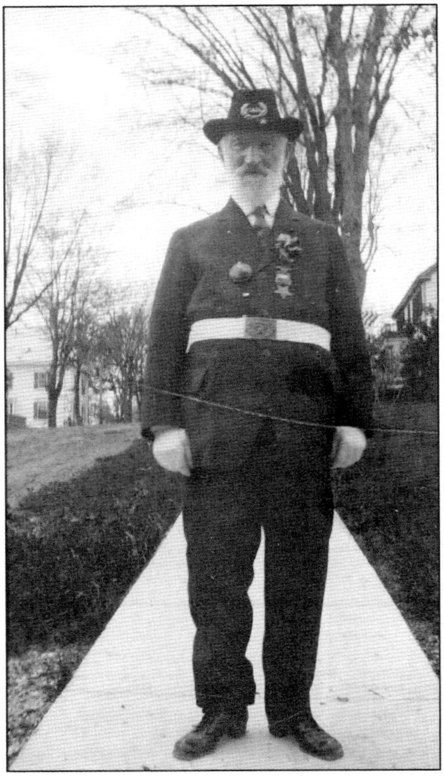

Dr. George A. Wheeler was the town doctor and a selectman for many years. A Civil War veteran, he served on the school board and was involved with every town committee requiring thoughtful consideration. The first town historian, he wrote *Castine, Past and Present* and *History of Castine*. He had a reading knowledge of eight languages, and at the age of eighty-five, began to study Russian (see pp. 25 and 27).

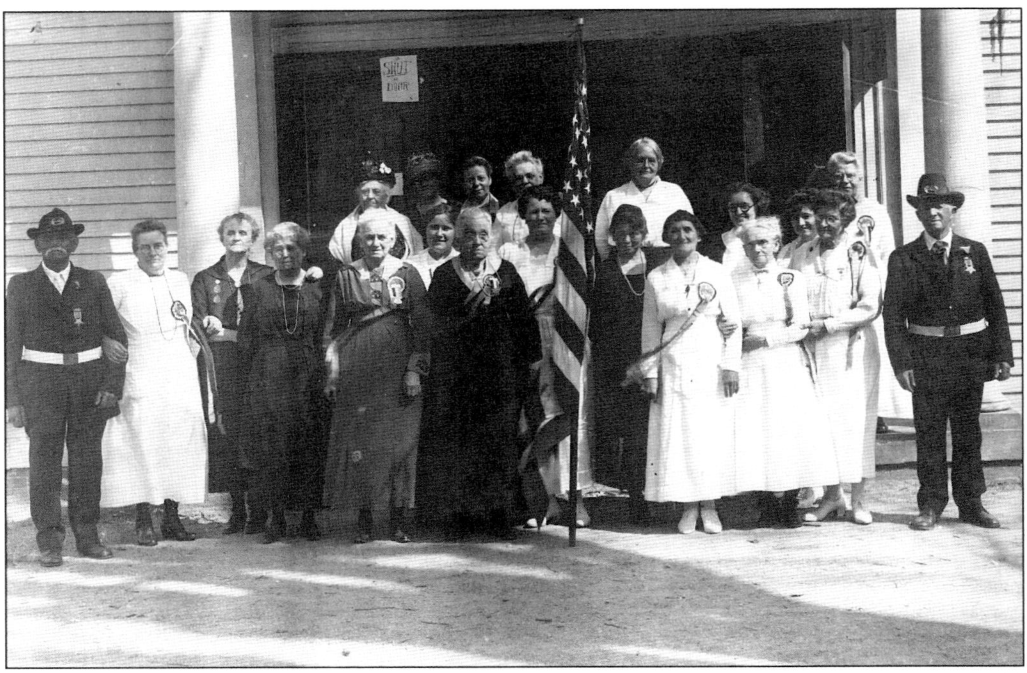

Civil War veterans and war widows are shown here *c.* early 1900s, in front of Emerson Hall, which was built as the town hall in 1901.

Four

Working Castine

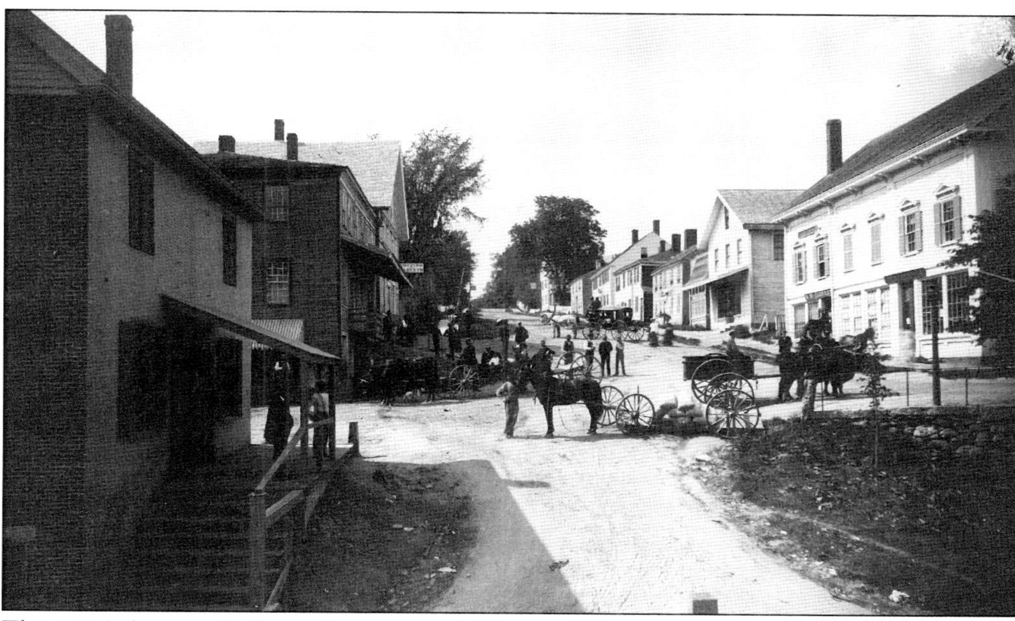

This 1885 photograph shows the commercial heart of Castine.

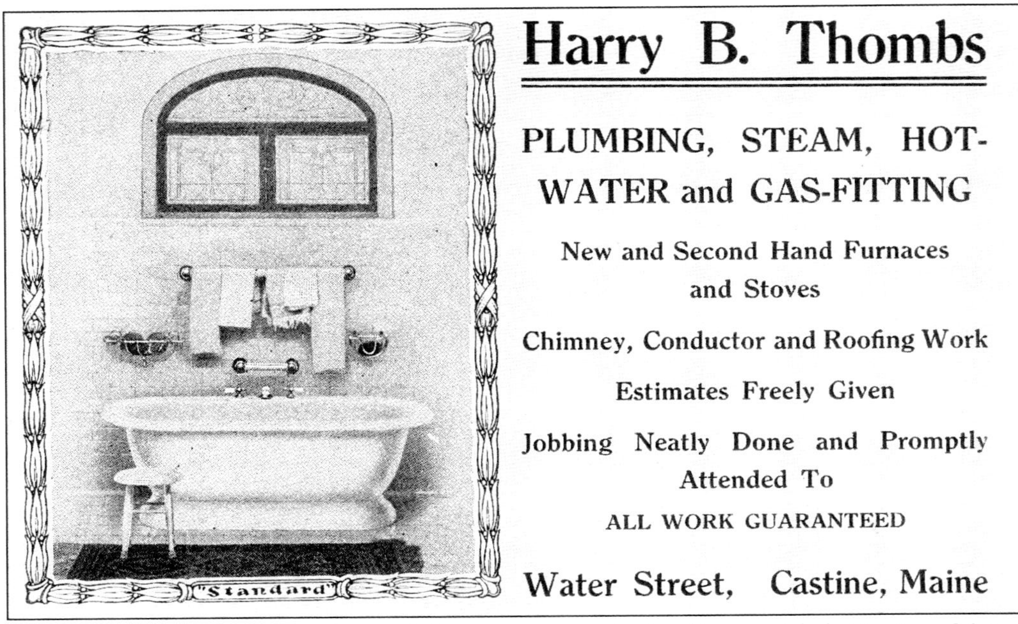

This advertisement appeared c. 1911 in a souvenir booklet entitled *Castine, Maine, Ancient Pentagoet*.

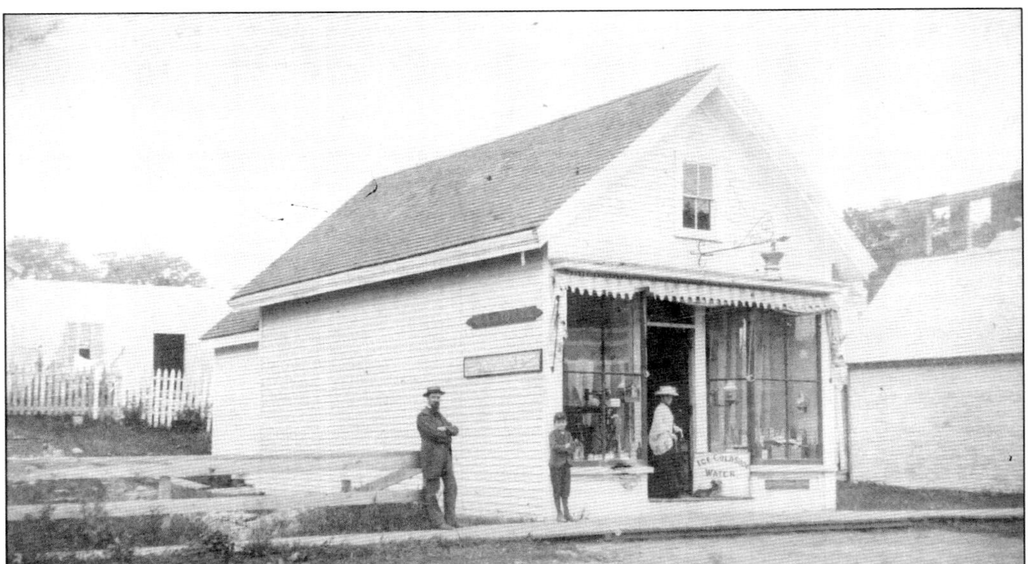

The building that housed Willis Avon Ricker's drug store on Water Street, shown here *c.* 1880, was torn down in the 1940s.

Al Clark and his wife Marion conducted a successful business for many years in their general store on Water Street, selling groceries, hardware, stoves, and patchwork quilts made by Marion in her "spare time." Clark also owned the Shetola House and a farm on Route 166, which he bought so that he could have a supply of fresh produce to sell. He had several vessels, including a 36-foot sloop for sailing parties from the hotel. He and his wife raised seven foster sons (see p. 115).

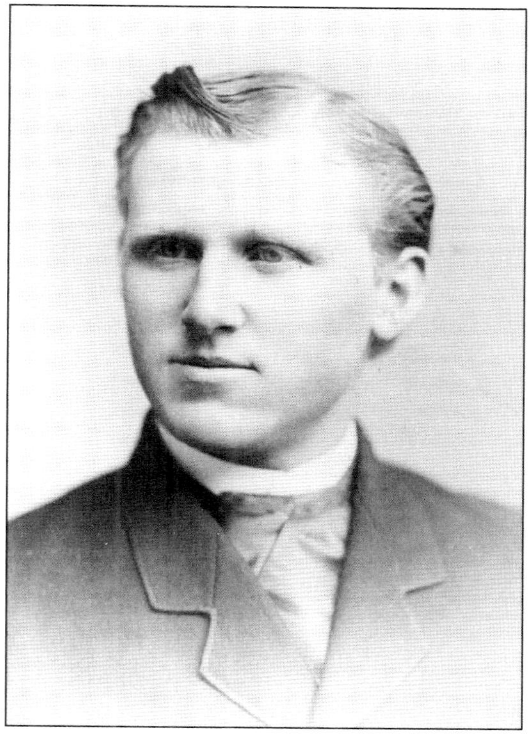

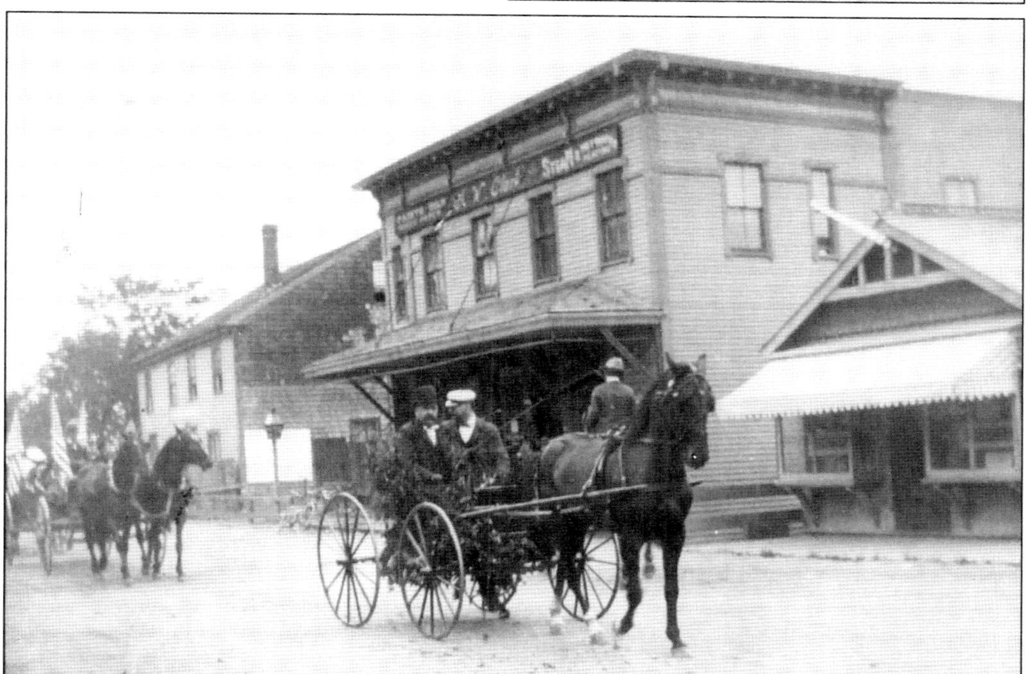

This little building on Water Street was built in 1882 to house the Walter Bartram Barbershop. In 1892 it became a telephone office with ten subscribers. The large building next to it was A.W. Clark's.

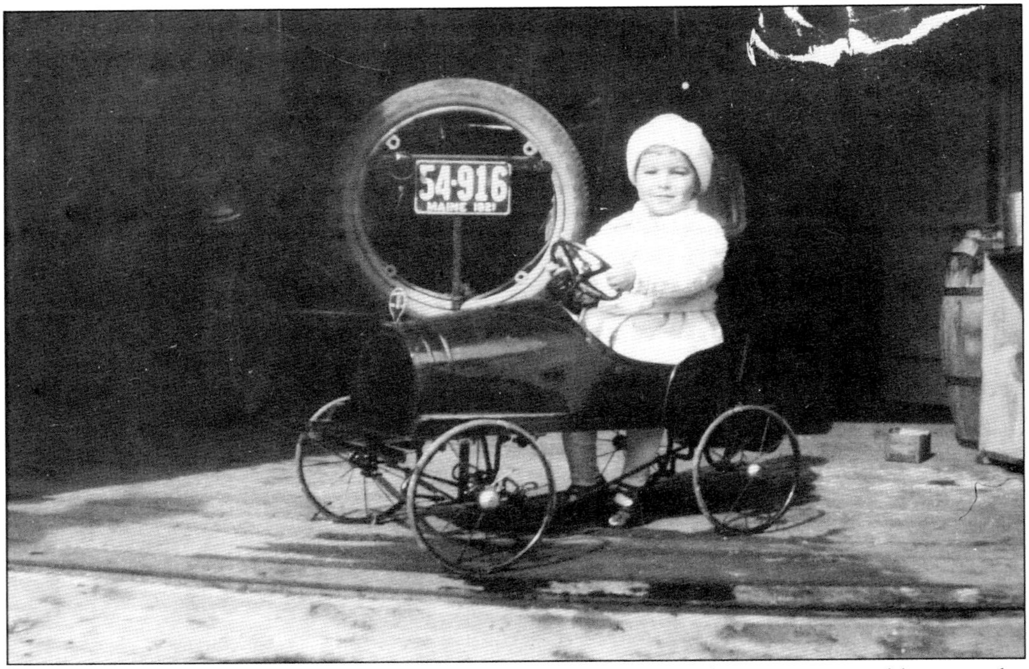

It seems fitting that little Ken Hooper was photographed sitting in his own convertible, since the Hooper family was so involved in different aspects of transportation in Castine over the years.

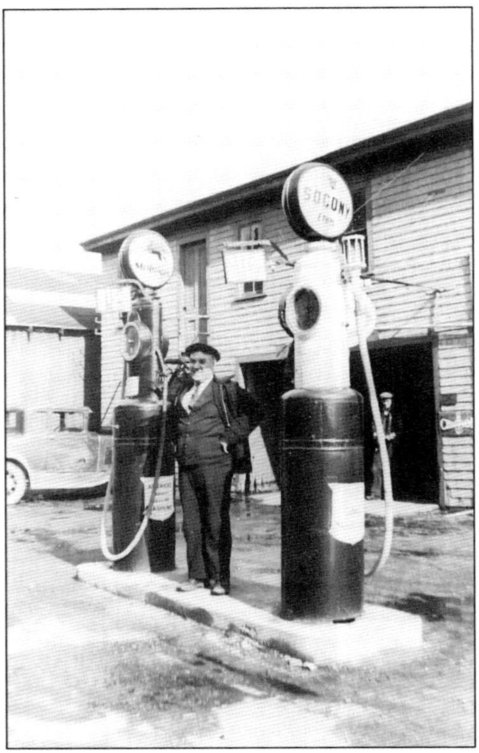

The Hooper family, who ran the livery stable in the 1800s, managed to adapt to the changes brought in the twentieth century and ran this garage for many years on Sea Street. Merton Hooper is at the pumps, *c.* 1930, when regular gas was 20¢ a gallon and hi-test was 22¢.

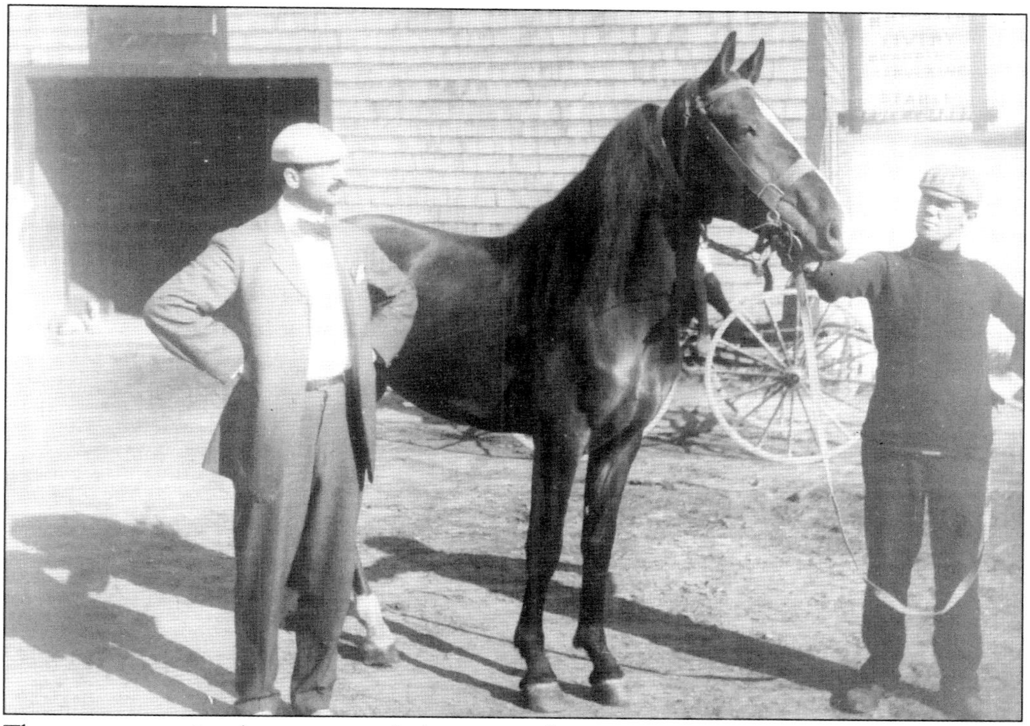

These men are in the process of choosing a horse to rent in 1911 from the Hooper Livery Stable.

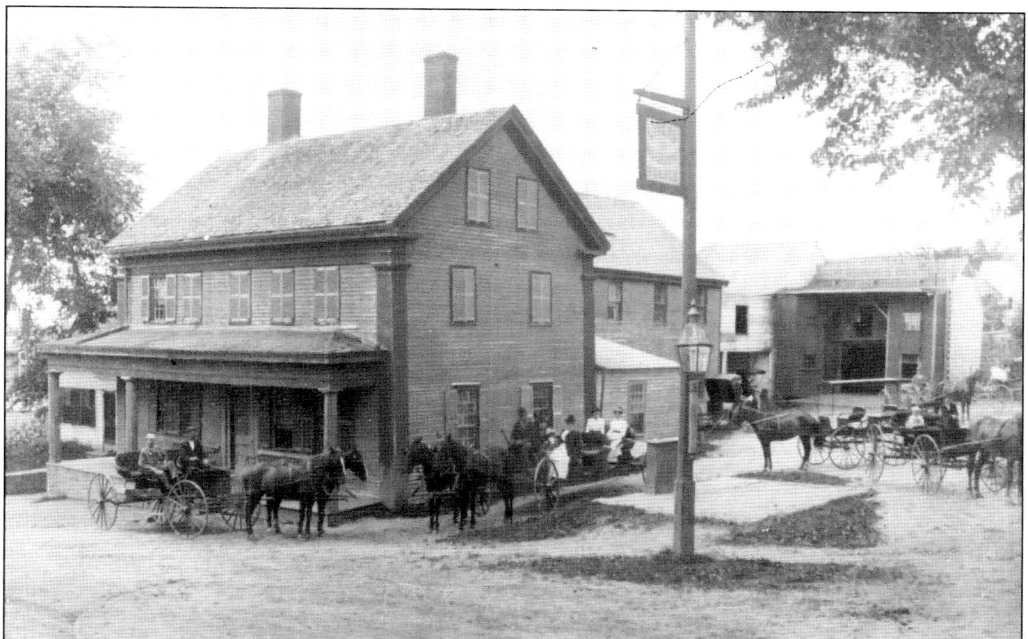

The William Hooper Livery Stable and Boarding House on Main Street is shown here. The Hoopers made carriages, and rented buckboards, carriages, and horses in the late 1800s.

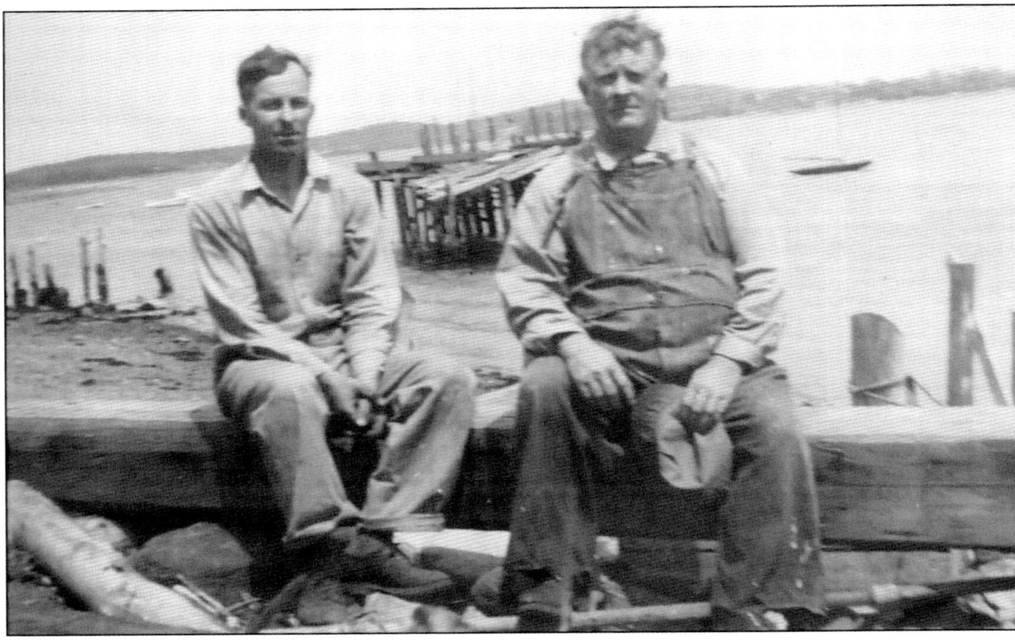

Mace Eaton (right), with his son Alonzo, was one of the last shipwrights in Castine. Mace came to Castine in 1925 with his wife and five children from Deer Isle. He built boats on the beach in front of his house near the site of the present Castine Yacht Club, including the *Arlene Booth*, c. 1926, a 56-foot schooner—his first big boat (see below). In 1939 he purchased what is today Eaton's Boatyard. The large building on the shore of the harbor had been used as a salt shed, a lumber yard, a stable, and a creamery. Enlarged since the early days, the boatyard has continued to the present. Mace designed and built the Castine-class sailboats, beginning with 16-foot boats in 1937. Later modified to 18-foot boats, the daysailers still comprise the racing fleet of the Castine Yacht Club (see p. 66).

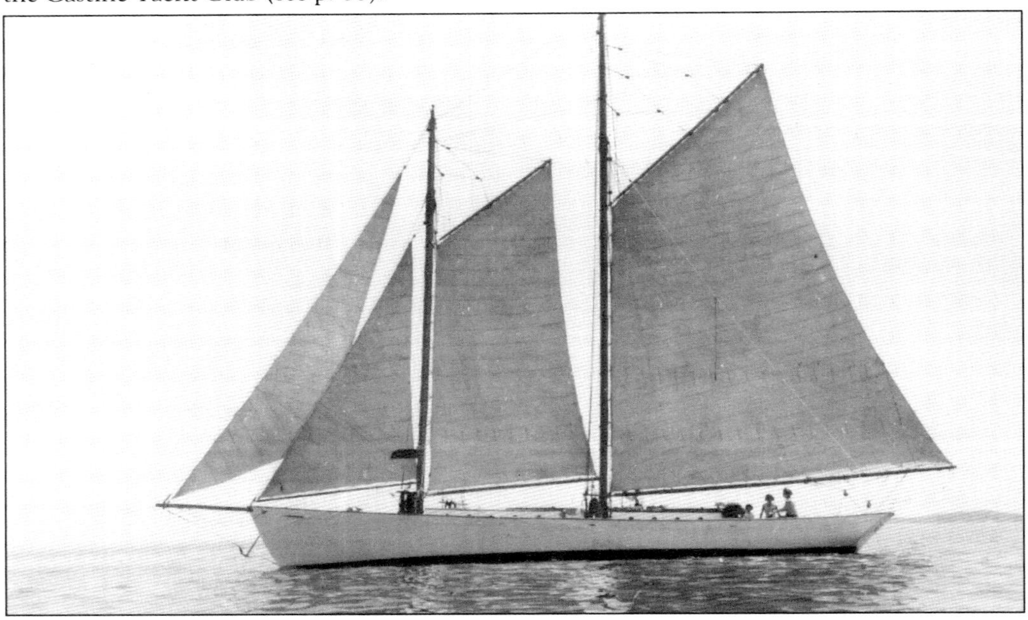

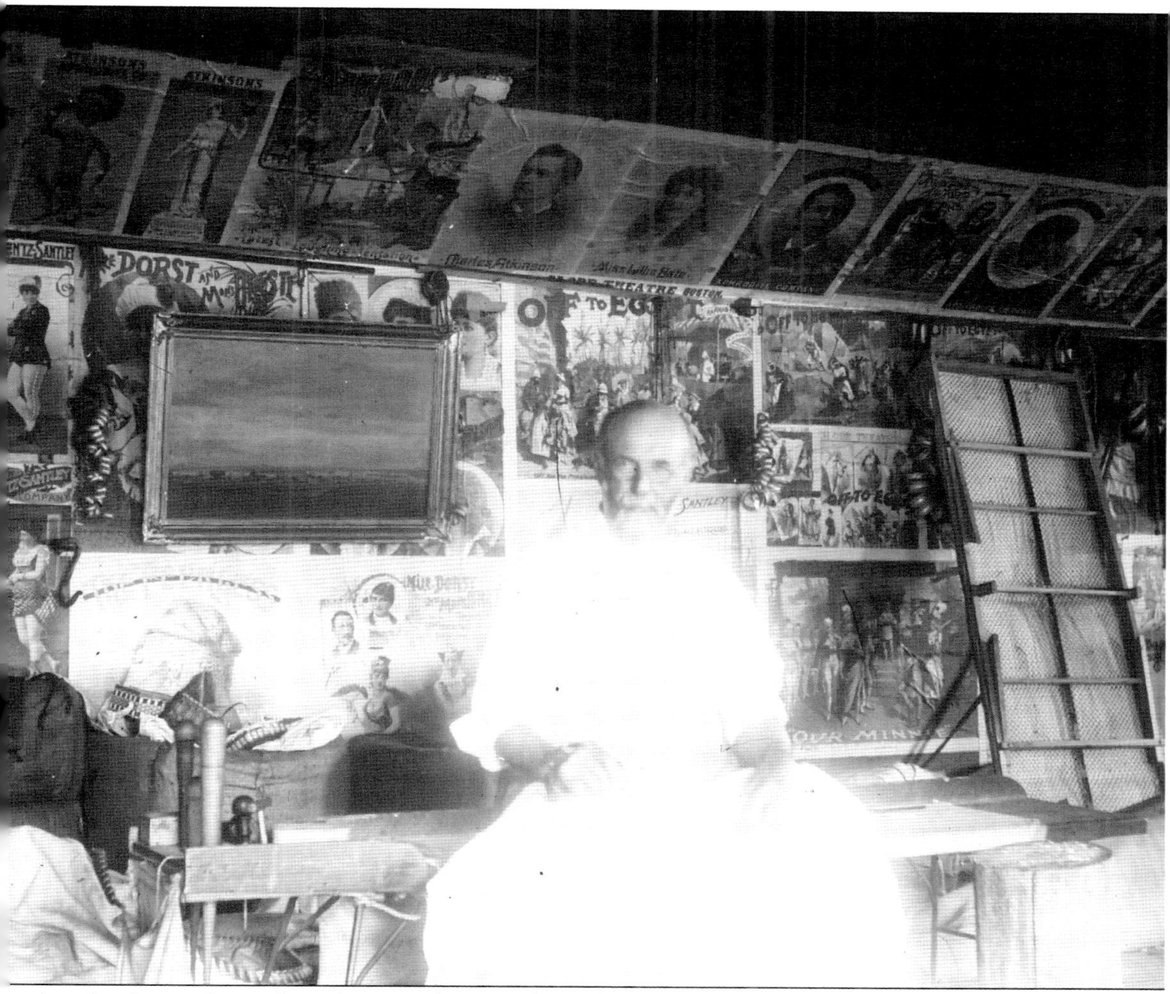

A sailmaker is shown here busy working in the sail loft upstairs at Dennett's Wharf. In the background are vaudeville posters brought back from Boston by sea captains for Millard Dennett. The painting on the left, *Castine from Ft. George* by Fitz Hugh Lane, is one of many he painted in the Castine area. Why it's in the sail loft is a puzzle.

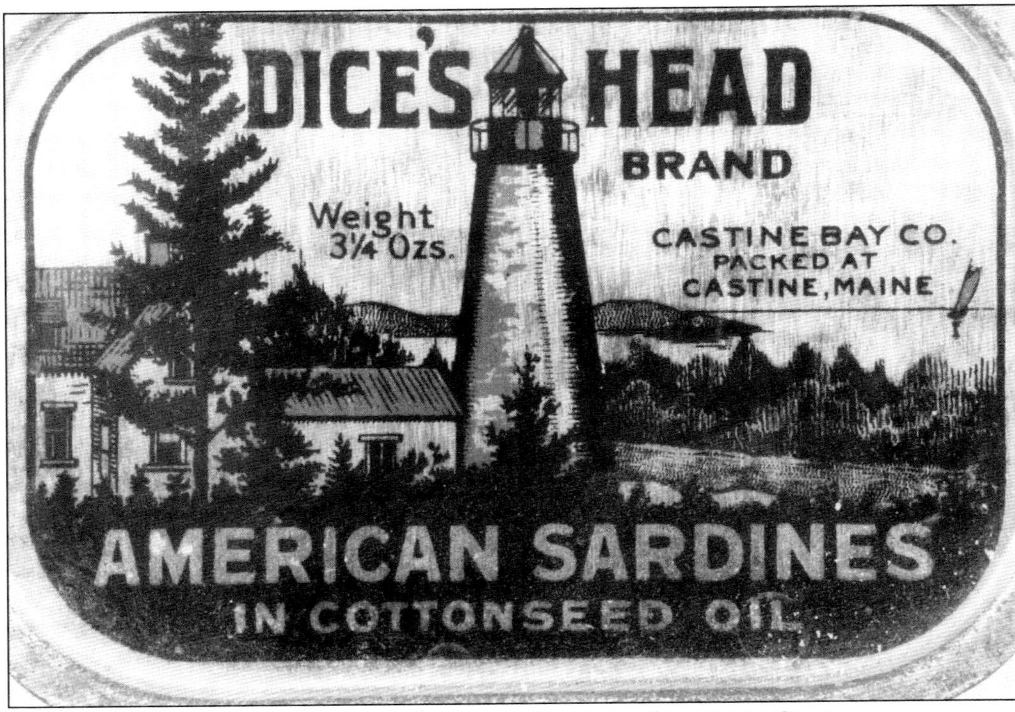

The Castine Bay Company was one of many small canning factories in Castine.

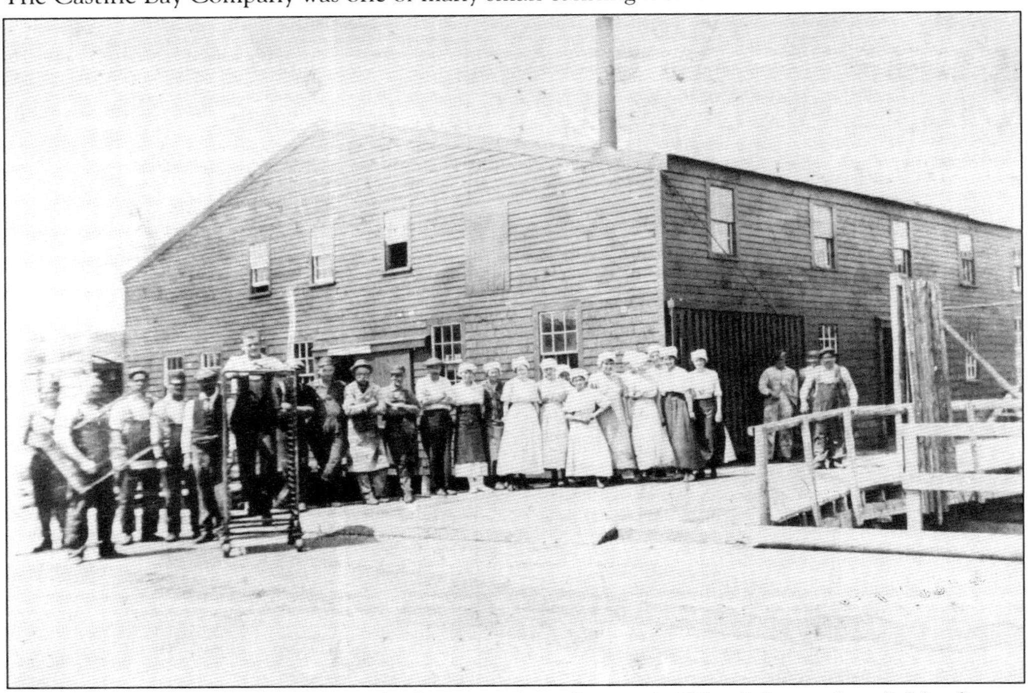

The Castine Sardine Factory was built in 1919 on Sargent's Wharf. It employed fifty-five to sixty people. It was in operation until 1939. Many residents still remember the sardine factory, and not fondly.

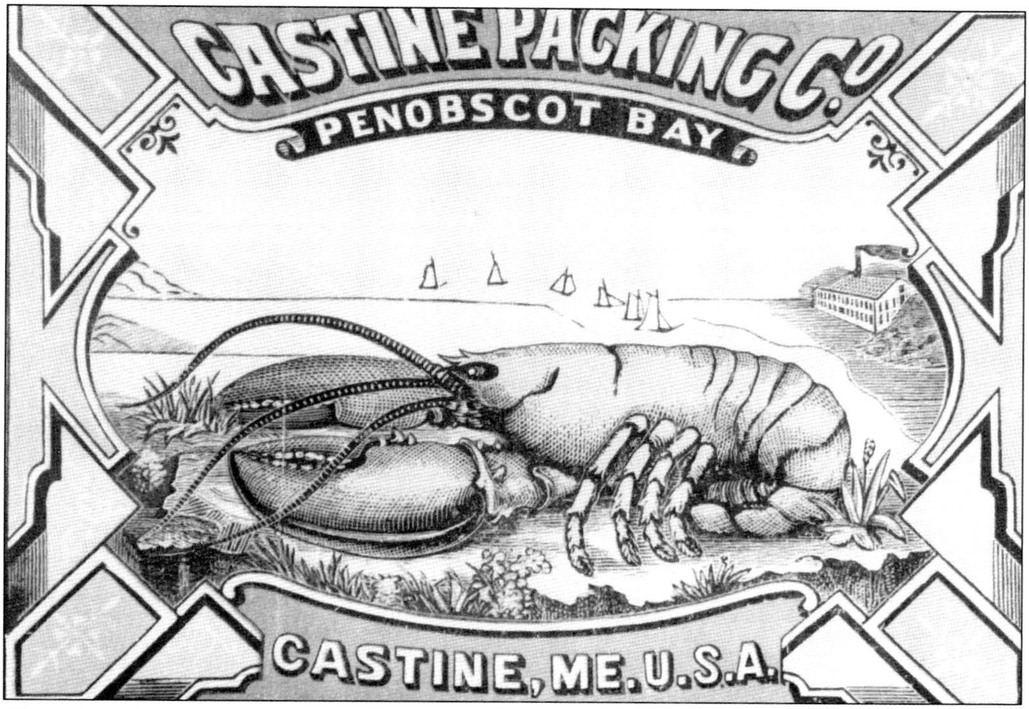

There have been several canning factories in Castine over the years, dating back to the 1870s. These businesses canned sardines, lobster, salmon, herring, fruit, and even mutton. One was the A.H. Mayo Canning Factory, which operated on Sea Street from 1910 until 1920.

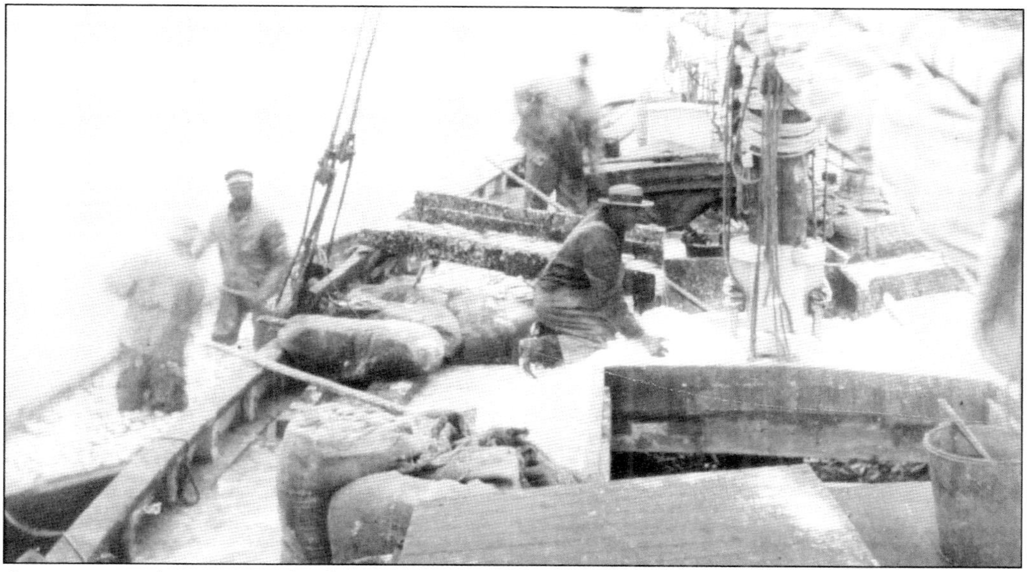

Castine served as a port of call, customs district, and salt depository for this part of the world. With all this activity, there were times when there were up to five hundred vessels in the harbor. Salt was transported and stored here from Liverpool, England, and Cadiz, Spain. Fisherman working the Grand Banks used this salt to preserve their catches. This photograph shows herring being salted right off the ship.

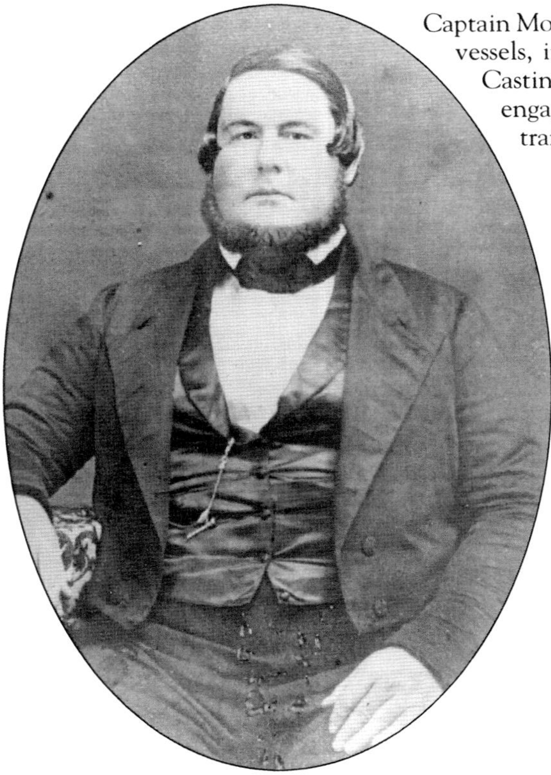

Captain Moses Gay Jr. (1816–1859) was master of many vessels, including the square-rigged *Adams*, built in Castine in 1840. Large sailing ships like the *Adams* engaged in extensive and highly-profitable transatlantic trade.

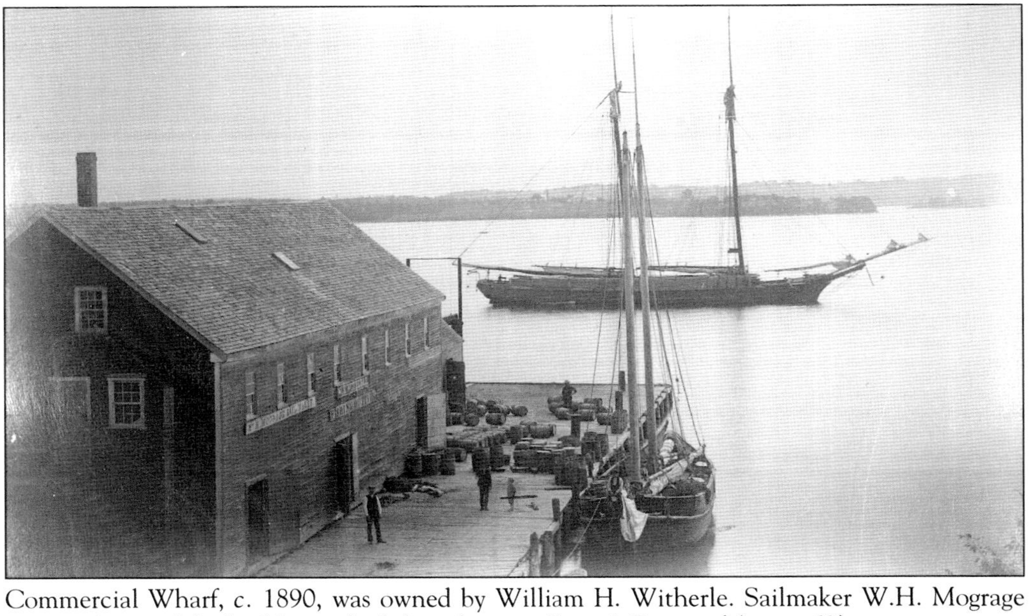

Commercial Wharf, *c.* 1890, was owned by William H. Witherle. Sailmaker W.H. Mograge occupied part of the building, which later became Eaton's Boatyard (see p. 62).

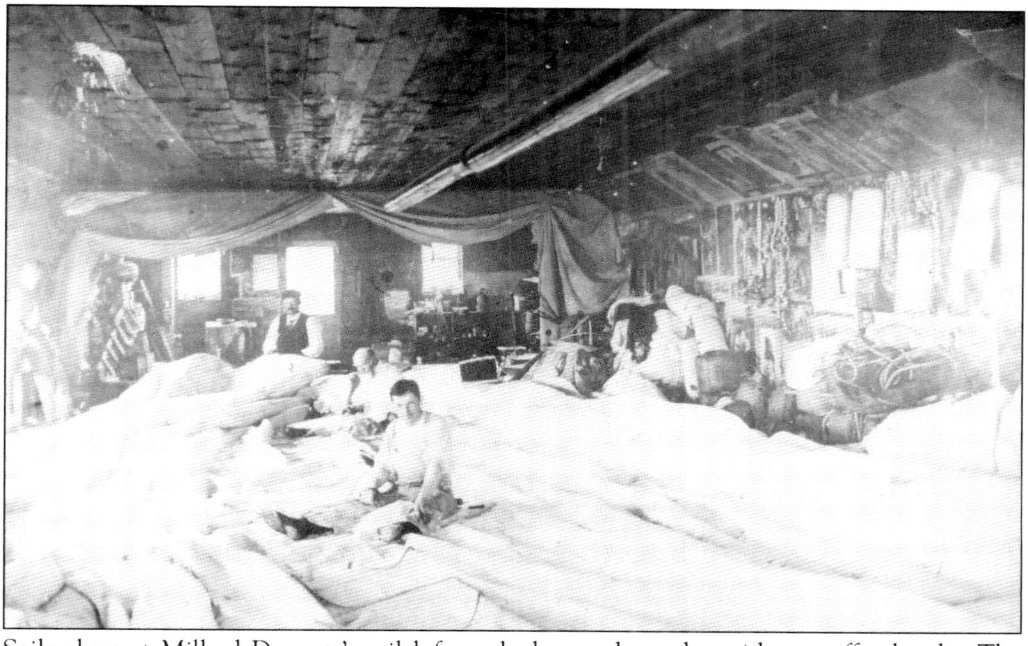

Sailmakers at Millard Dennett's sail loft worked a ten-hour day without coffee breaks. The prevailing rate was 1 1/2¢ a yard for sewing, which was all done by hand. A good sailmaker could sew 300 yards a day.

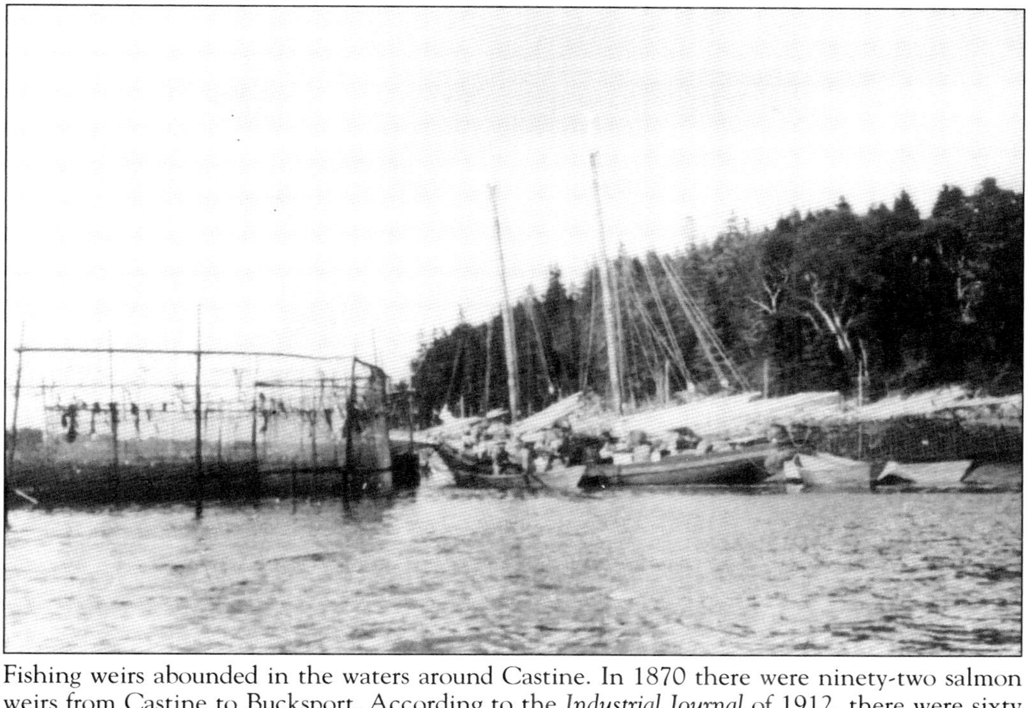

Fishing weirs abounded in the waters around Castine. In 1870 there were ninety-two salmon weirs from Castine to Bucksport. According to the *Industrial Journal* of 1912, there were sixty herring weirs in Bagaduce waters. A weir off Dyce's Head once held the record for a yearly catch of salmon, having taken in over 1,600 pounds of fish.

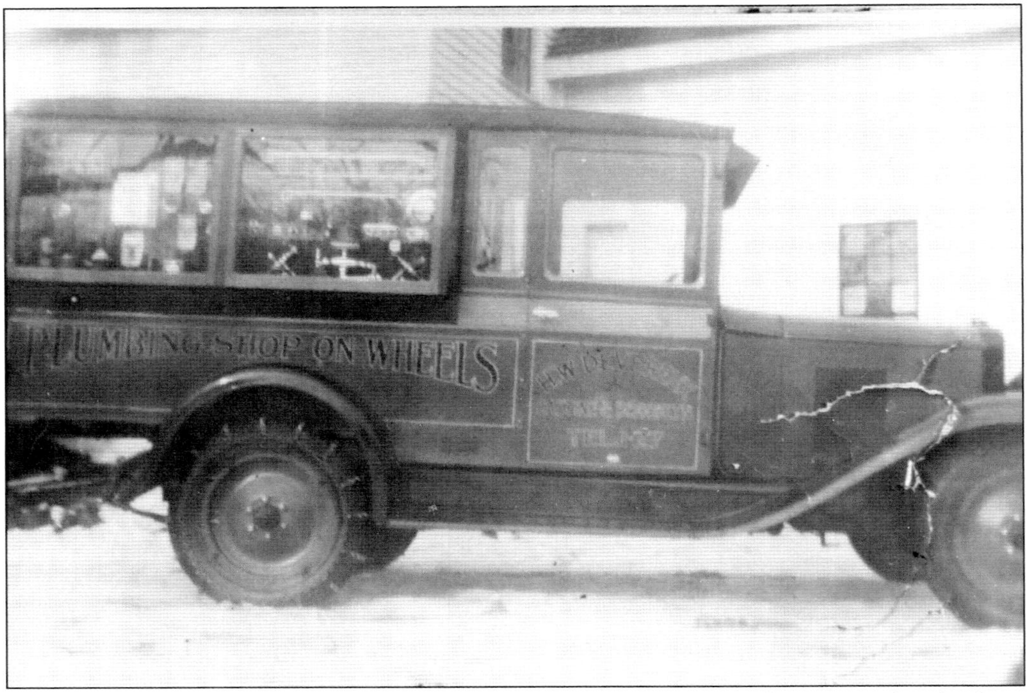

The "Plumbing Shop on Wheels," owned by H.W. Devereux, stood ready to cover the plumbing needs of this rural community.

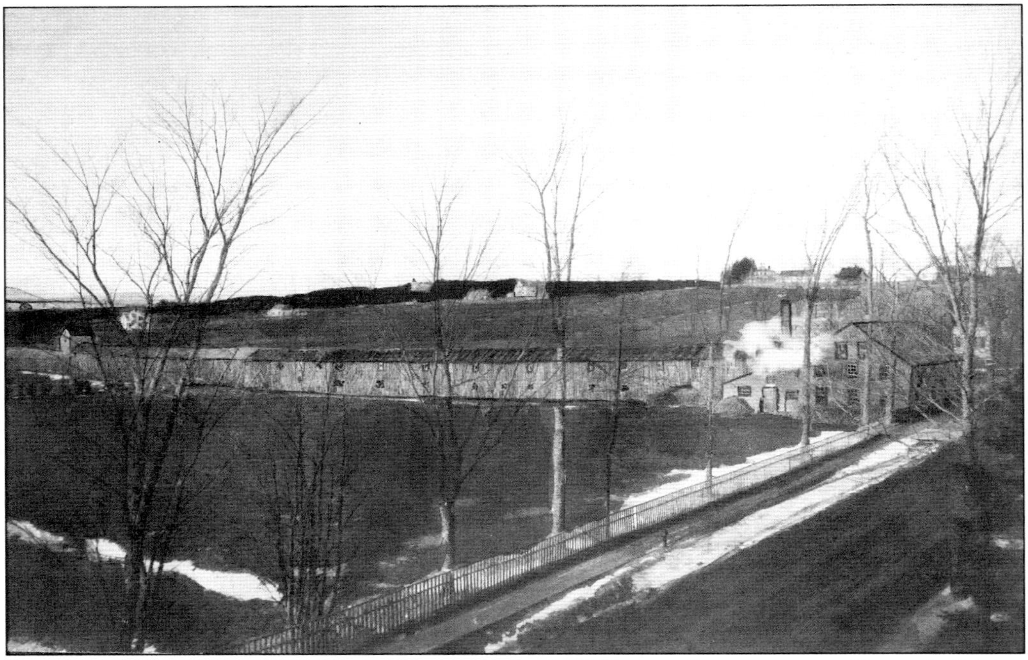

Known as the Old Rope Walk, the factory of the J.W.Dresser Company actually made fishing line known as Castine Cod and Mackerel line. There were several rope walks in various locations around town; this one stood where Richie Field at Maine Maritime Academy is now.

Alva Clement and Noah Brooks Hooper cut ice at the Castine Reservoir on Battle Avenue in the 1920s. February was ice-cutting month in Castine. Large blocks were cut from local freshwater ponds and hauled to the foot of Green Street. From there the ice cakes were unloaded onto a sluice which led to the ice shed, located on the right side of the coal wharf. The ice was preserved in sawdust for use in homes, hotels, and stores during the summer.

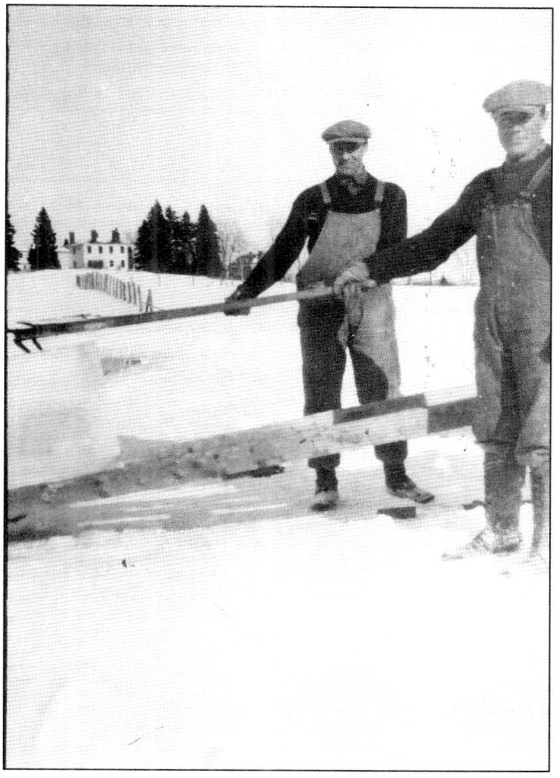

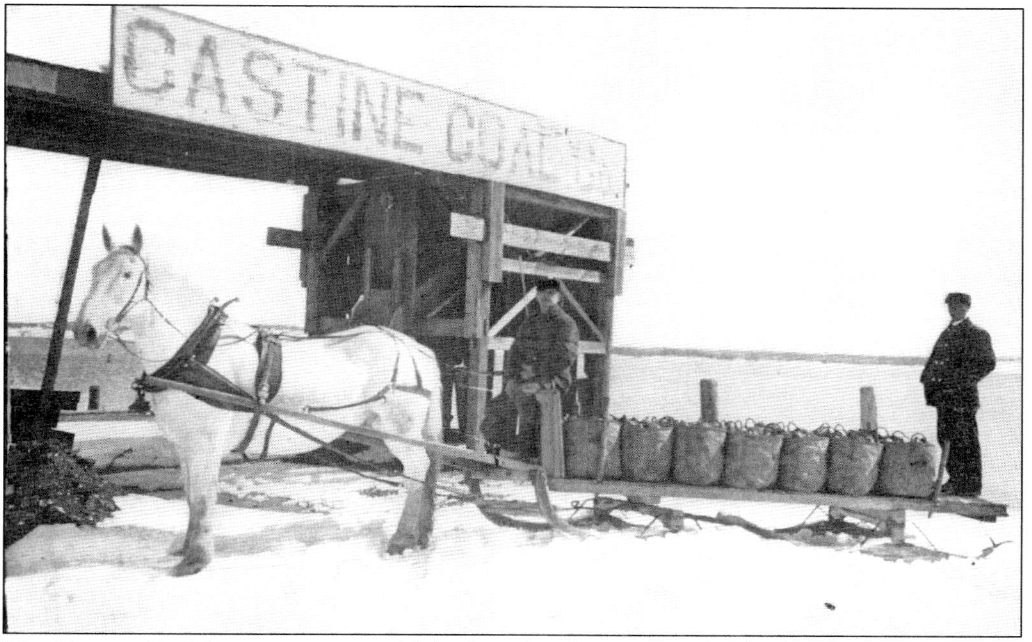

The Castine Coal Company was established on Sea Street in 1883. The building, owned at the time by Clarence Wheeler, collapsed in 1943 when 1,800 tons of coal were placed on the wharf.

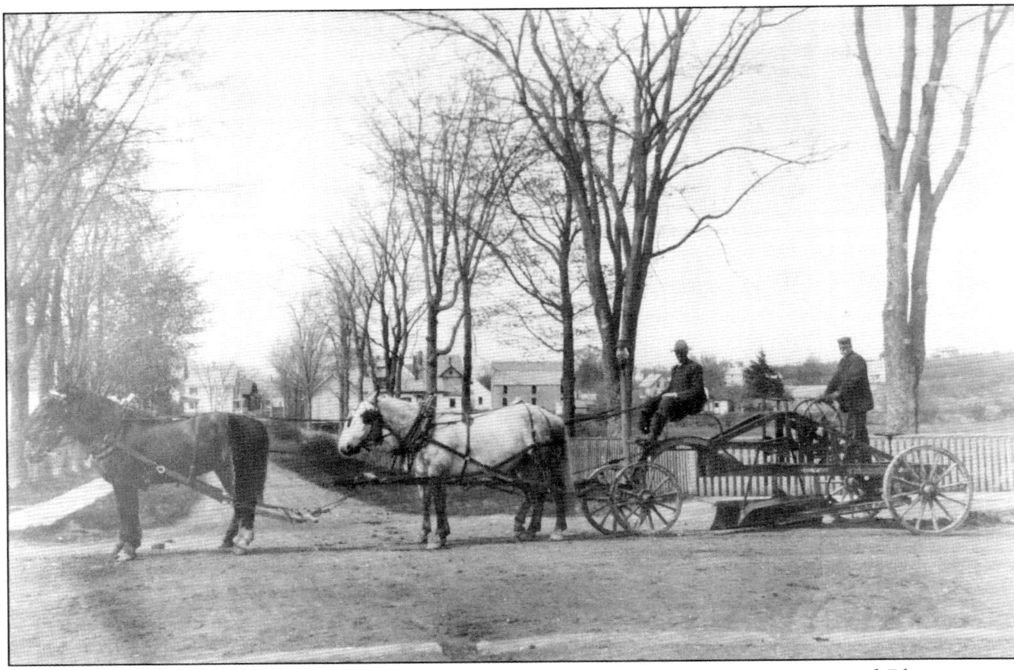

This crew was smoothing the ruts on the unpaved road at the intersection of Pleasant and Court Streets, *c.* 1905.

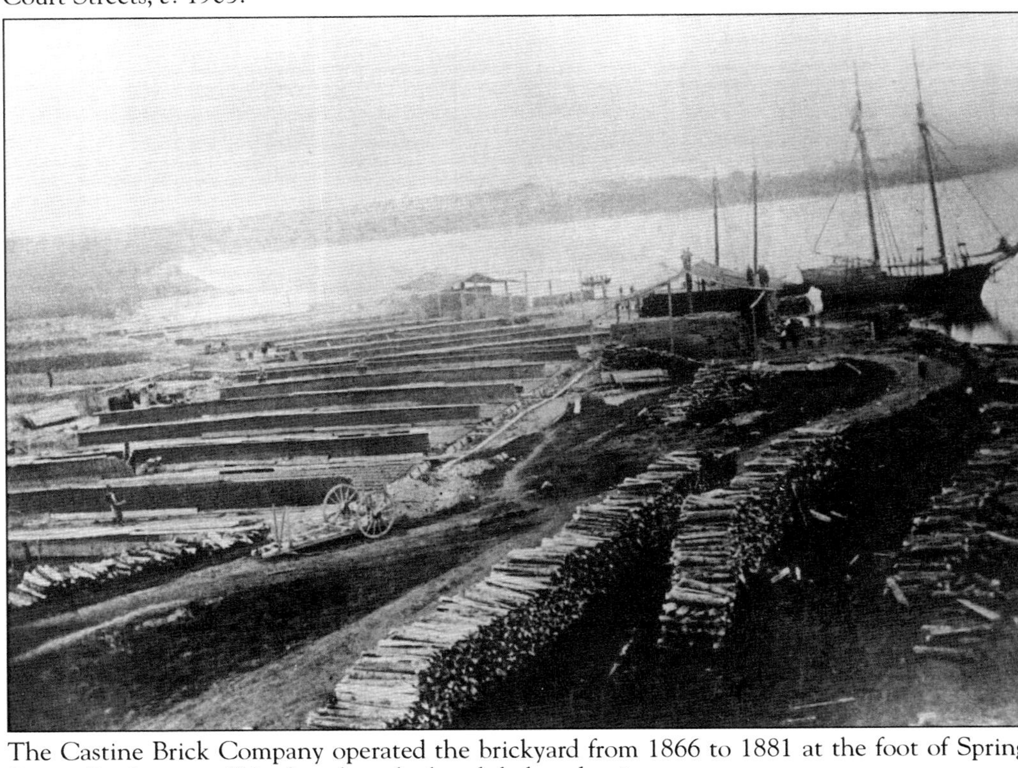

The Castine Brick Company operated the brickyard from 1866 to 1881 at the foot of Spring Street. Bricks can still be found on the beach below the site.

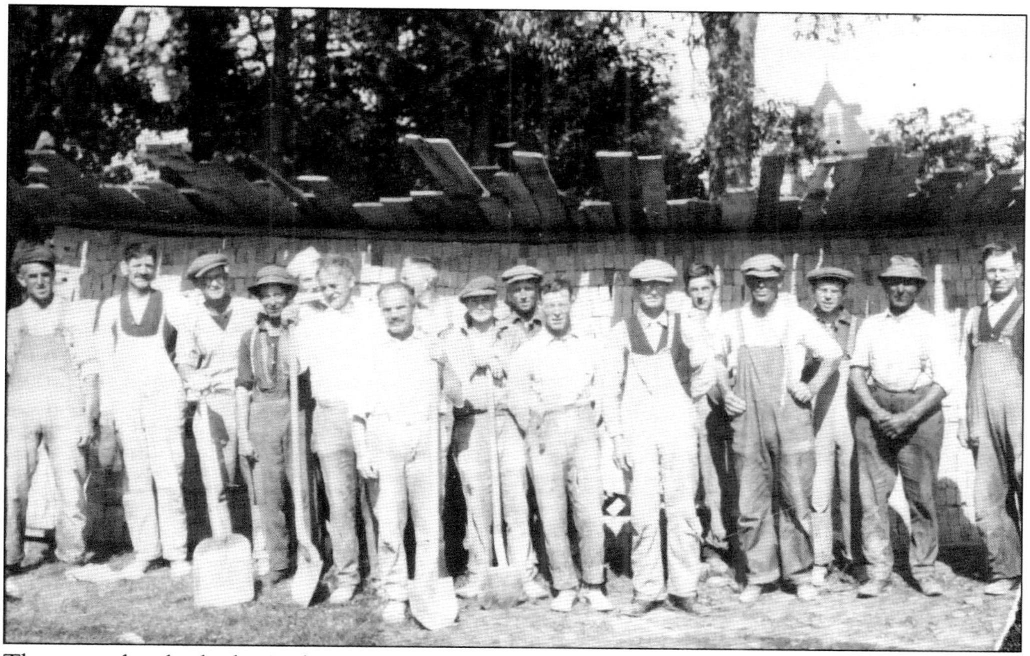

The crew that built the Wilson Museum on Perkins Street in 1920–22 included Russ Sawyer, John Gardner, Leon Littlefield, Roy Bowden, Leland Perkins, Will Steele, Pearl Colson, George McKinnon, Walter Farley, William Clark, Arthur Morey, Fred Connor, and Norm Grindle.

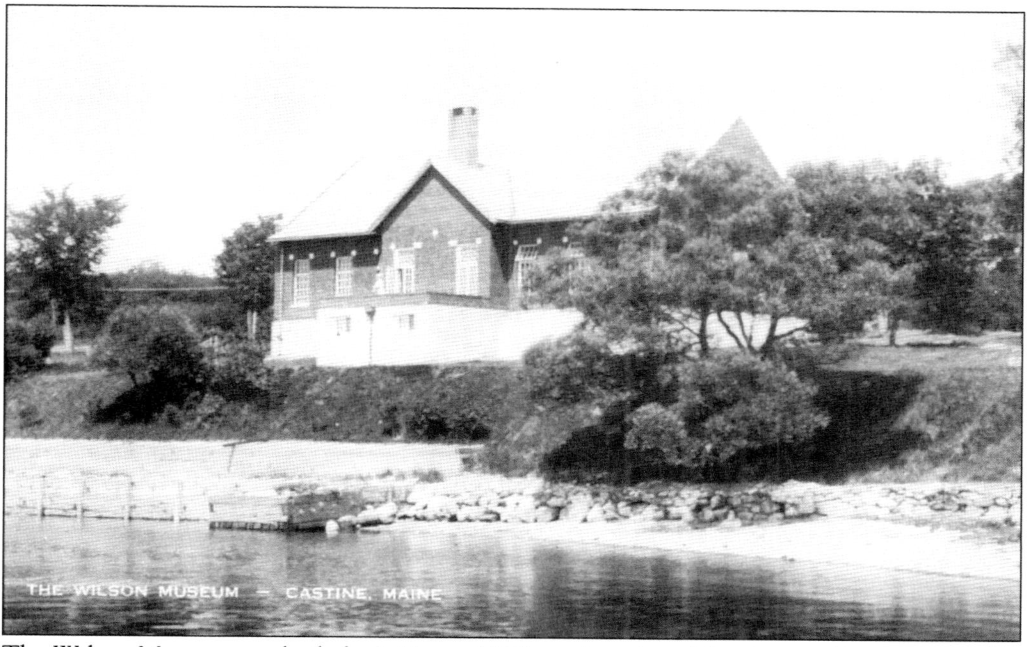

The Wilson Museum was built for J. Howard Wilson, founder of the Castine Scientific Society in 1921, and houses his collection "to show the antiquity of Man."

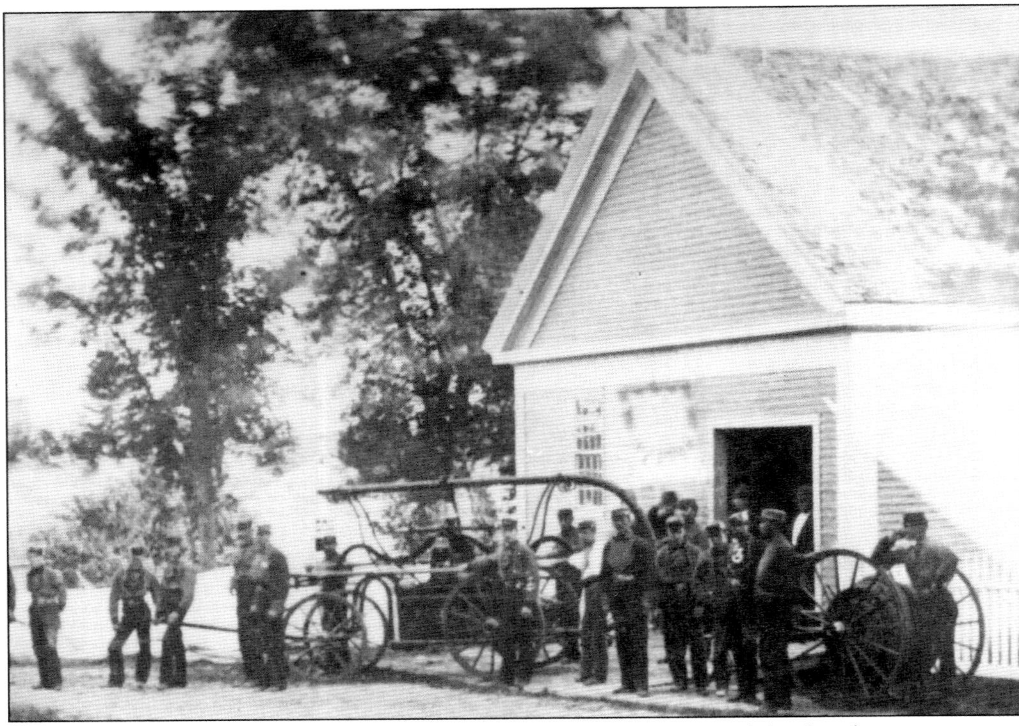

At the annual town meeting in 1872 the selectmen and engineer of the fire department were authorized to purchase a new fire engine for $1,000. In 1873 a vote was approved to use the former Western Schoolhouse on lower Pleasant Street for an engine house.

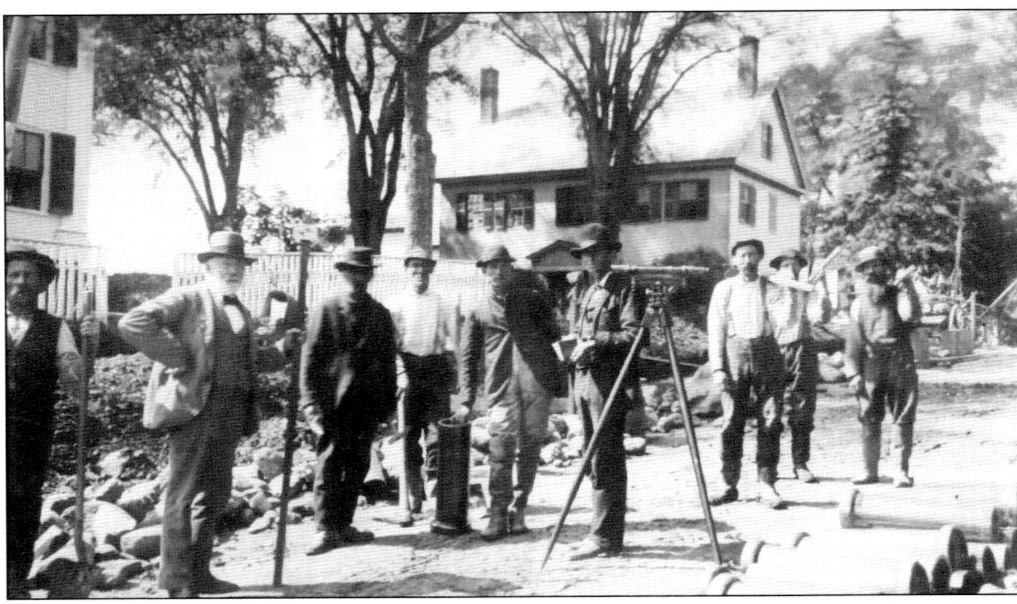

Workers installed the sewer line to the Eastern State Normal School from the middle of upper Main Street, c. 1895. Gas street lights were installed in town in 1910, and were replaced by electric street lights in 1917.

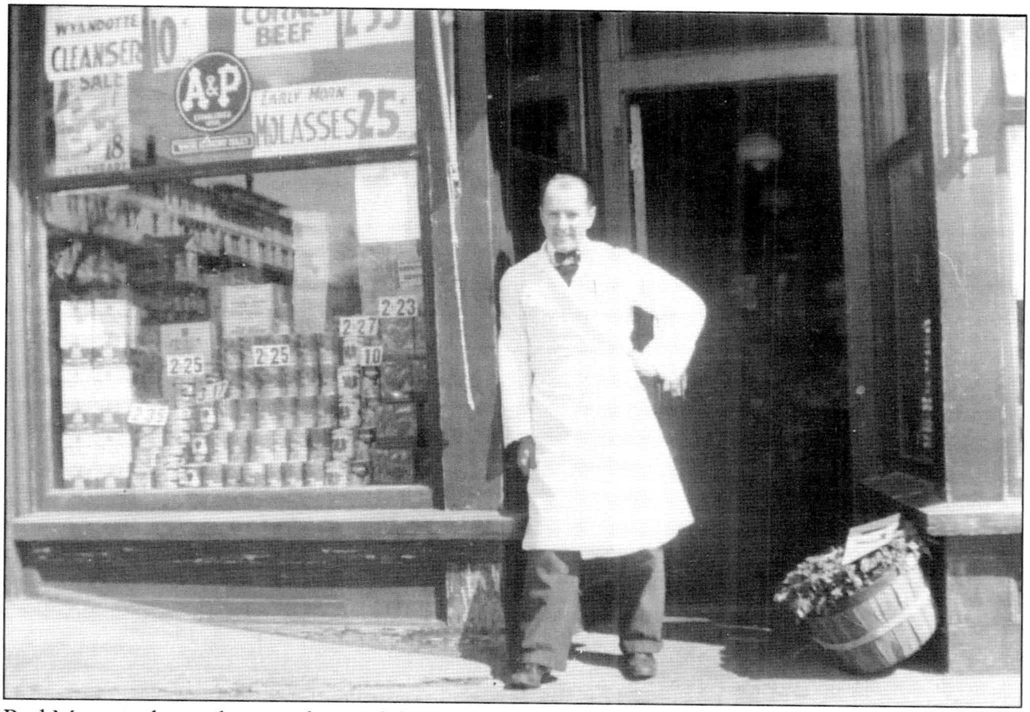

Bud Mayo is shown here in front of the A&P on lower Main Street in the late 1930s.

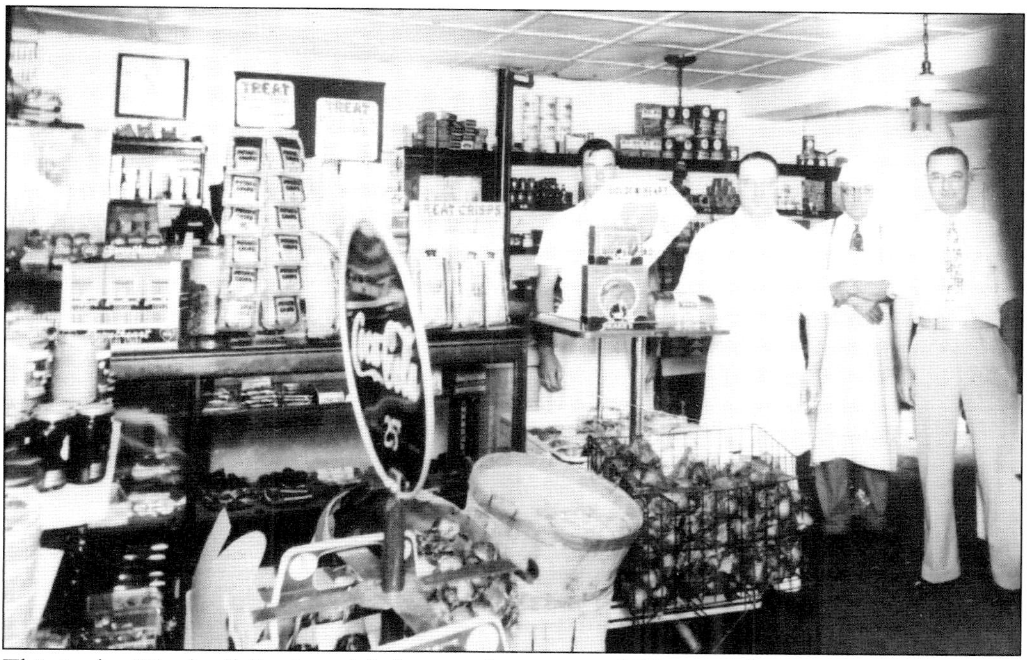

This is the Wardwell Sanitary Market on the corner of Water and Main Streets, c. 1920s. Horace, Gus, Frank, and Ralph Wardwell are pictured. At this time Castine had five grocery stores, two meat markets, a bakery, and a fruit store.

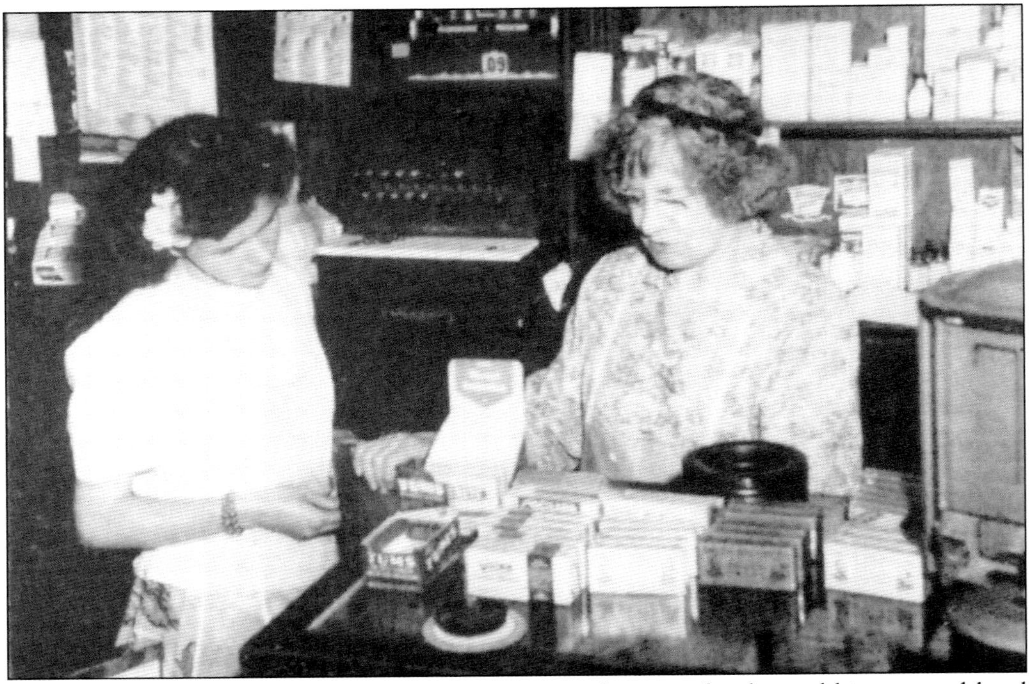

"Ma" McLeod's sandwich shop on Main Street was a hangout for the midshipmen and local teenagers in the 1940s and '50s.

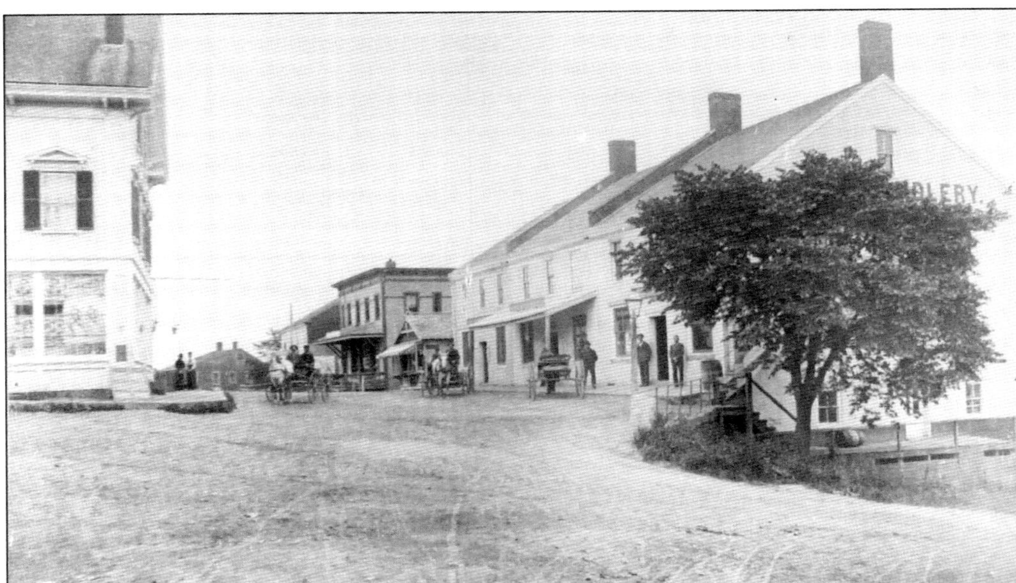

Looking up N.E. Water Street in the late 1800s, the Village Drug Store is on the left. Pictured on the right, from right to left, are: the J.W. Dresser Ship Chandlery & Groceries; Isaiah Shepherd & Hooper Groceries & Confectionery; Witherle & Co. Groceries; the Walter Bartrum Barbershop; Moses G. Gray Stoves, Tin, & Hardware; James B. Crawford Books; and the William Witherle Building.

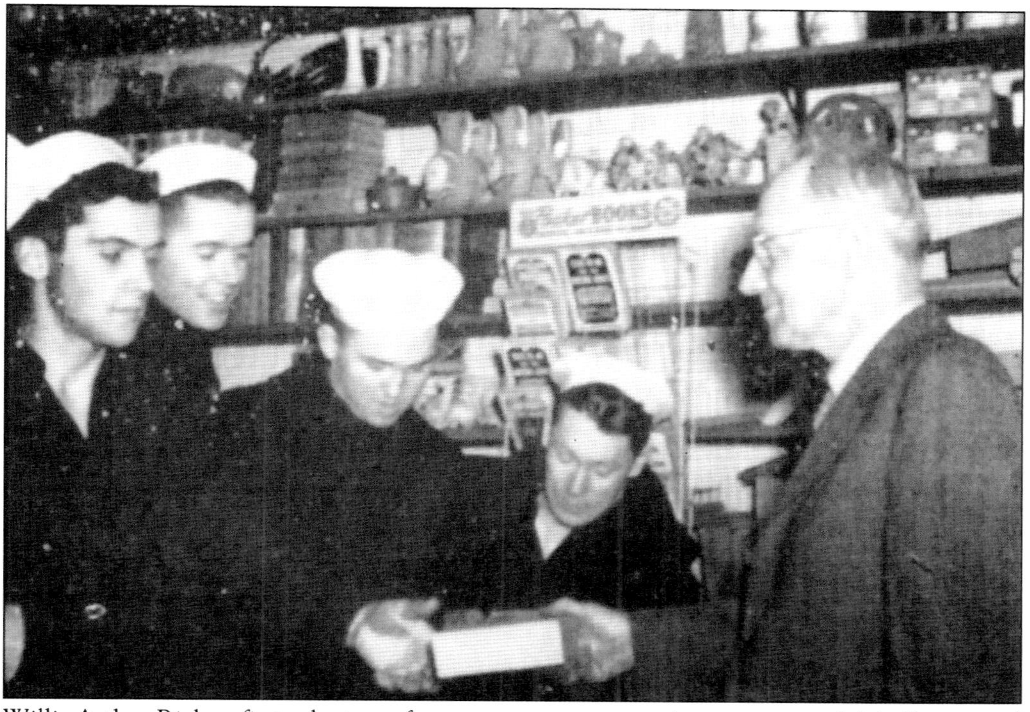

Willis Arthur Ricker, first selectman for many years, ran a stationery store on Main Street, and was happy to cater to the tastes of Maine Maritime Academy students, who became a familiar sight in town in the 1940s.

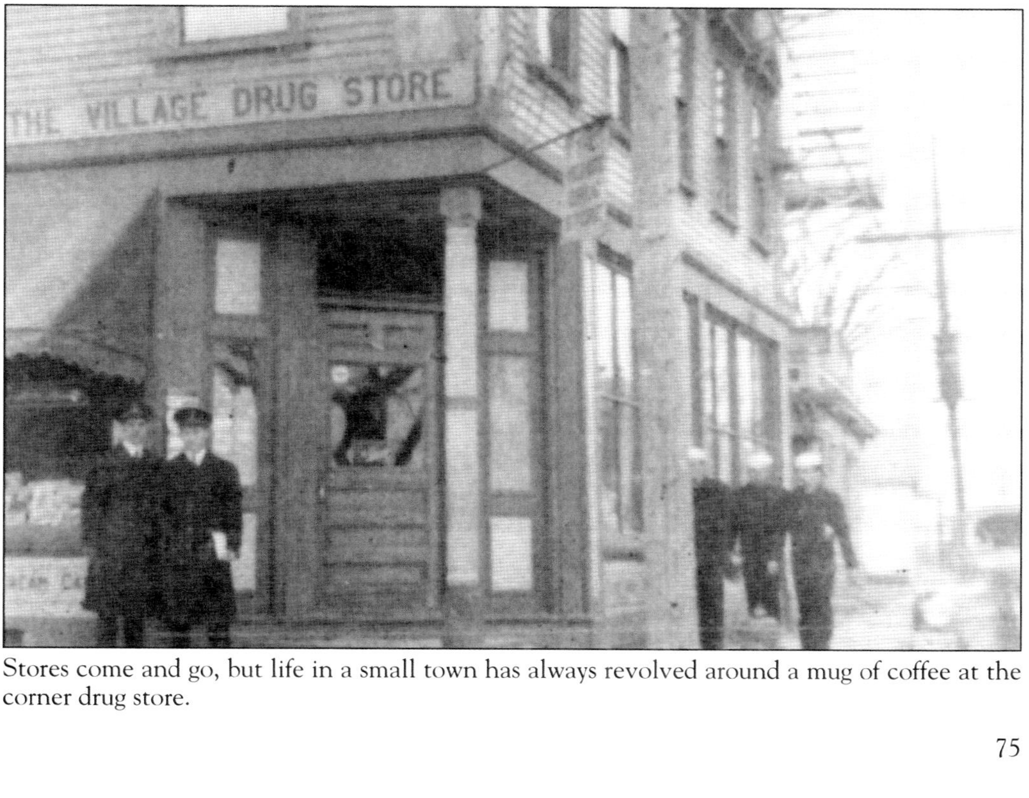

Stores come and go, but life in a small town has always revolved around a mug of coffee at the corner drug store.

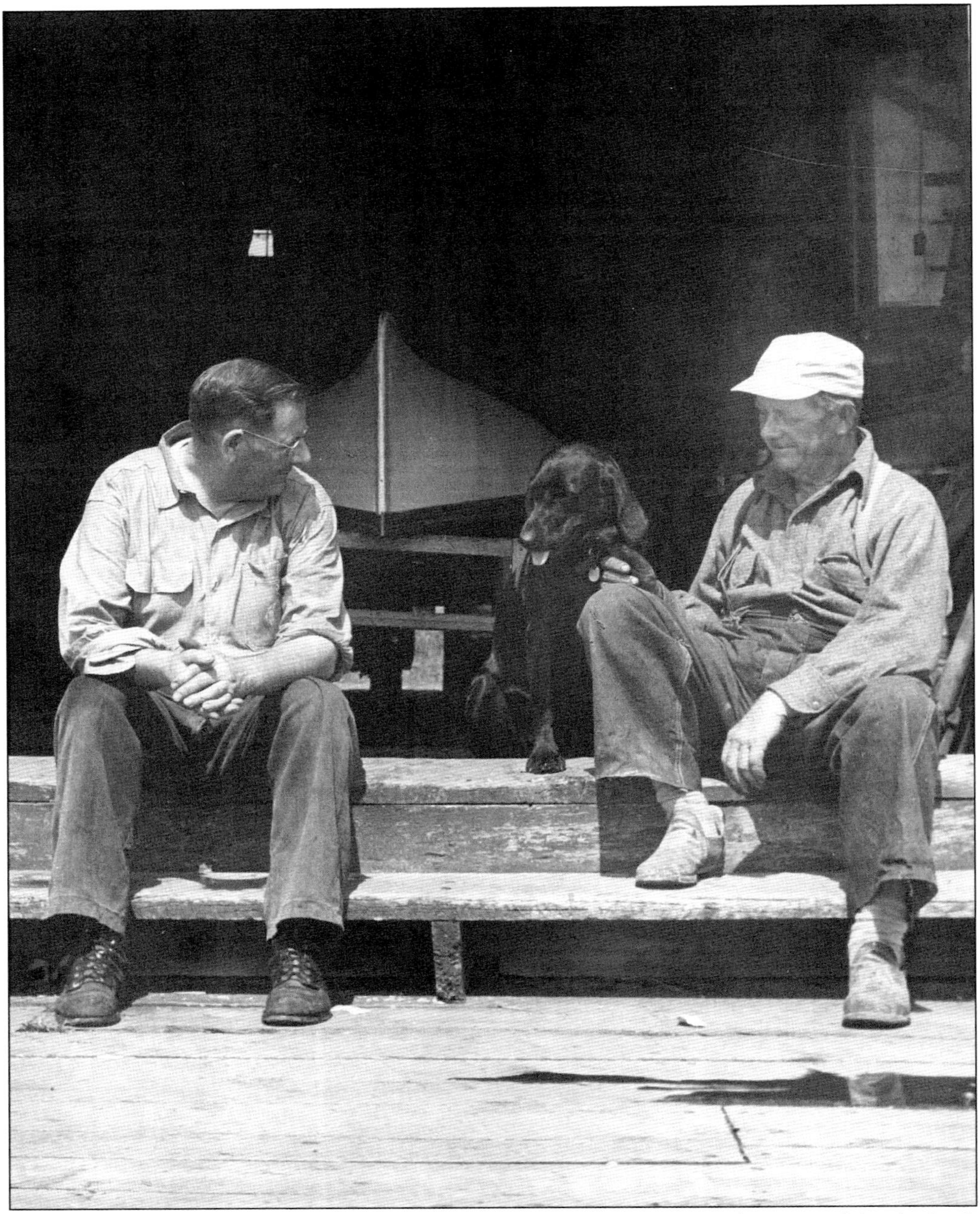

Joe and Jake Dennett at Dennett's Boat Yard, a popular place to pass the time of day for both locals and folks "from away," from the 1930s to the 1970s.

Five

Along the Waterfront

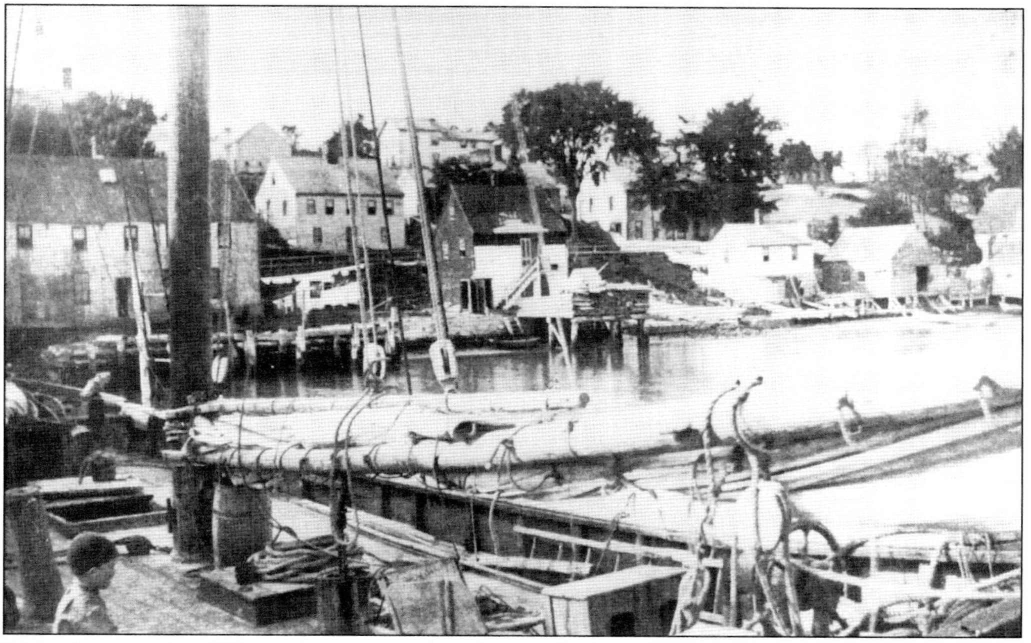

This photograph of Water Street was taken from a dock on Oakum Bay.

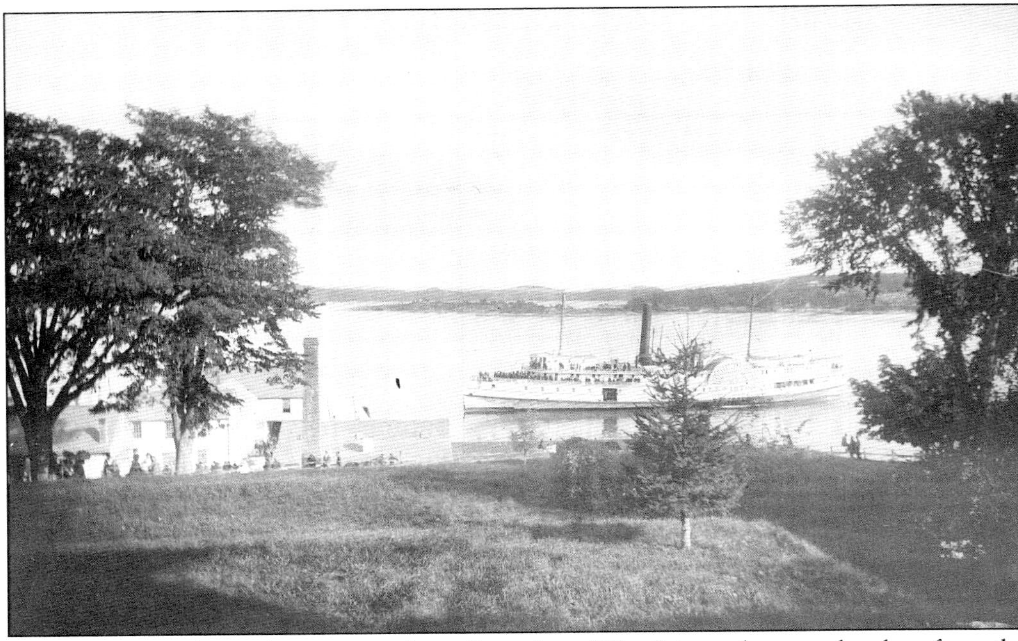

The *Lewiston* is shown here approaching Steamboat Wharf, in a photograph taken from the lawn of the Acadian Hotel. The docking of steamers in the late 1800s and early 1900s drew large crowds. Steamboat Wharf was located where the Maine Maritime Academy wharf is today.

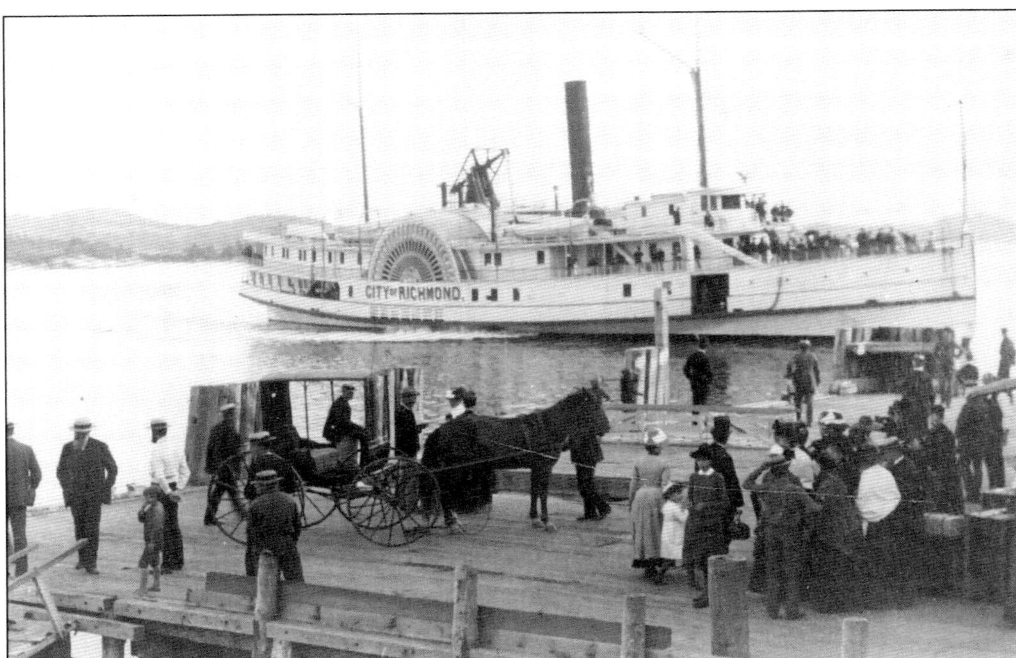

This is the steamer *City of Richmond*. From the 1860s through the 1920s many steamers made Castine a port of call. At the height of the summer as many as seven steamers called daily at Castine.

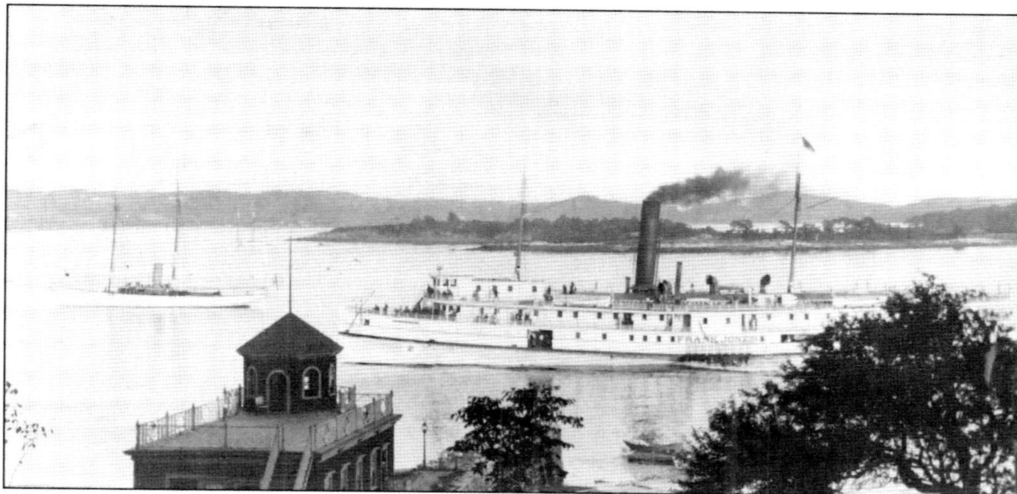

The steamer *Frank Jones* passes the Grindle tea house and dock on Perkins Street, c. 1900. This steamer connected with the Maine Central Railroad in Rockland. Others steamers connected with the Boston-Bangor boats.

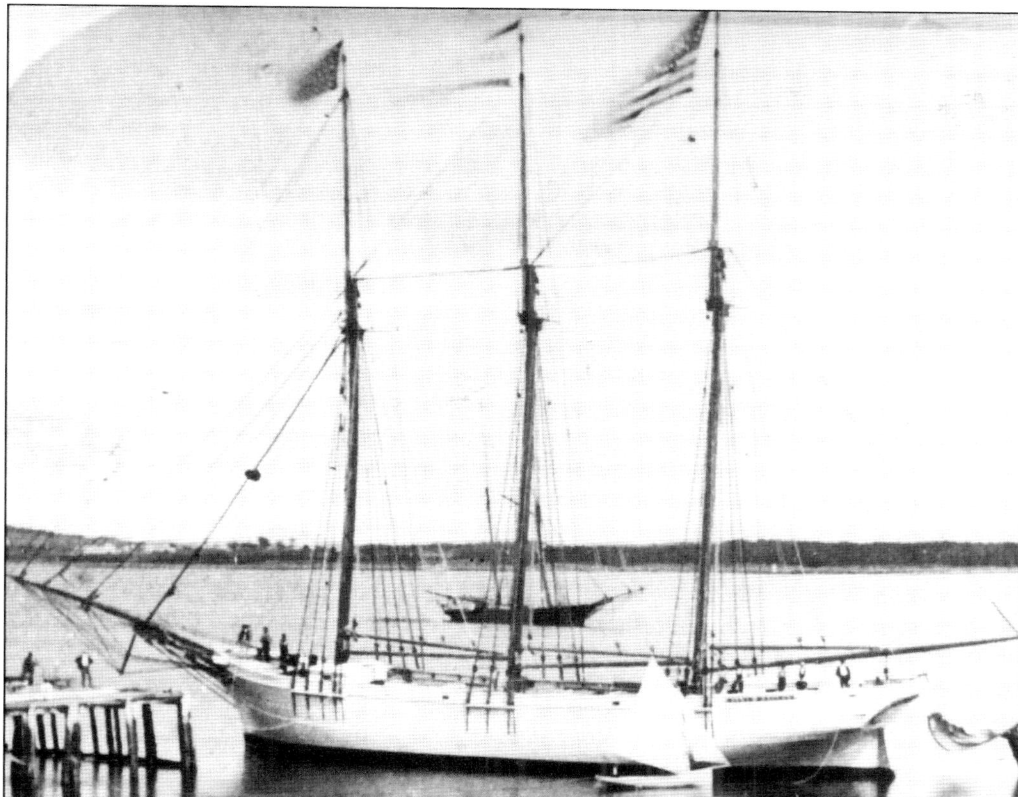

The *Annie W. Barker* was built in Castine in 1873. Between 1792 and 1887, 121 ships were built by various shipyards in Castine. For many years it had a customs house and was a port of entry for the United States. Castine merchants carried on a brisk trade with the West Indies, Liverpool, Cadiz, New Orleans, and other ports.

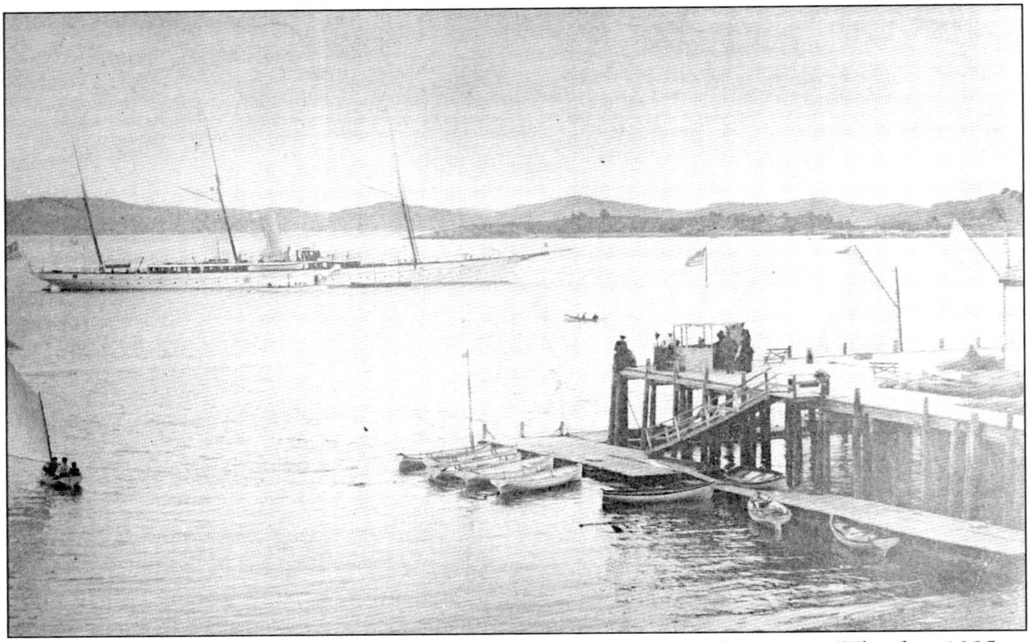

Financier Jay Gould's huge yacht *Atalanta* was photographed from Dennett's Wharf, *c.* 1885.

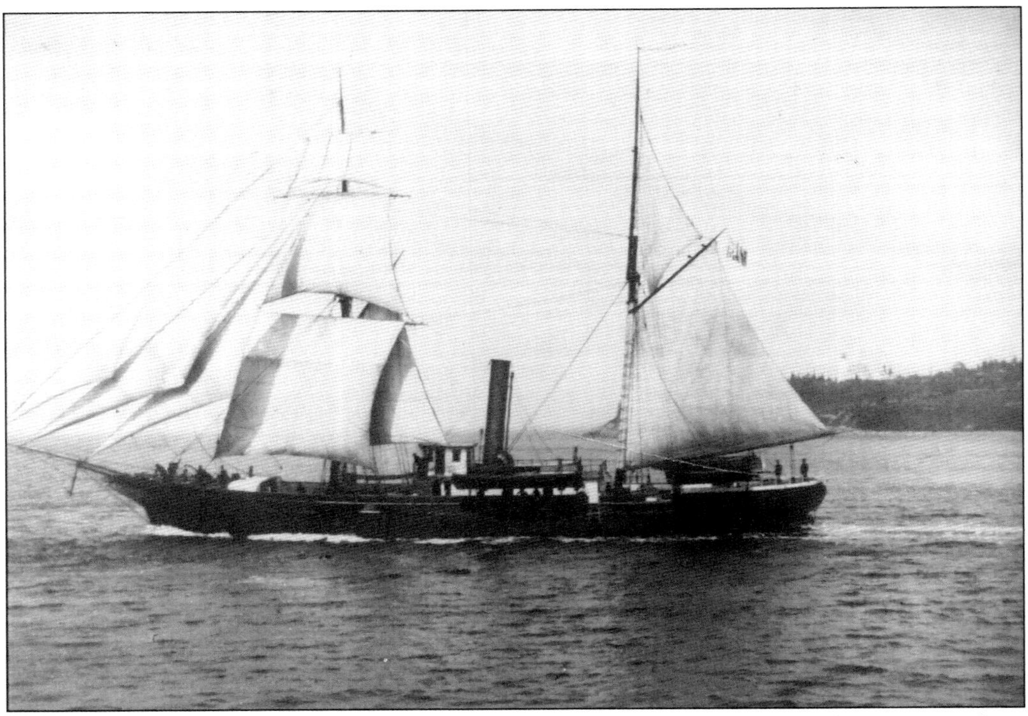

The revenue cutter *Levi Woodbury* is shown here in Castine Harbor in the late 1800s. These boats were the forerunners of the U.S. Coast Guard.

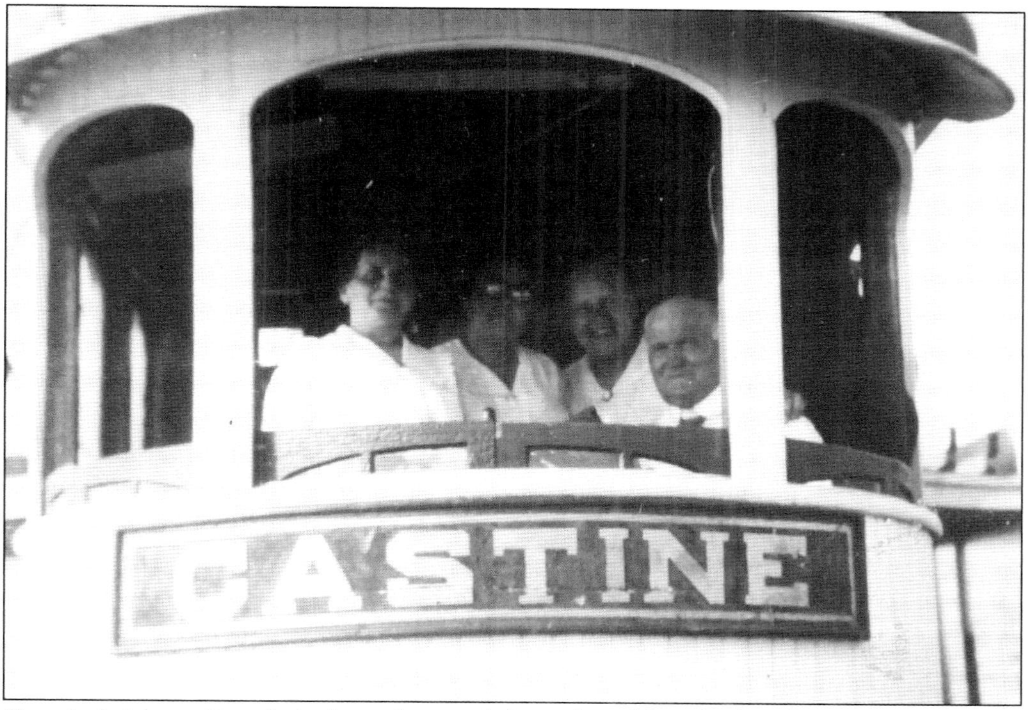

Captain Leighton Coombs is shown here with his wife and friends aboard the *Castine*, c. 1920. The *Castine* was a Penobscot River excursion steamer built in 1889, which traveled between Rockland and Bangor, and Belfast and Castine. She sank in 1935 off Vinalhaven.

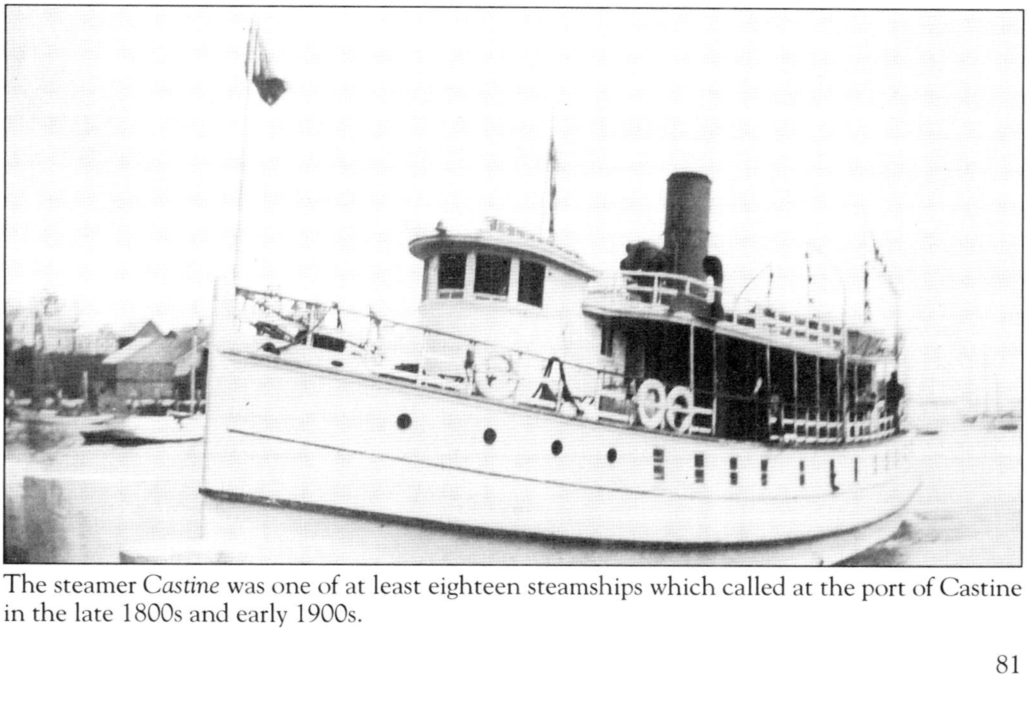

The steamer *Castine* was one of at least eighteen steamships which called at the port of Castine in the late 1800s and early 1900s.

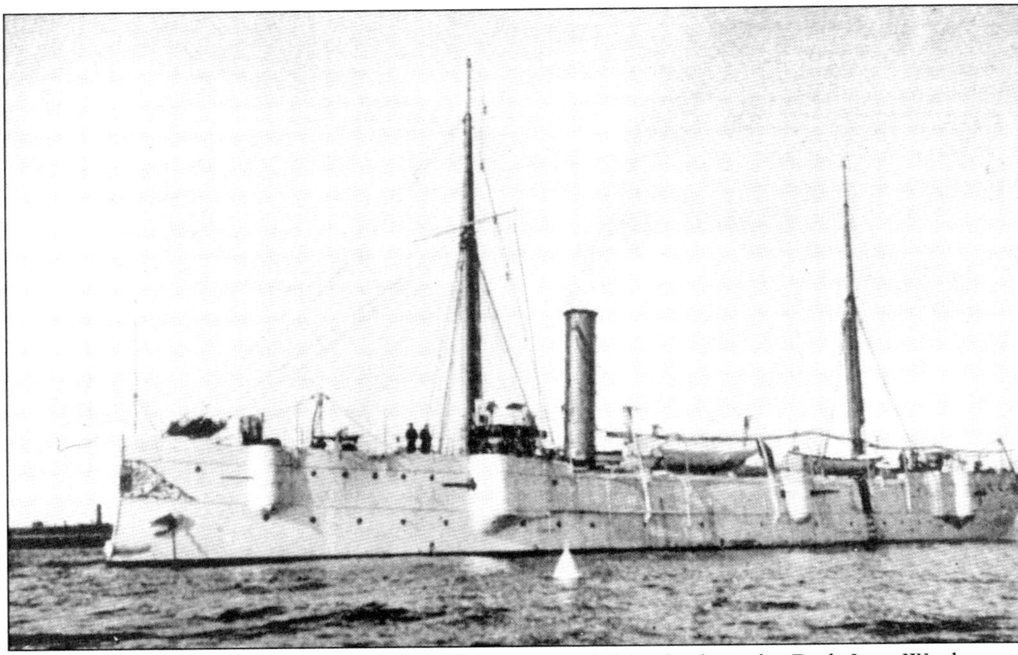

The gunboat USS *Castine* was one of the first two steel ships built at the Bath Iron Works.

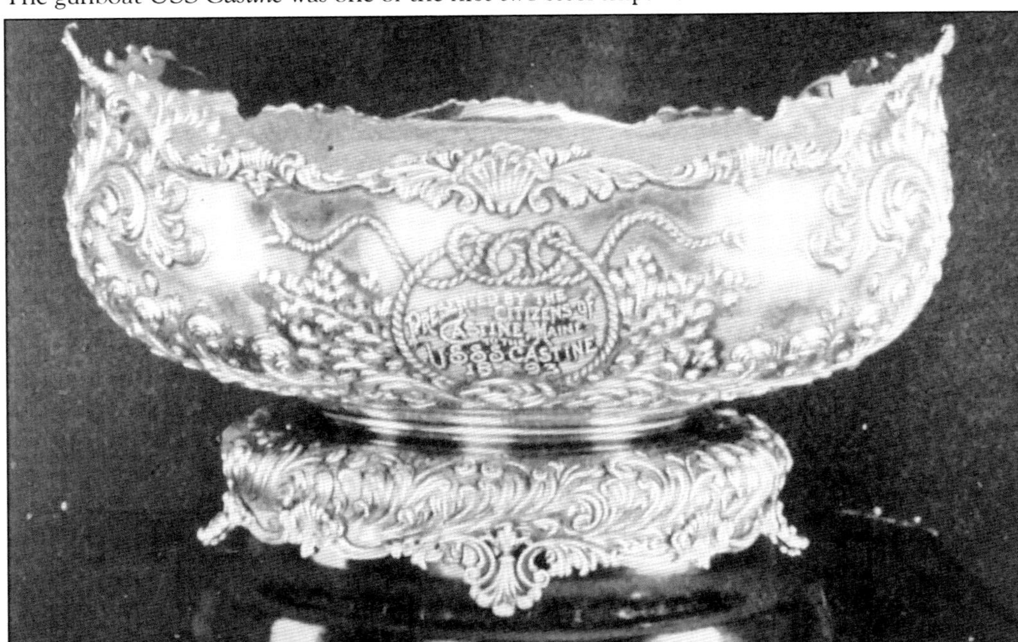

This silver fruit bowl was presented to Commander Thomas Perry of the USS *Castine* by the town on December 31, 1894, during a three-day celebration in honor of the ship's visit. In return, the pennant from the USS *Castine* was given to the town as a souvenir of the ship's first cruise.

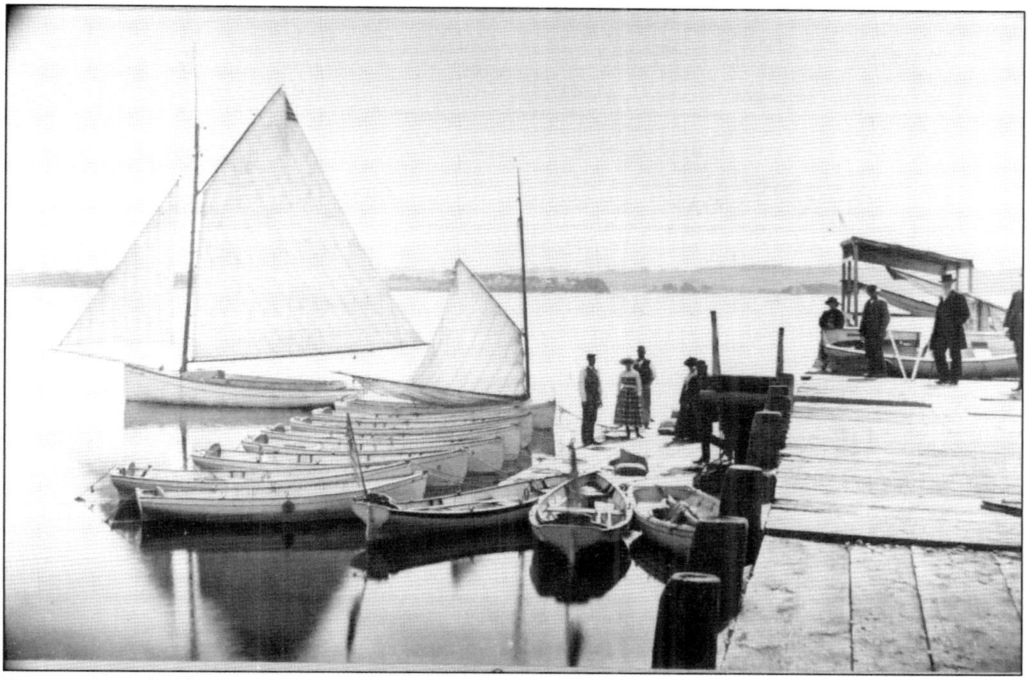

Dennett's Wharf rented launches, catboats, rowboats, and canoes to summer visitors, and provided lessons for the novices. Upstairs in the old building was a sail loft and downstairs was a bowling alley.

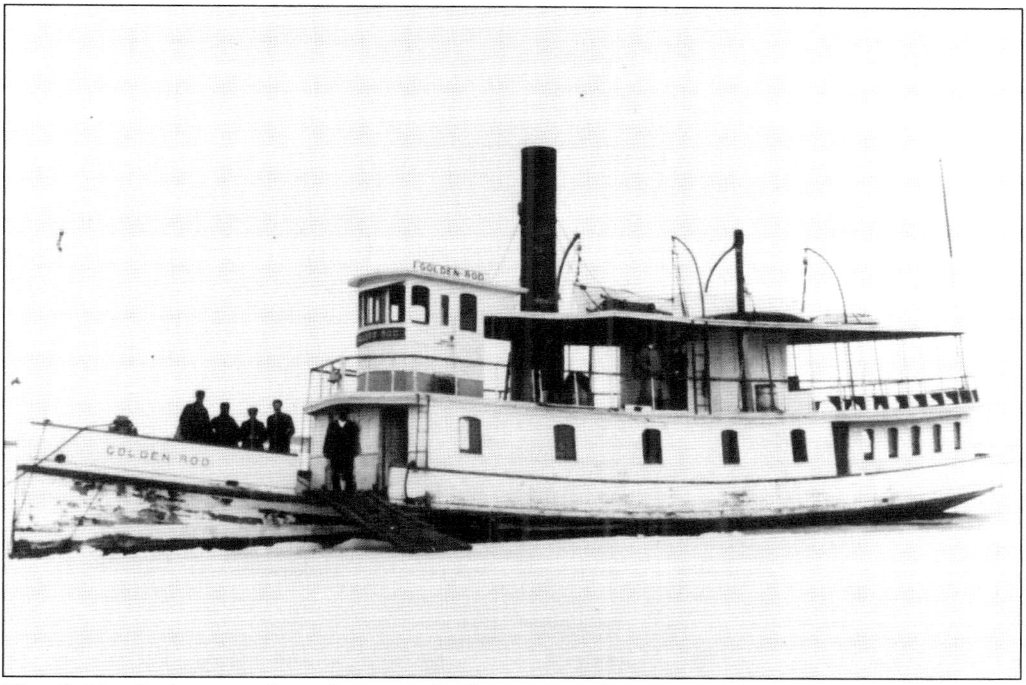

The *Golden Rod was* stuck in the ice at Belfast on March 8, 1907. This vessel was a Penobscot River excursion steamer. She sank in Castine Harbor across from Eaton's Boatyard in 1938.

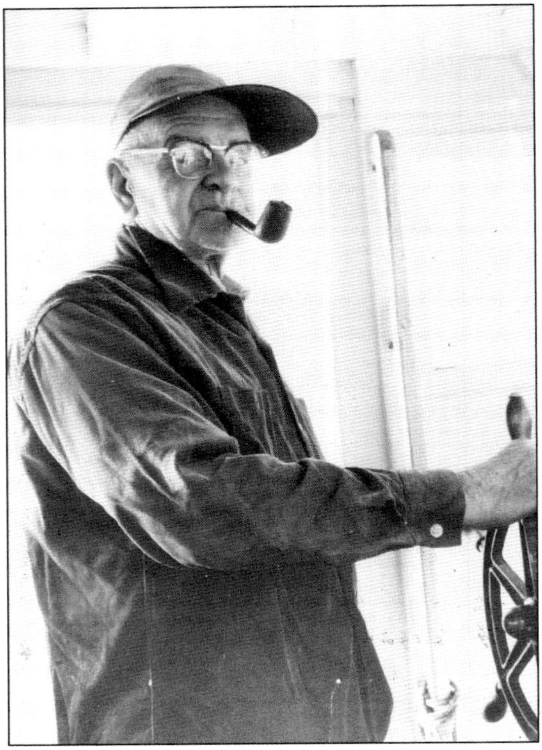

Captain Ladd piloted the mail boat *Hippocampus* from the 1930s to the 1950s.

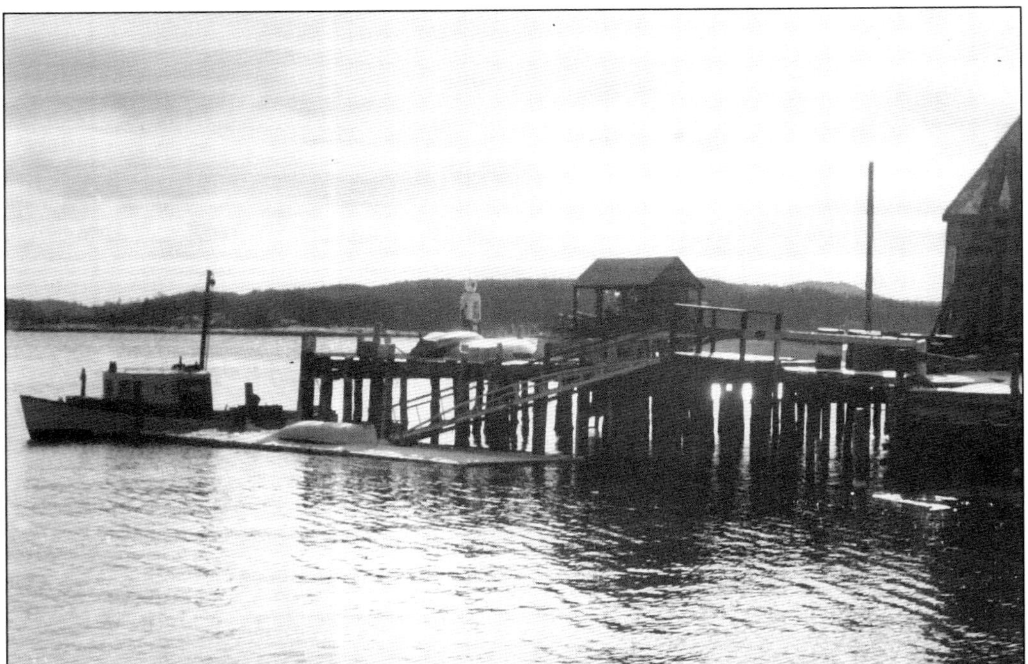

The *Hippocampus* was the last of the mailboats, bringing mail and passengers to Castine and other ports in Penobscot Bay. It is shown here at Dennett's Wharf in 1945.

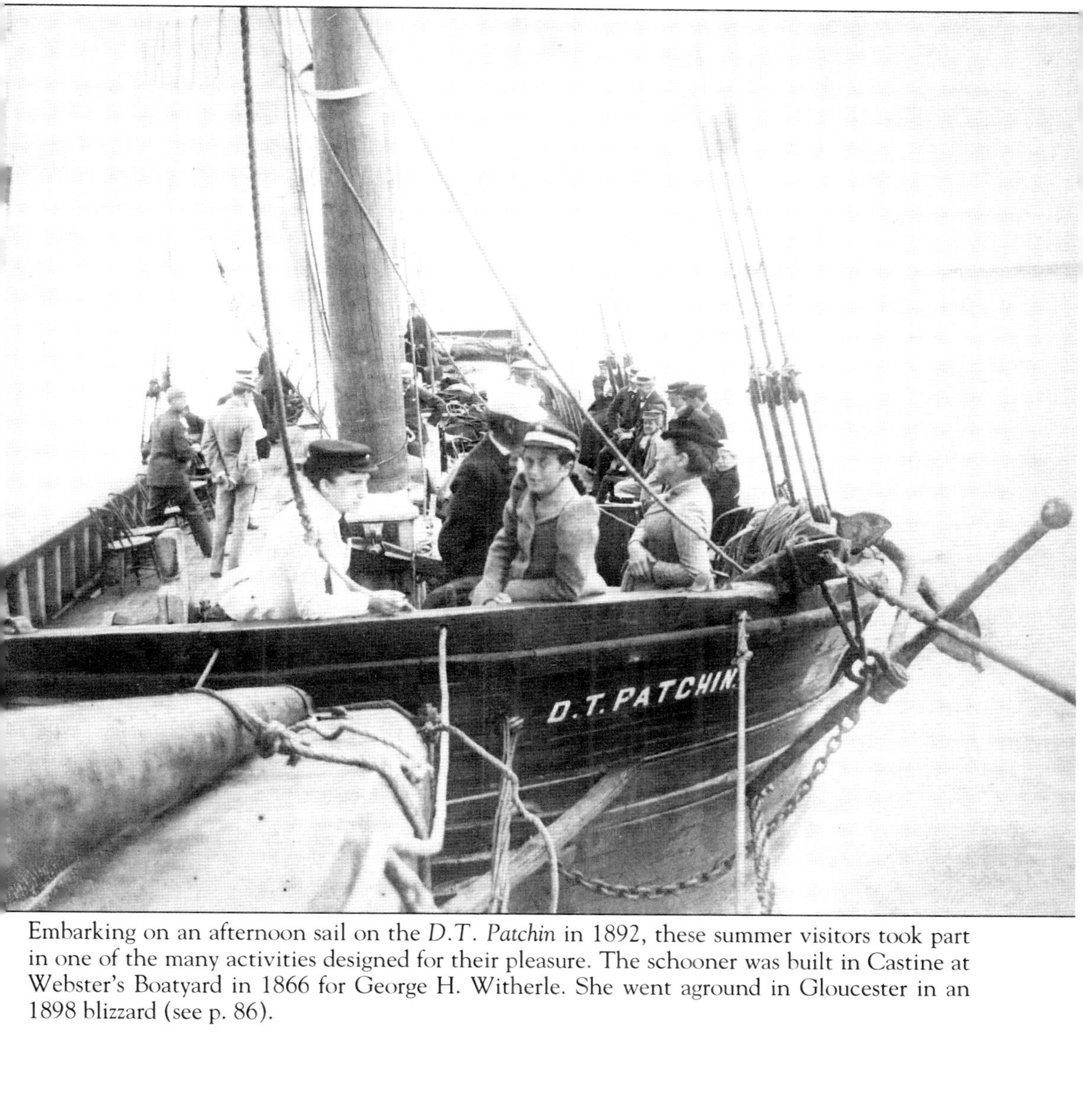

Embarking on an afternoon sail on the *D.T. Patchin* in 1892, these summer visitors took part in one of the many activities designed for their pleasure. The schooner was built in Castine at Webster's Boatyard in 1866 for George H. Witherle. She went aground in Gloucester in an 1898 blizzard (see p. 86).

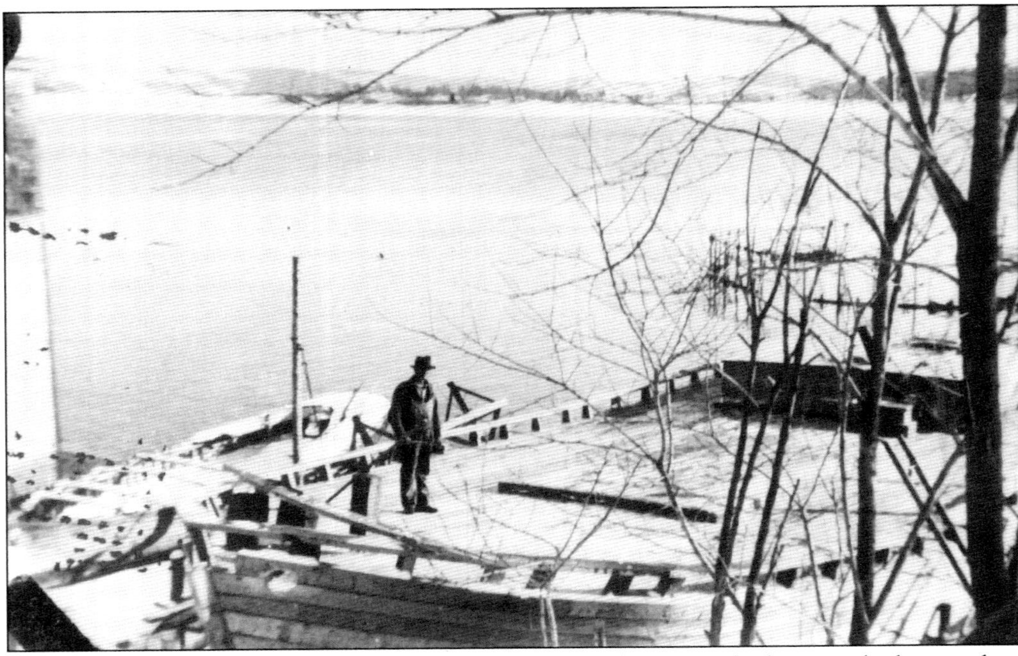

Captain Jim Webster's boatyard on Perkins Street in the late 1880s had its own little cog wheel railway to carry lumber down the bank from the street. Two and three-masted schooners were built here.

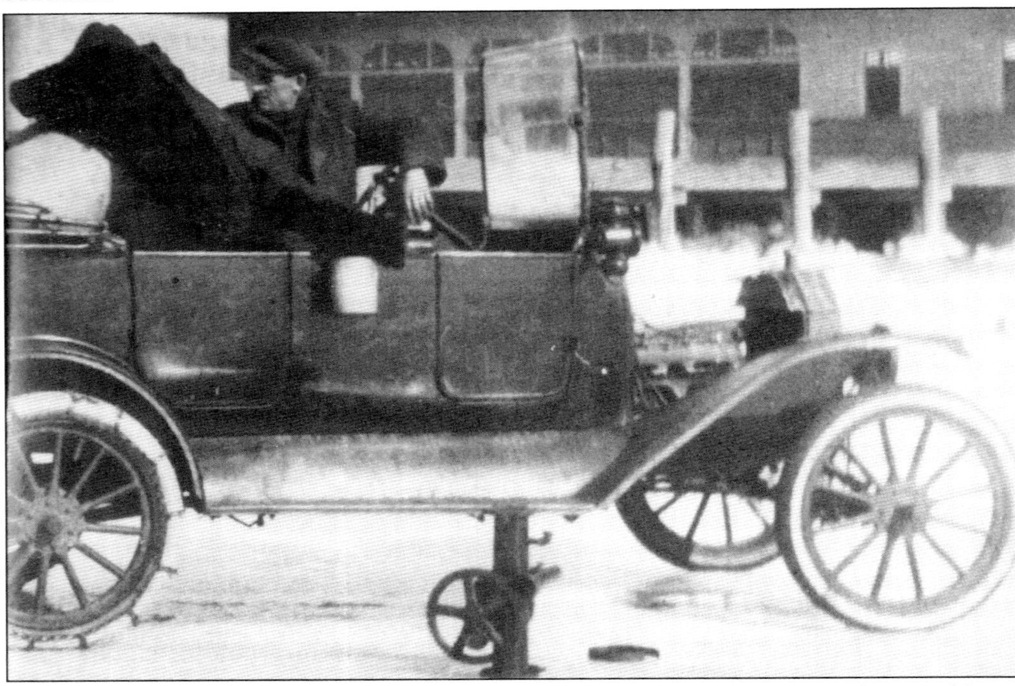

Captain Albert Gray of Harborside drove his Model T Ford Pathfinder across the ice of frozen Penobscot Bay to Belfast in February 1918. Penobscot Bay was frozen over in 1915–16. Hundreds of people crossed the bay that winter on foot, bicycle, and in carriages.

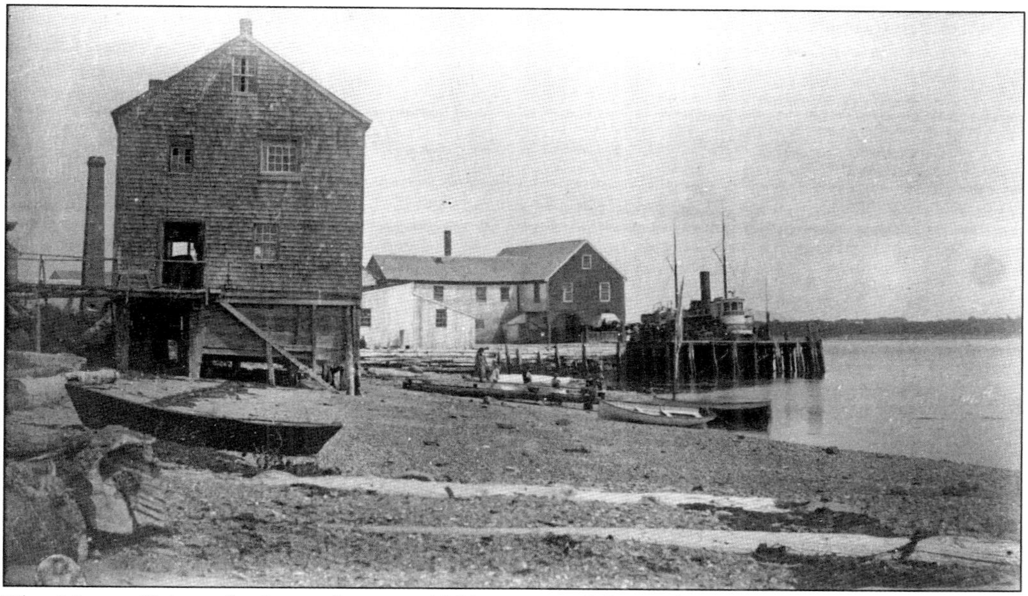

The Noyes Shipyard, shown here c. 1881, operated from the 1820s to the 1880s. In the mid-1800s, Castine was the second wealthiest town per capita in the United States, due to several factors; the prime one being the fact that six shipyards were in operation continuously.

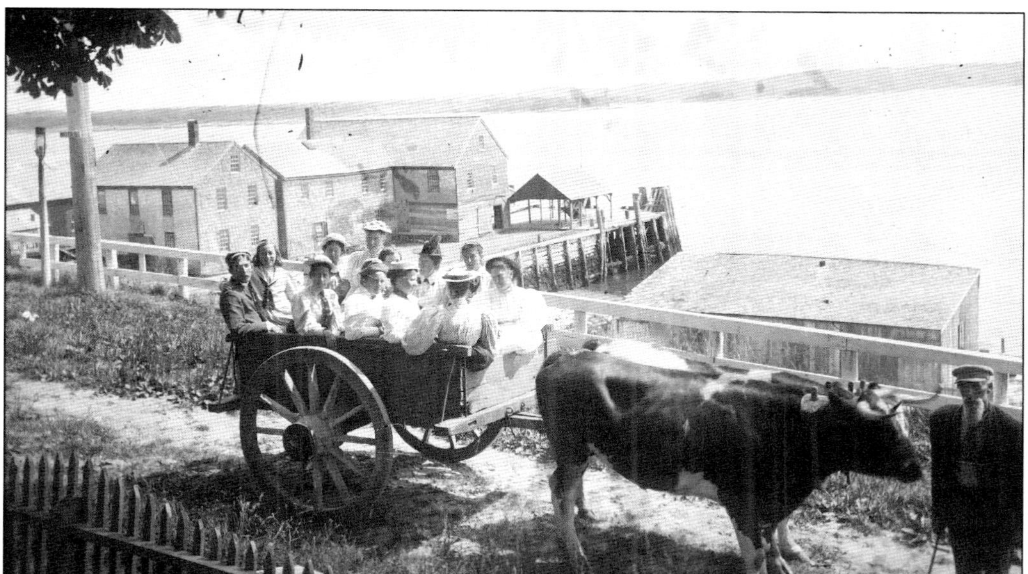

Mr. Veazie gave rides to the summer visitors in his ox-drawn cart. This photograph was taken from the stairs of the Acadian Hotel. Across the way the old Steamboat Wharf can be seen.

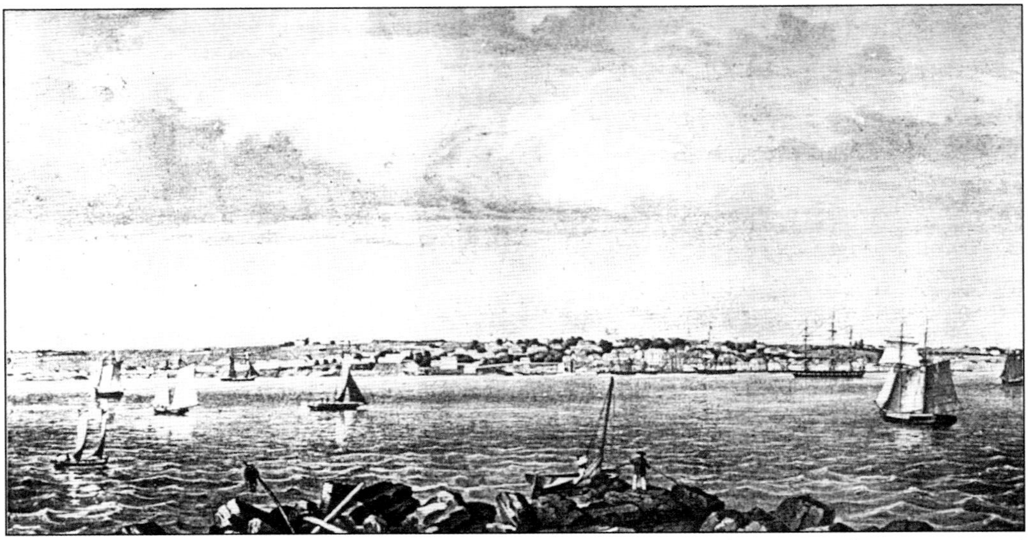

This lithograph, *Castine from Hospital Island*, was created in 1855 by Fitz Hugh Lane, a noted American Luminist painter of the nineteenth century. Lane was one of the most famous summer visitors to Castine. This scene includes a dozen sailing vessels in Castine's harbor; the two square riggers with their sails furled on the right are probably the *Adams* (built in Castine in 1840) and the *William Witherle* (built in Castine in 1851). There is a side-wheel steamer docked at the wharf. Although no one knew it at the time, the appearance of the steamer portended the end of the day of sail, and with it, the end of Castine's golden years of seagoing commerce.

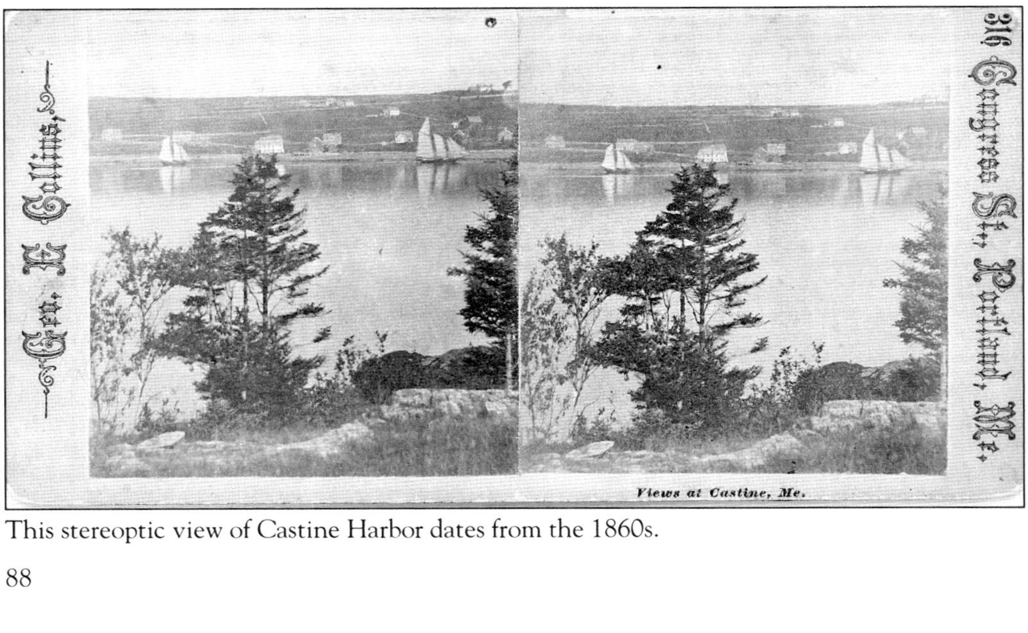

This stereoptic view of Castine Harbor dates from the 1860s.

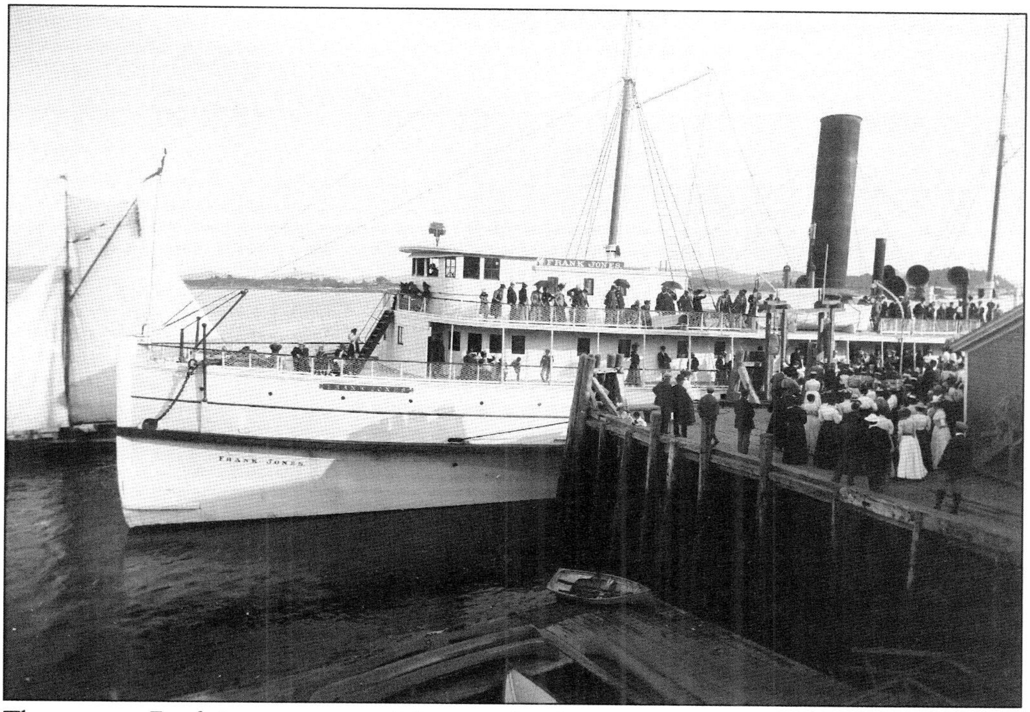

The steamer *Frank Jones* was one of the most handsome steamers in the area. It was built in 1892 in Bath, and at the time it was the only modern side-wheeler with electric lights.

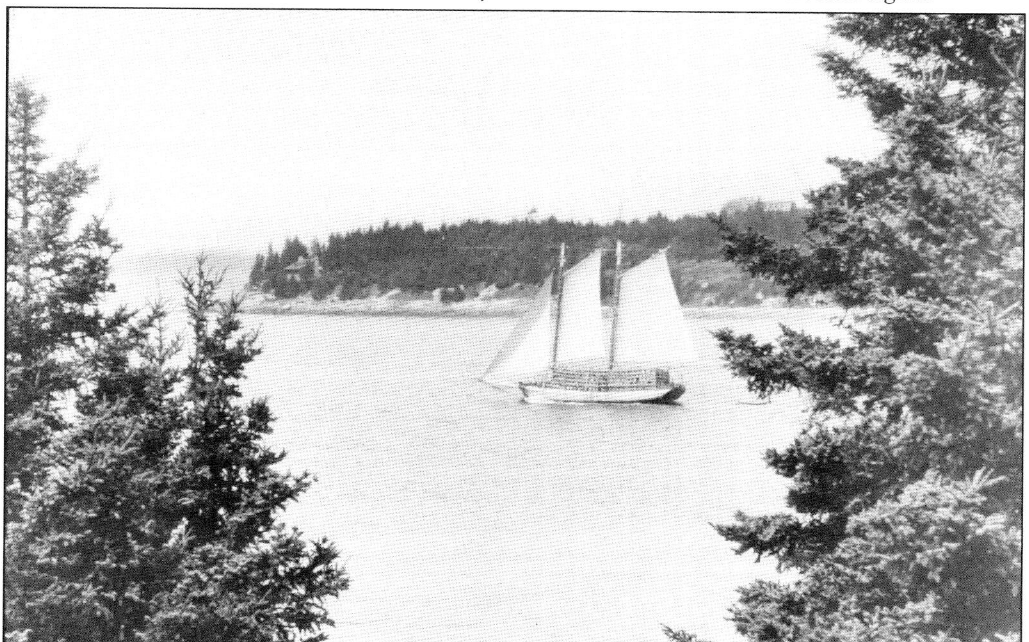

This coastal schooner is headed out with a load of lumber bound for lime kilns at Rockland. These "coasting" schooners were the workhorses of nineteenth-century Maine, carrying fish, salt, ice, coal, and bricks, as well as wood.

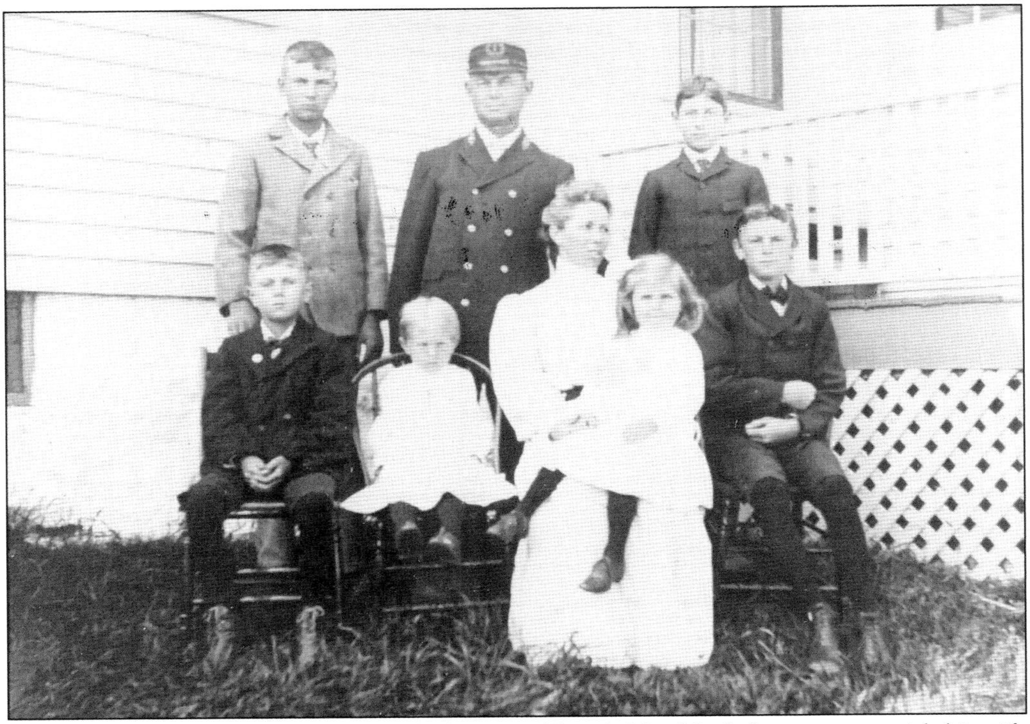

Captain Edward Treworgy Spurling, the keeper of Dyce's Head Lighthouse, poses with his wife Gertrude and their family, including daughter Bea (seated in the front row, second from the left), *c.* 1905.

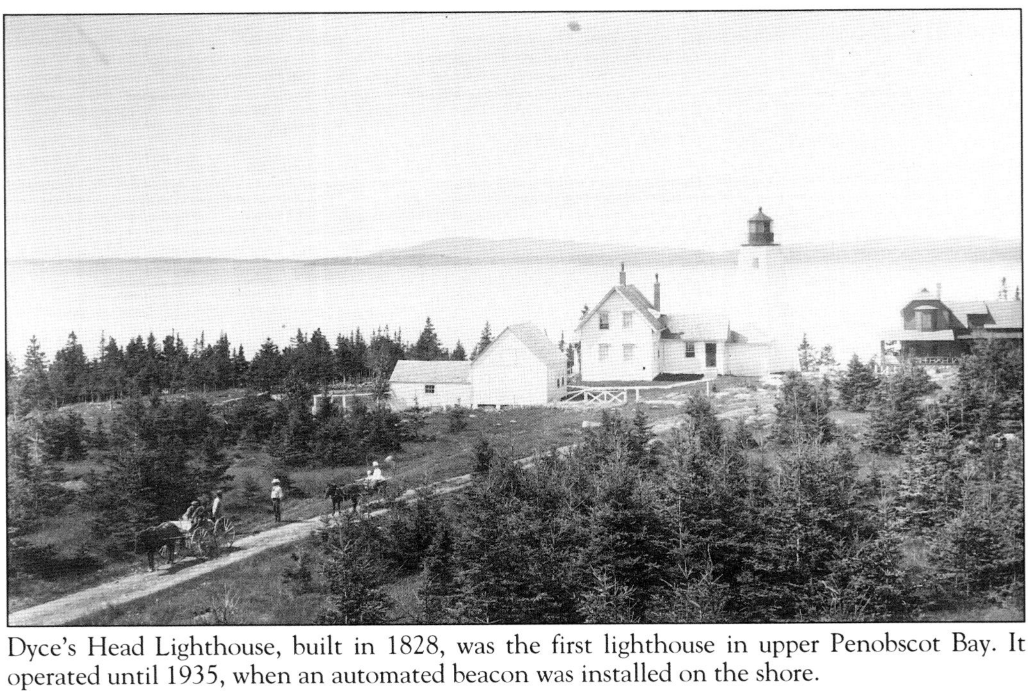

Dyce's Head Lighthouse, built in 1828, was the first lighthouse in upper Penobscot Bay. It operated until 1935, when an automated beacon was installed on the shore.

Six

Summer Fun

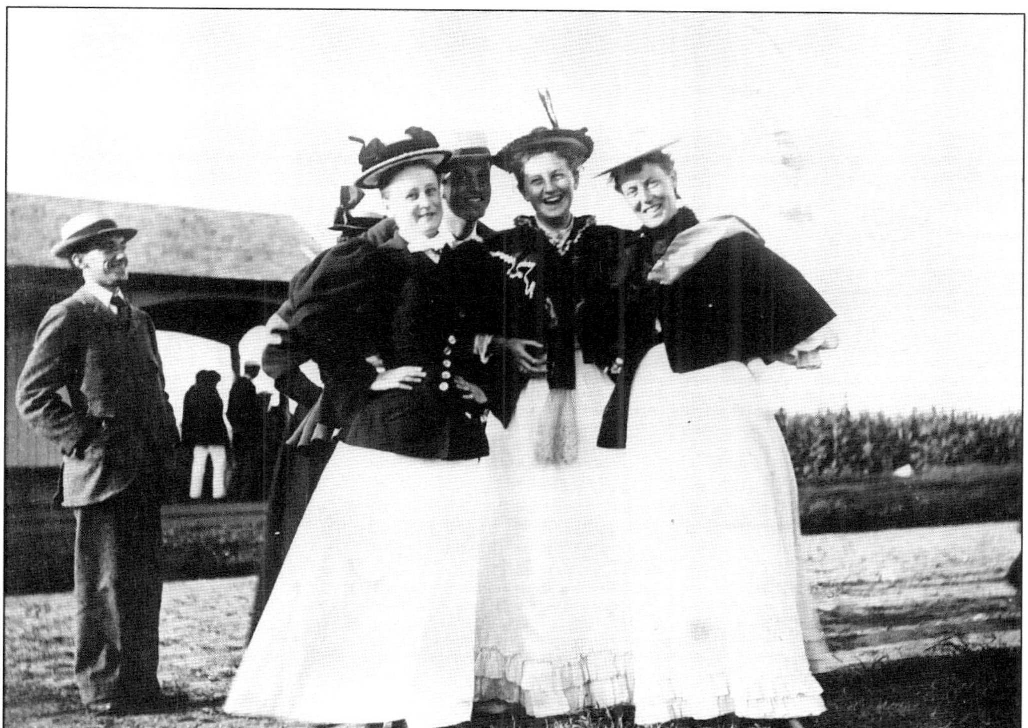

Tennis was very popular in Castine. Edith Blake MacPherson, Henry Blake, Alice Blake Newell, and Hattie Symonds Whipple stand at the edge of the tennis court at "Belmont Cottage" on Perkins Street, *c*. 1901. The young man on the left was a guest at "Dome of the Rock," a popular hotel near Witherle Park from the 1880s until it burned in 1903. It advertised tennis for its guests but neglected to tell them that it had no courts of its own.

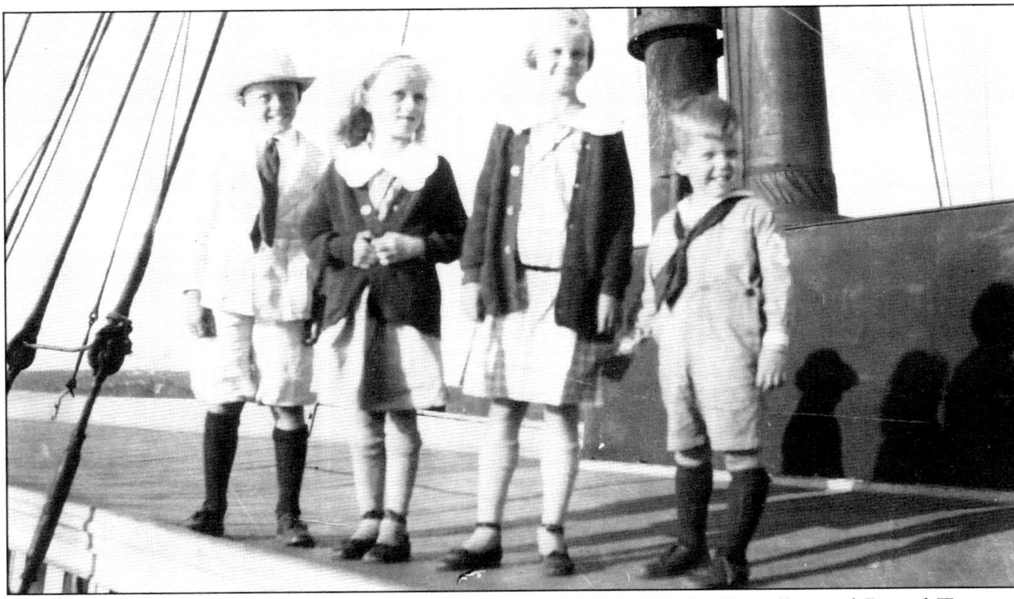

Summer residents Ed Tenney, Betty Taylor Foote, Barbara Taylor Prindle, and David Tenney, c. 1920, came to Castine each summer by steamer from Boston. Steamboat transportation lasted until the 1930s. The last Boston boat sailed December 28, 1935. The *Castine* was wrecked off Vinalhaven that year, the *Golden Rod* stopped sailing, and the *Pemaquid* had already gone south to take on another route.

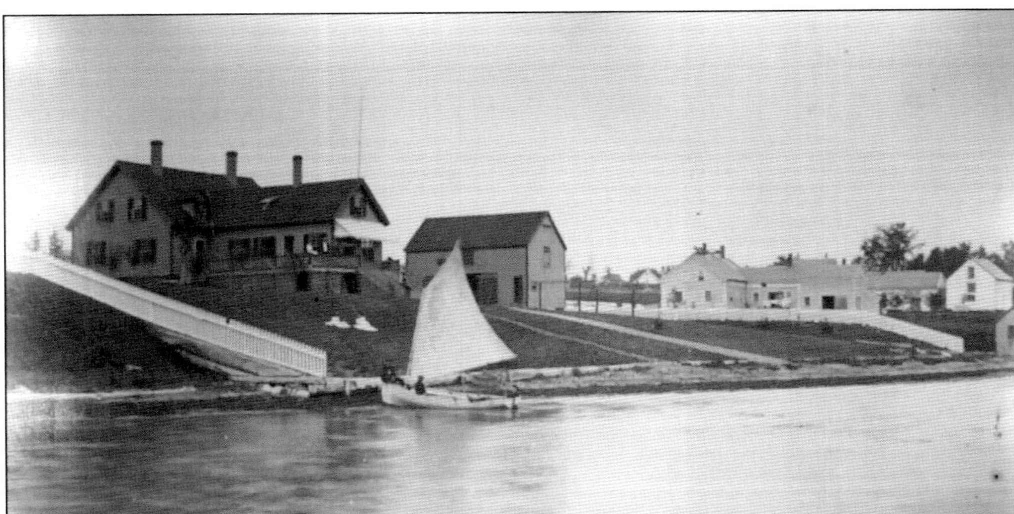

The first summer home in Castine was built in 1876 for Judge Henry Goodenow of Bangor. He, his wife, and his six children formed a lively nucleus of Bangor summer visitors, who were soon followed by cottage builders from all over New England and beyond.

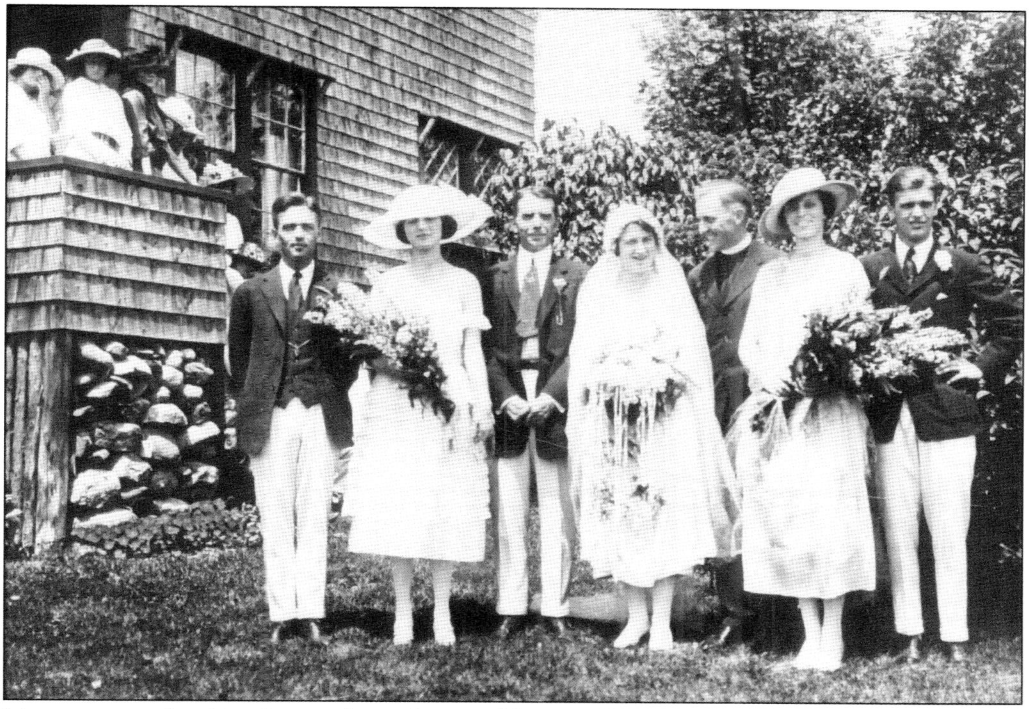

Many summer families chose to have their weddings in Castine, a custom that continues today. The bride and groom shown here on their wedding day, July 20, 1921, are Mary Mikell and Oliver Hart. The Reverend Hart later became the Bishop of Pennsylvania.

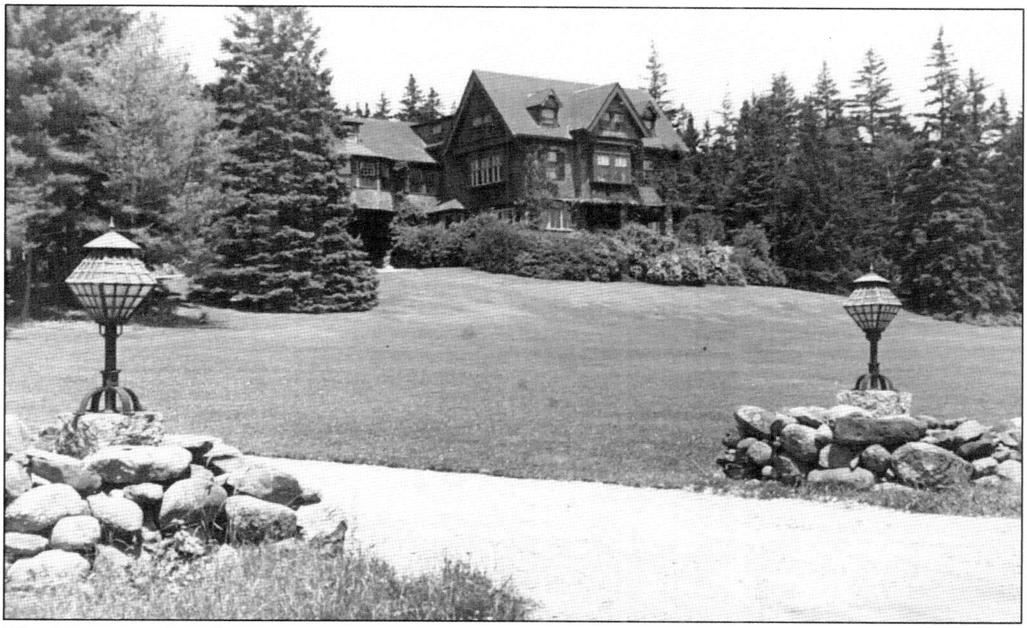

The Manor on Battle Avenue was originally built in 1895 as a cottage for Commodore Fuller of the New York Yacht Club. It was enlarged and remodeled in the late 1890s by the McClintocks of Pittsburgh. The Art Deco entrance lamps burned kerosene.

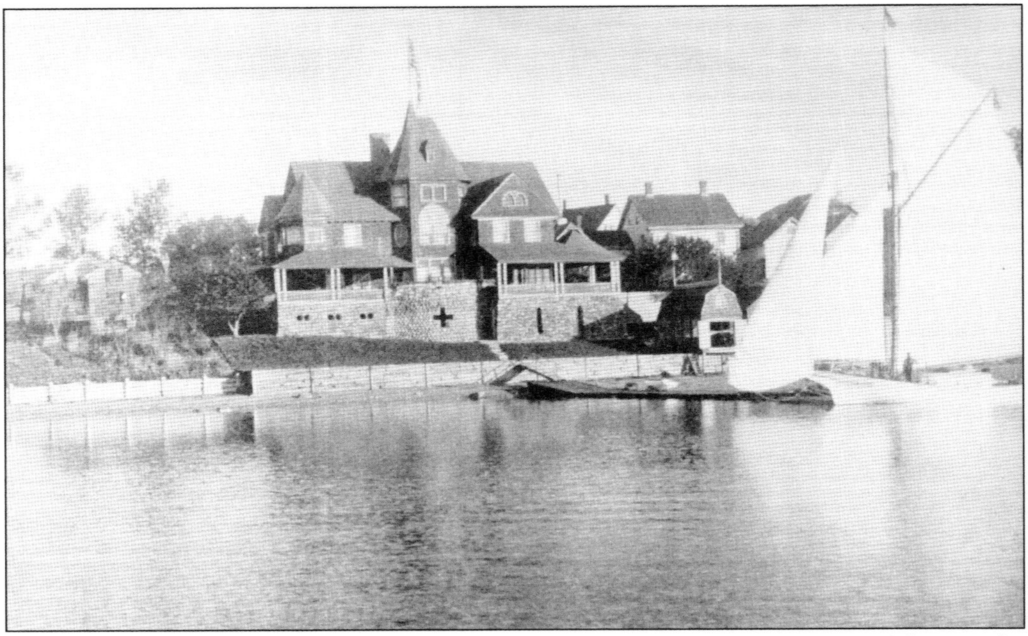

Dr. George A. Wheeler described the home that was to become Holiday House as follows: "The Agoncy cottage, on Perkins Street, just east of the old French fort, is the property of Colonel A.K. Bolan, of New York. It is a handsome and commodious house, and has a superb water front, with a full view of the harbor. The grounds towards the street are tastefully laid out, and there is a fine beach in front. The stables are at the southern end of Court Street, but within a reasonable distance from the house. This cottage was built in 1893. Colonel Bolan has become a permanent citizen of the town."

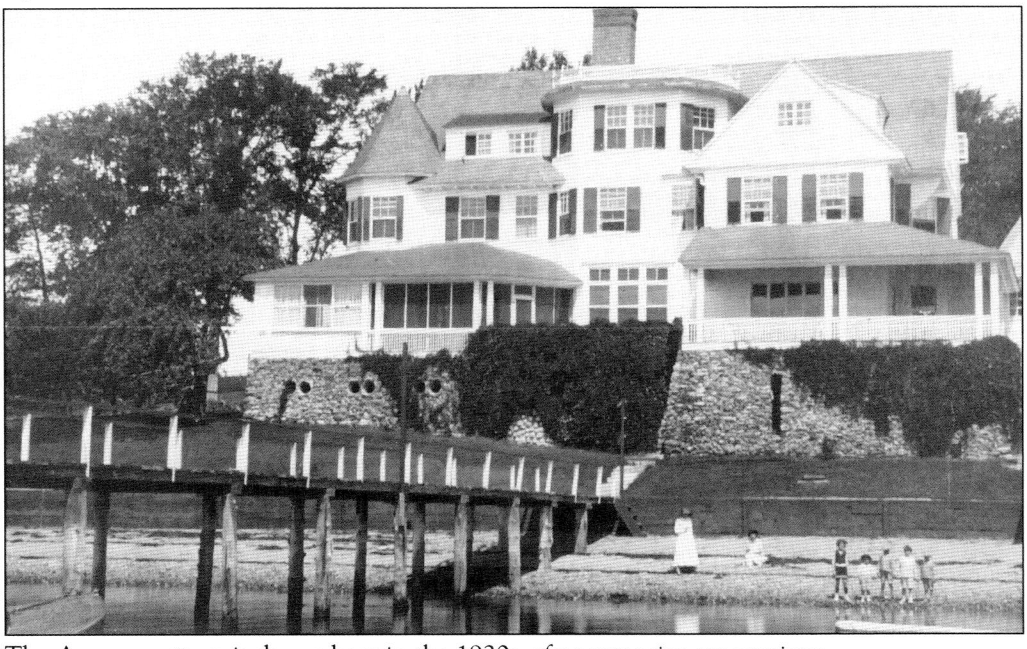

The Agoncy cottage is shown here in the 1920s, after extensive renovations.

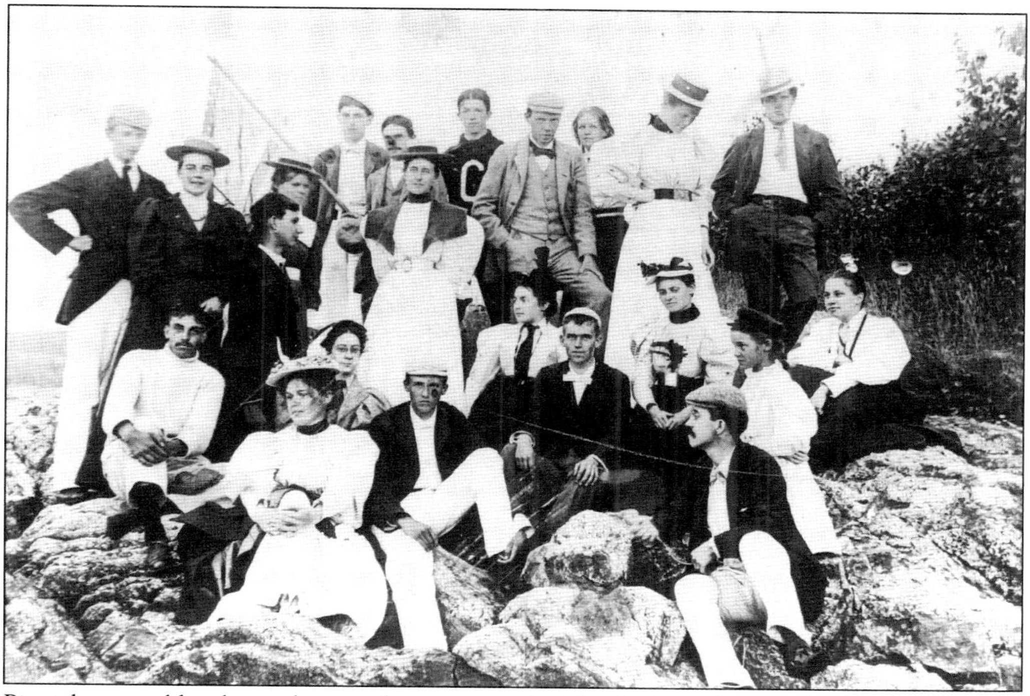

Picnickers would go by rowboat or sloop to a nearby island, where they would eat clams steamed in sea weed with sweet potatoes and a lobster or two snuggled beside them. Bacon and green ears of corn were sometimes roasted in the embers of a bonfire.

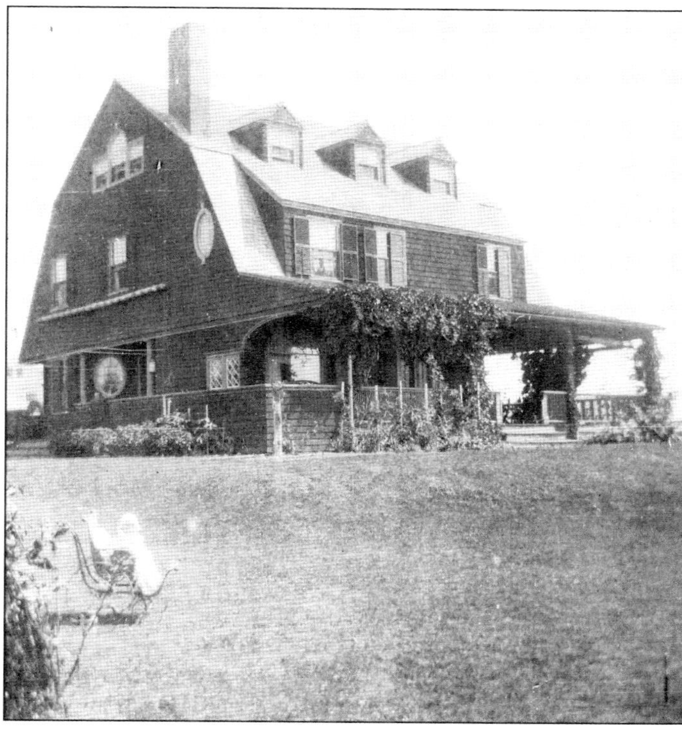

Thomas Blake built his summer cottage, "Belmont Cottage," in 1891–92. The gambrel-roofed, shingle-style cottage was designed by noted architect W.R. Emerson. This design became famous along the New England coast. Hope MacPherson Brown is in the wicker carriage.

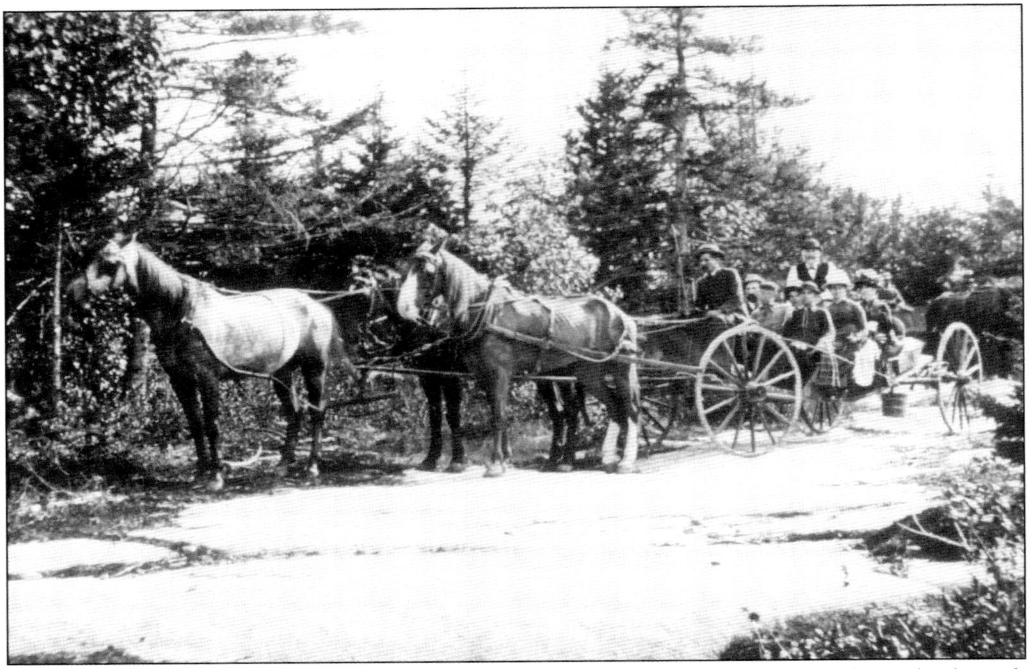

There were four nine-passenger buckboards in town that provided rides through Witherle Park and excursions to Brooksville on the ferry (see p. 123).

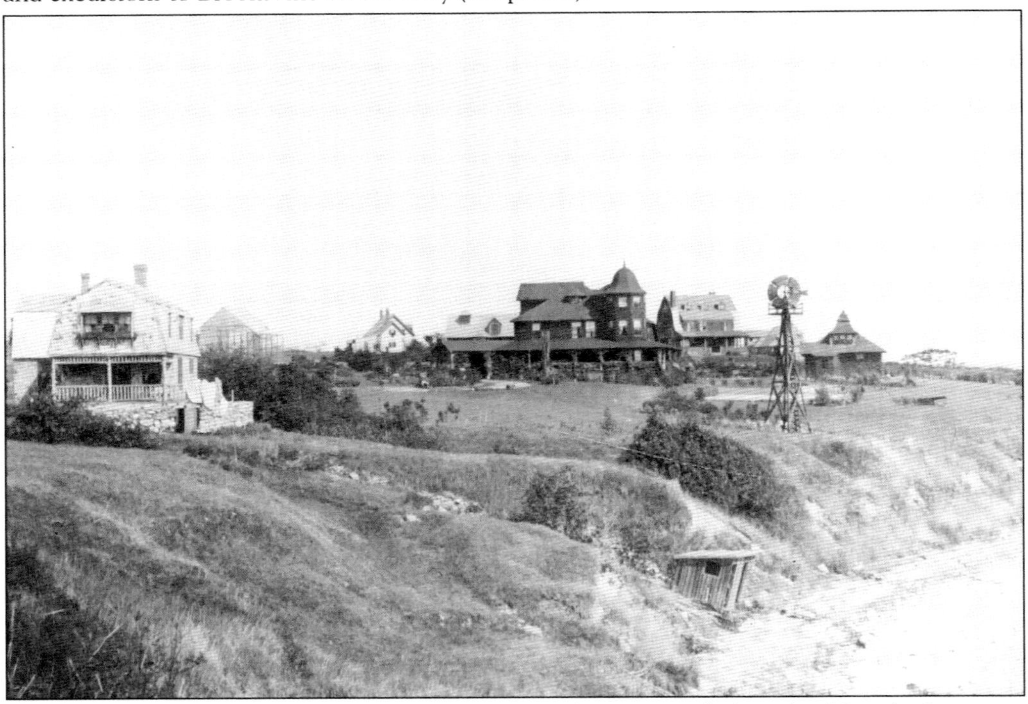

This photograph contains a number of interesting elements, including the "Carofan" cottage, the Blake tennis court, the Sylvester farm, "Otter Rock," the Solgar cottage (gone), and "Belmont Cottage." The windmills pumped water to the cottages from wells.

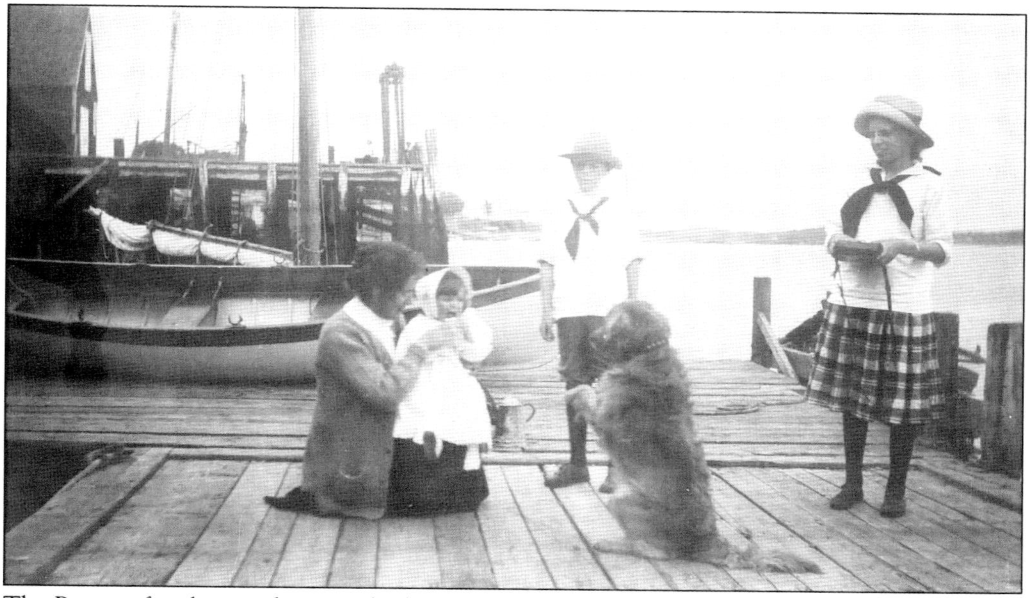

The Parsons family was photographed on a dock in 1910.

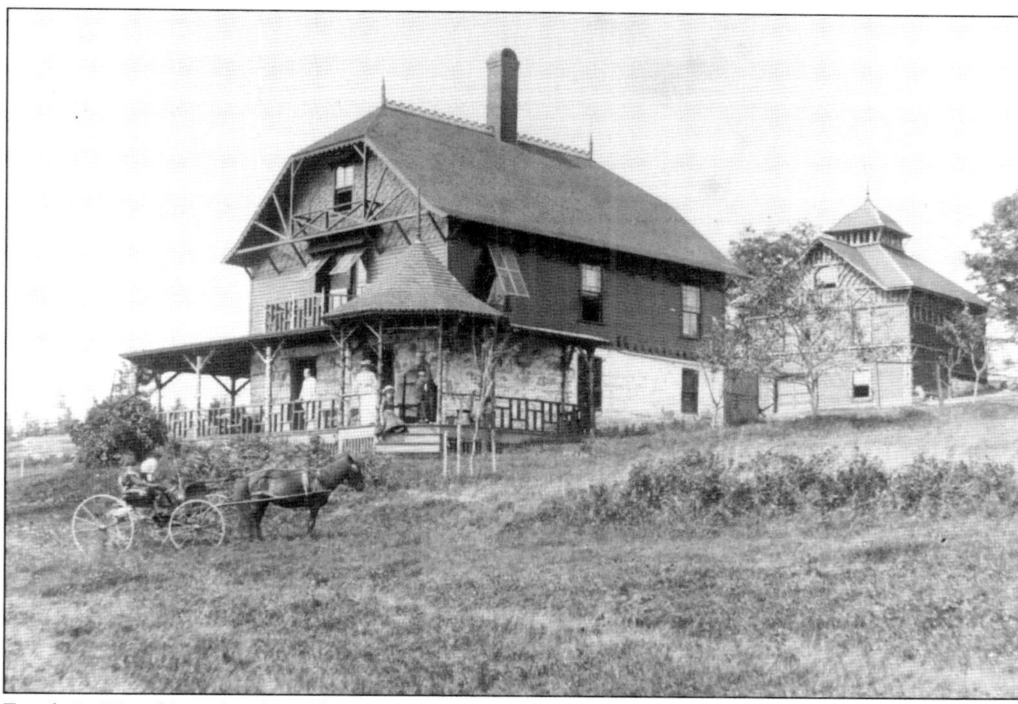

Frank P. Wood bought the old Witham farmhouse in 1884 in the southern end of town on what is now Perkins Street. The lower floor was made of stone and was at least one hundred years old at that time. An upper floor was added, with slabs covered with bark, making the "Stone Cottage" a very picturesque home. Mr. Wood also built several cottages to rent.

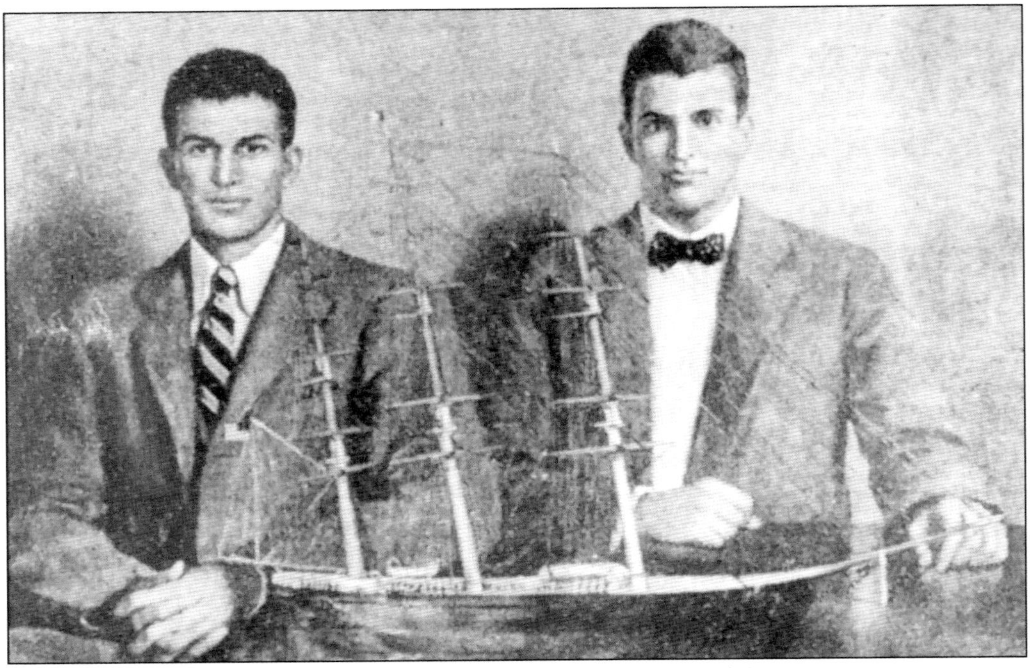

Richard Ames (1912–1935) and Henry Ames (1914–1935) hailed from a prominent summer family. They lost their lives while trying to save their father, Robert, when he was washed overboard in a storm off the coast of Newfoundland during a transatlantic race to Norway. Their mother, Margaret G. Ames, who continued to summer in Castine for many years, showed remarkable courage in the face of this triple tragedy and was a benefactor of the Castine Hospital and many other local projects (see p. 125).

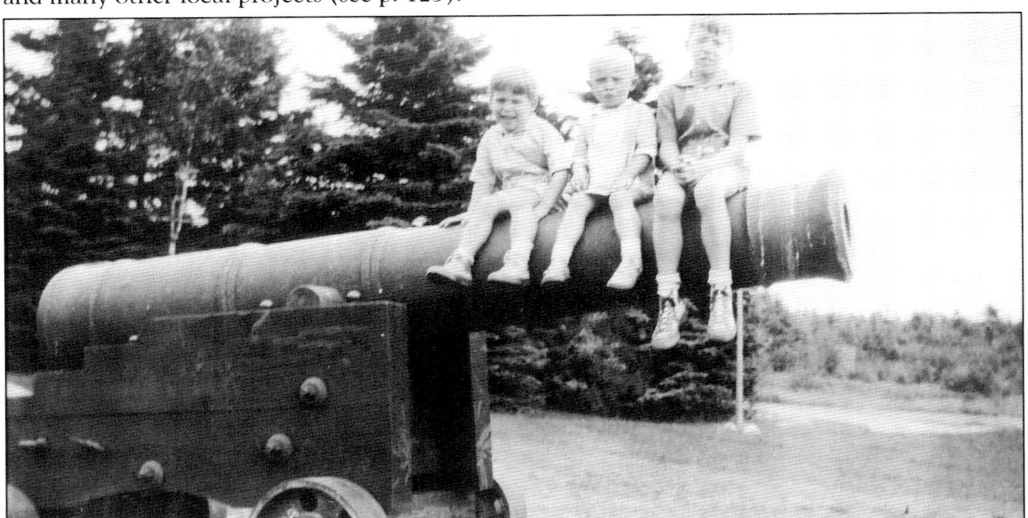

The cannon in front of the "Stone Cottage" on Perkins Street is one of five cannons in Castine. They are all relics of the War of 1812, except for the one in front of the town hall which was captured in the Philippines in 1889, and "loaned" to the town in 1901 by Commander Very of the gunboat USS *Castine*. The children are Francis "Buster" Brown (in the middle) and the Vetterlein brothers.

First Lady Eleanor Roosevelt, one of the many notables who came to Castine, visited often in the 1930s, staying with Molly Dewson and Polly Porter at "Moss Acre" (see p. 119).

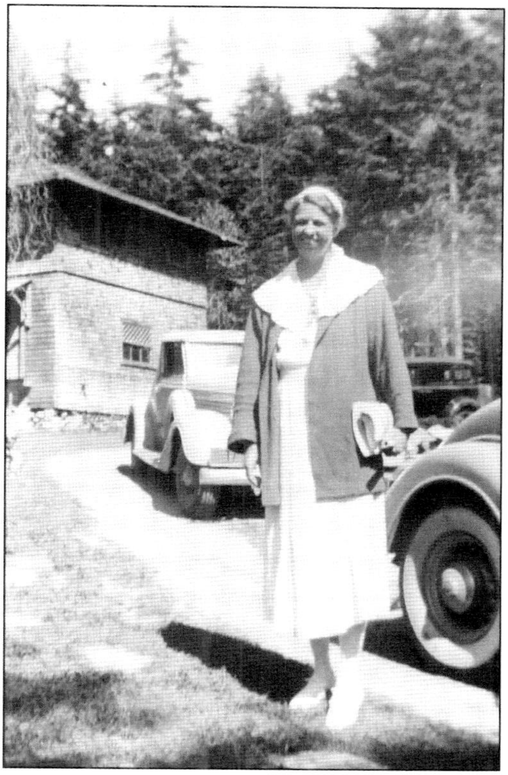

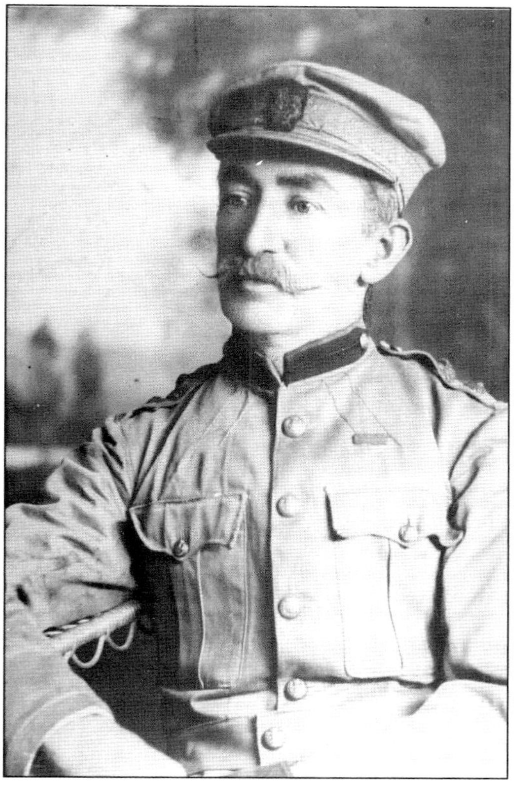

Lieutenant Colonel John Williams Castine, of Adelaide, South Australia, is a possible descendant of the Baron de St. Castin, through Anslem, the son of the Baron and Mathilde (the daughter of Madockawando, Chief of the Tarrantine). John visited Castine in 1923 with other members of his family and was royally treated by the townspeople at a banquet and reception given in honor of the family at the town hall.

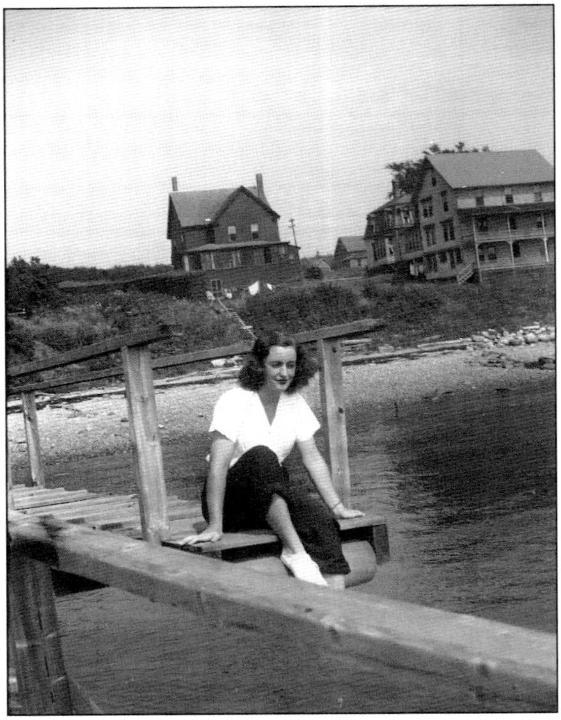

Long-time summer resident Barbara Young Tenney, *c*. 1938, poses on the Volkman's pier in front of some cottages on Perkins Street. The house on the right shows a large boarding house extension toward the water that has since been removed. Teachers and others came to Castine for their summer vacations and stayed in the various boarding houses around town.

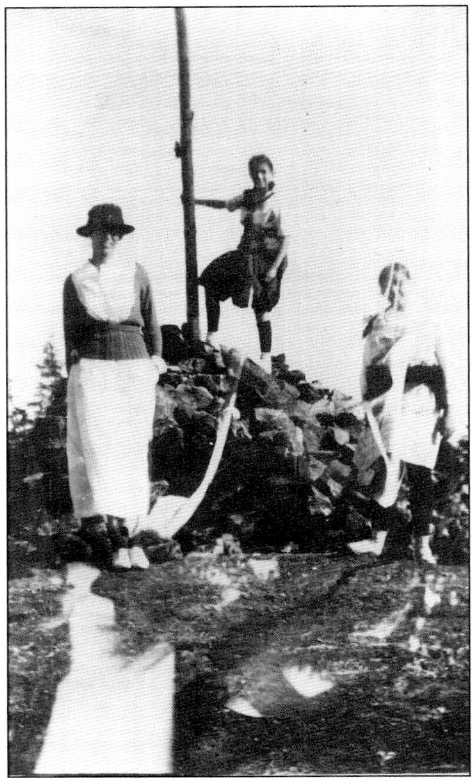

Hiking has always been a popular summer activity. This group stands proudly on the top of Blue Hill in 1919.

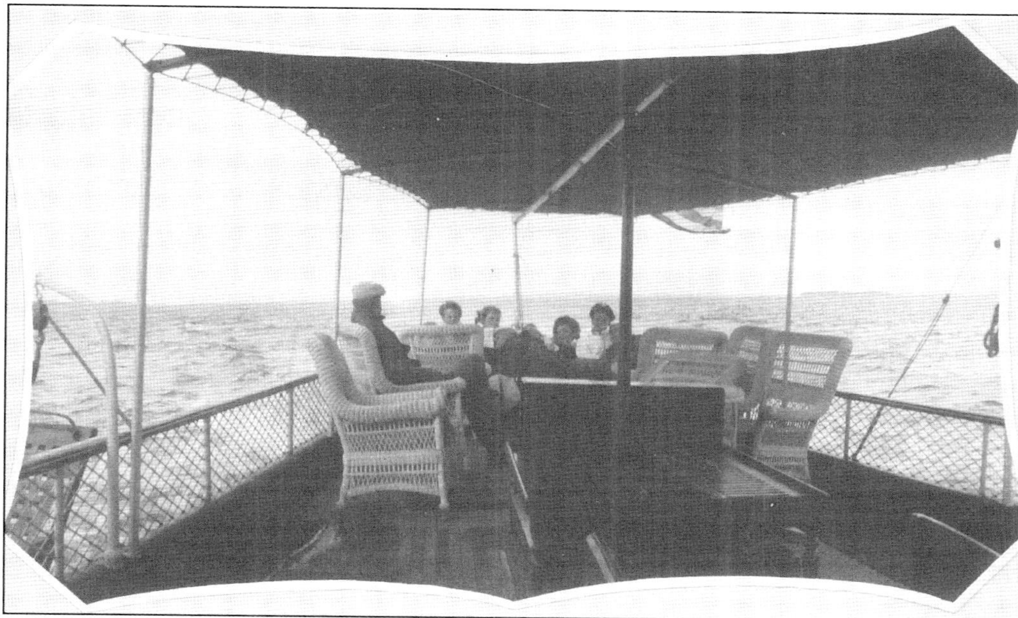

This beautifully-appointed yacht was photographed in 1910.

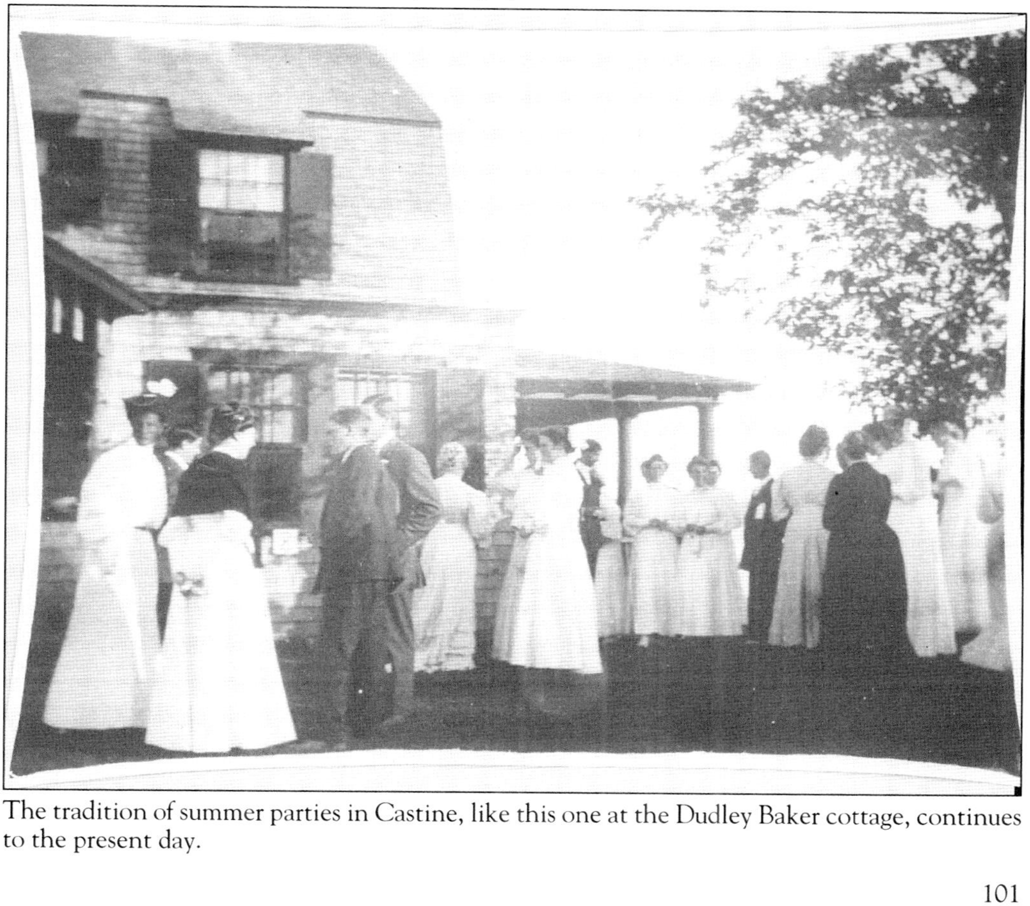

The tradition of summer parties in Castine, like this one at the Dudley Baker cottage, continues to the present day.

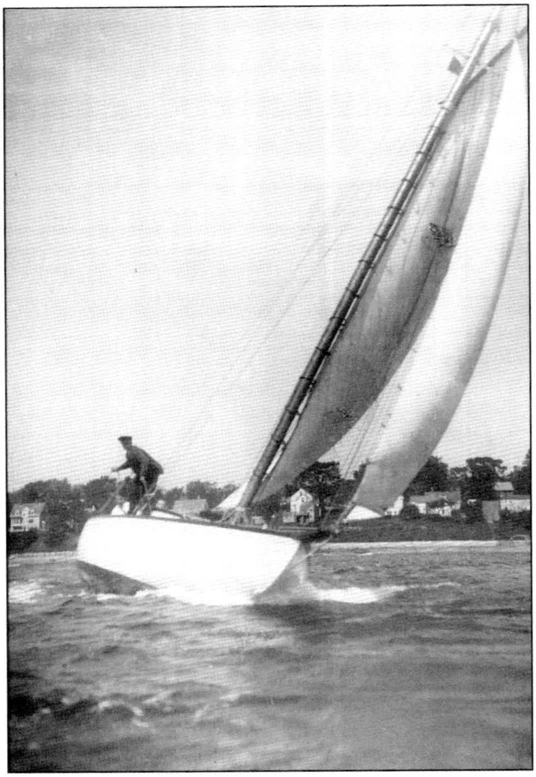

The sloop *Papoose* was first owned by Thomas D. Blake, and later sold to Dr. Alice North. The skipper was Captain Charles Patterson.

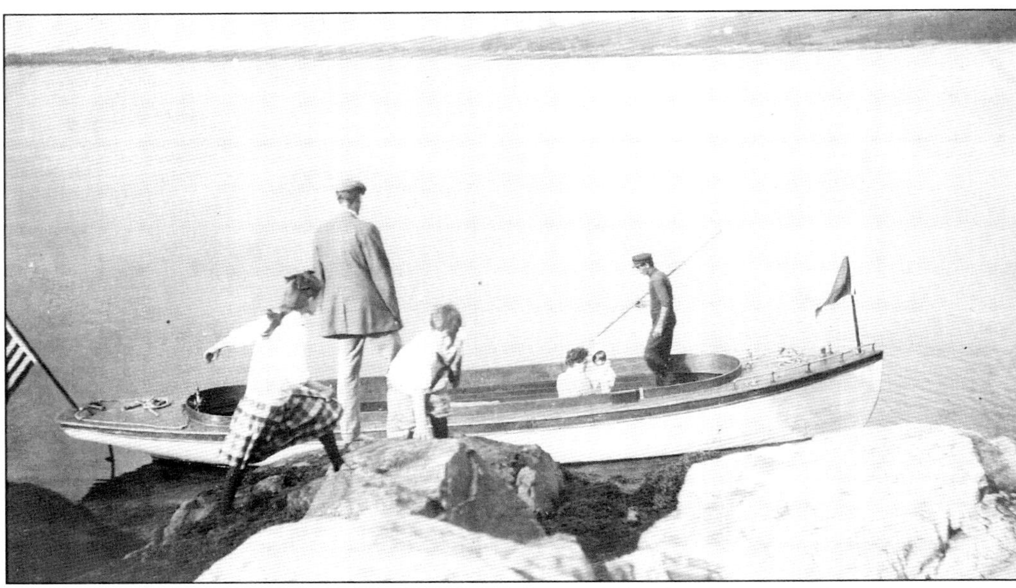

This group is boarding a launch on Nautilus Island, *c.* 1910, for the trip back to Castine. Even canoeists traveled far from the harbor, sometimes paddling around Cape Rosier.

Peggy Parsons Robinson (left) and Helen Goodwin Austin are shown here, *c.* 1910.

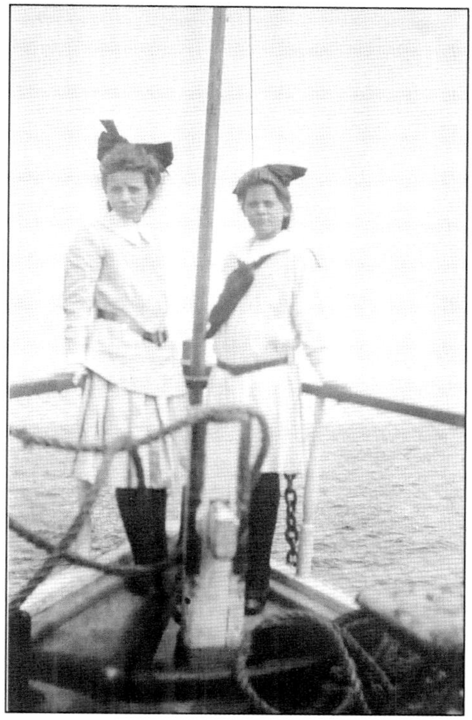

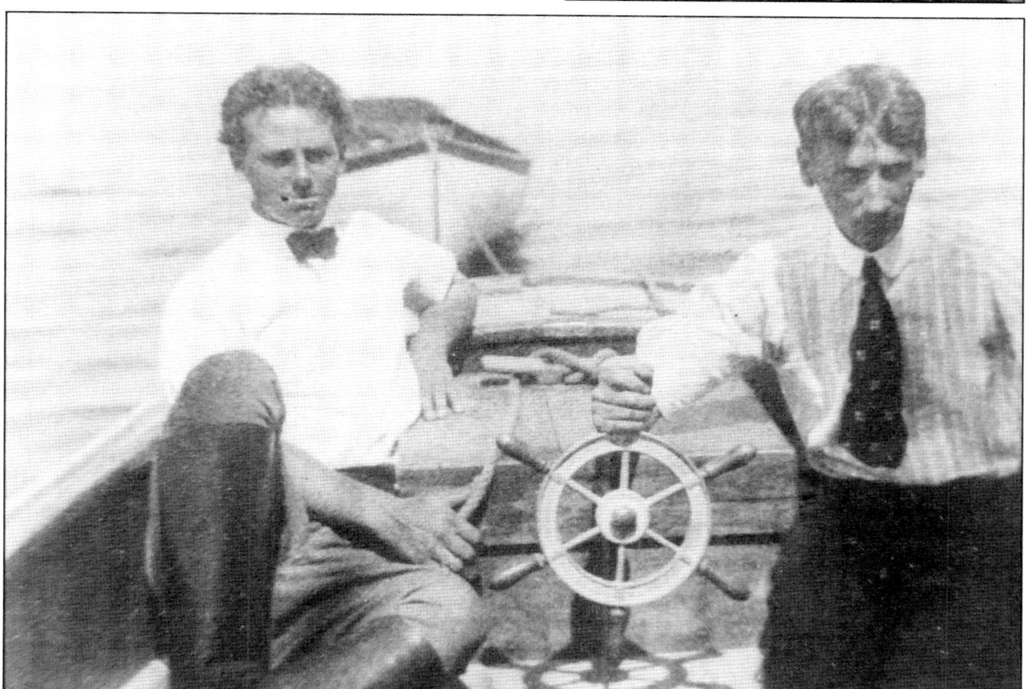

These two well-dressed men were photographed while out for a sail, *c.* 1900. Adventurous sailors in small sloops or catboats would brave the "Reach" to Deer Isle or further out at sea to Isle au Haut.

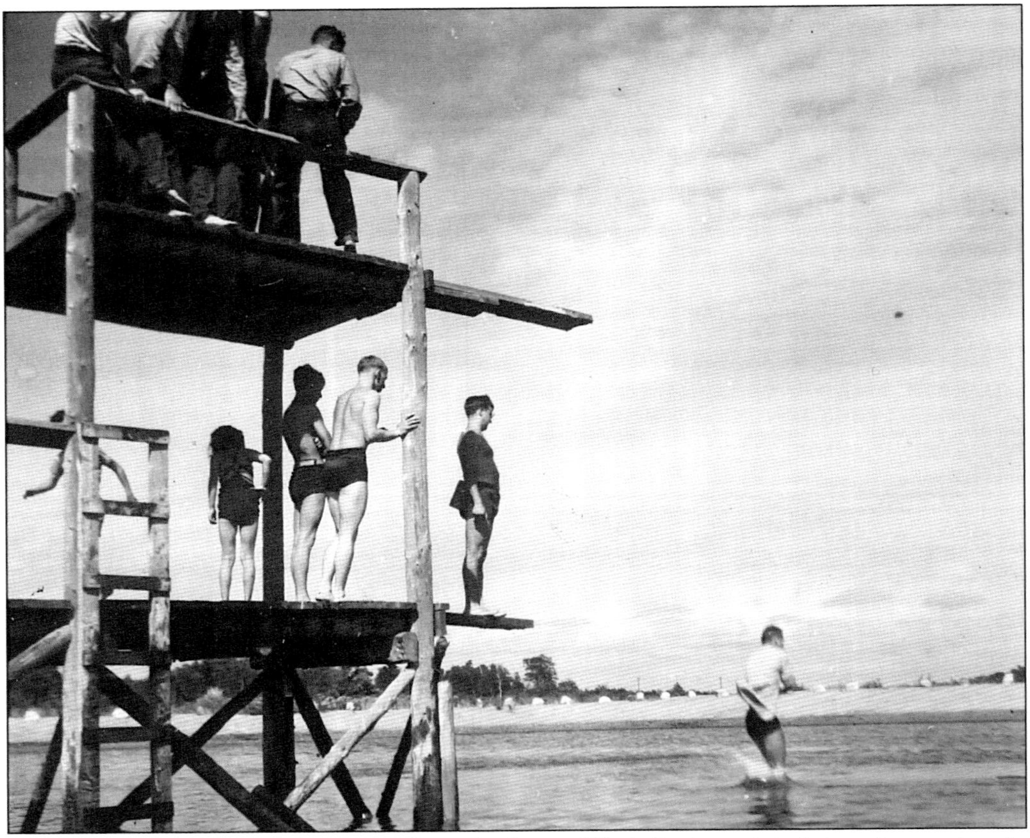

The Castine saltwater swimming pool was built as a Work Projects Administration project in 1934 during the depths of the Depression. It had a diving tower and was 170 feet wide and 470 feet long. Located across the road from the beach at Wadsworth Cove, it filled and emptied with the tides. The swimming pool remains a happy memory for the hundreds who swam there until it was closed in the 1960s.

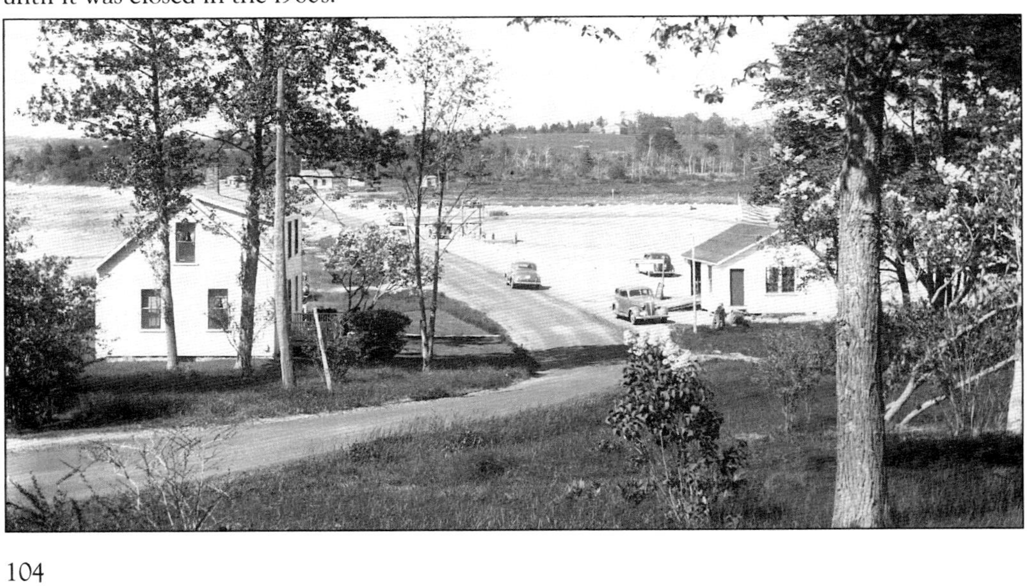

This precarious pyramid of swimmers was photographed in the 1920s.

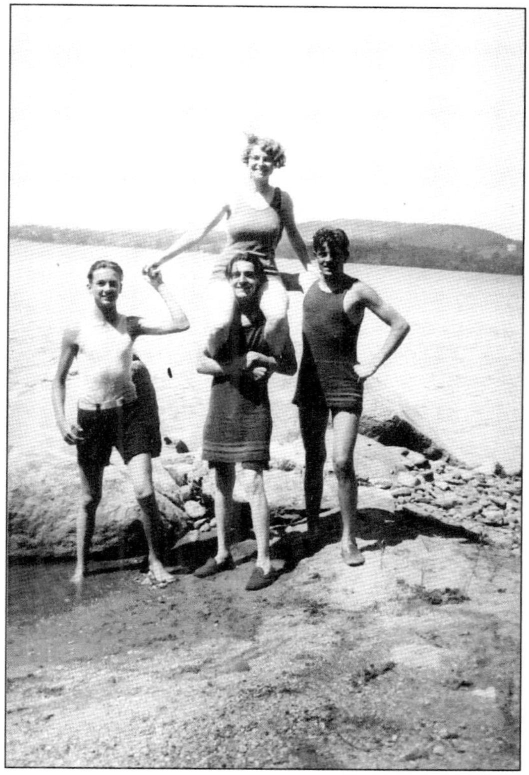

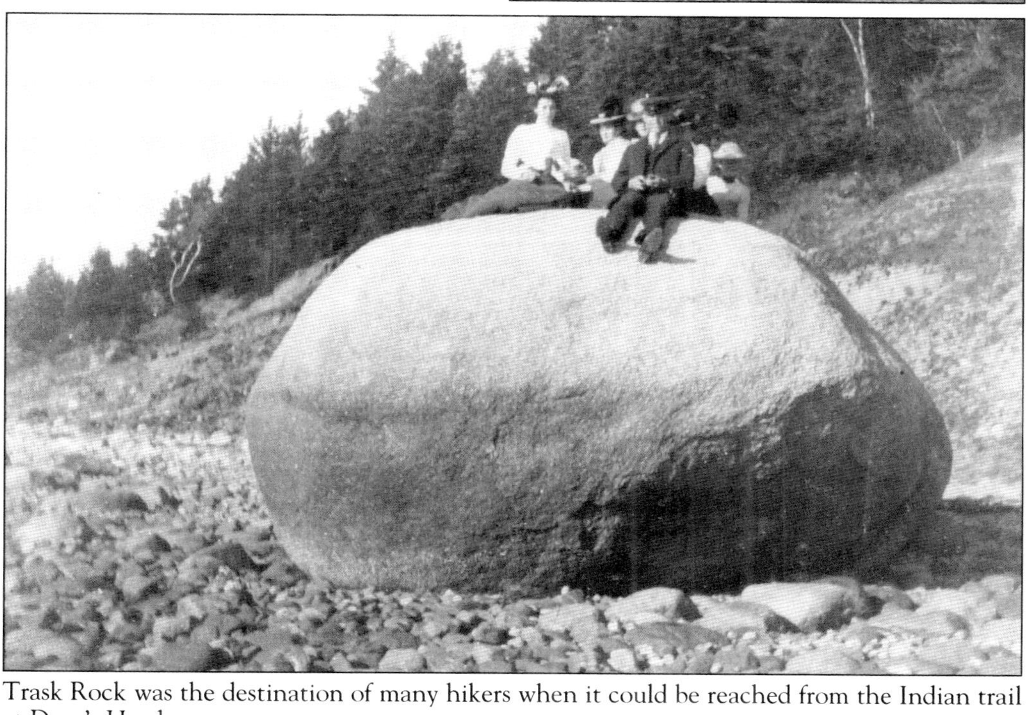

Trask Rock was the destination of many hikers when it could be reached from the Indian trail at Dyce's Head.

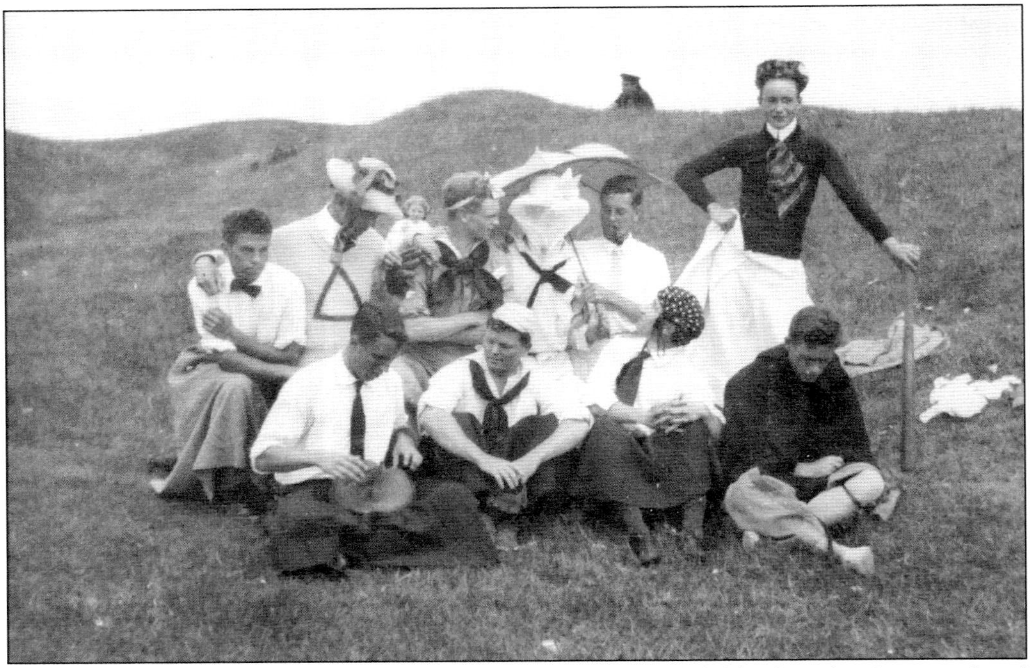

By the 1880s, the interior of Fort George was used as a baseball field, where local teams played neighboring teams. In this 1908 photograph, a men's team, handicapped in skirts, takes a break from an exciting game against the women. The teams were known as the "Paralyzers" and the "Pulverizers."

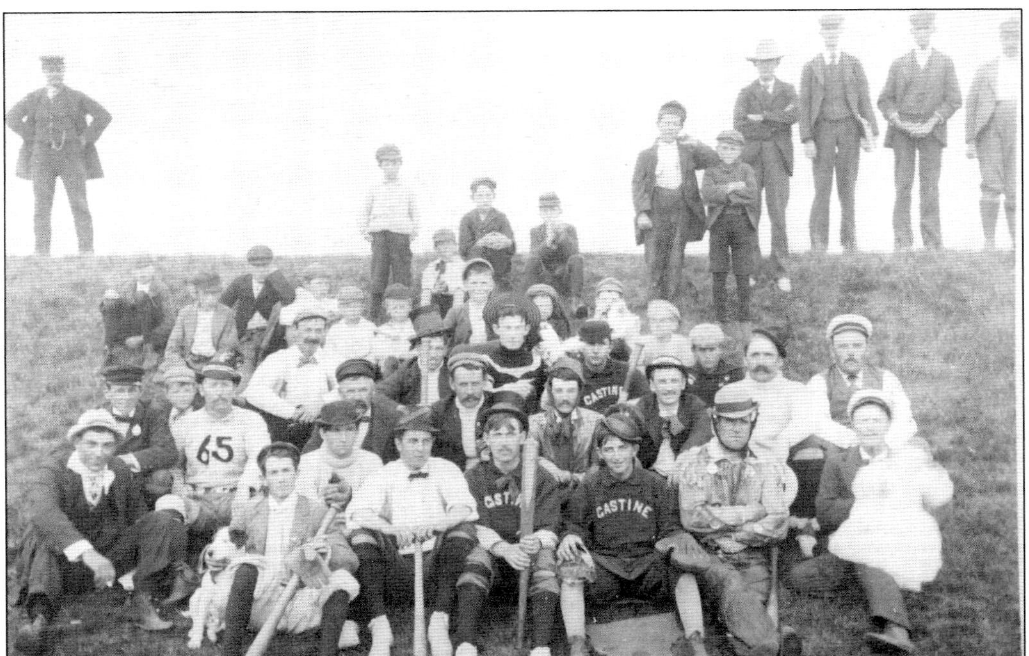

At this game in 1898, married men teamed up to challenge bachelors.

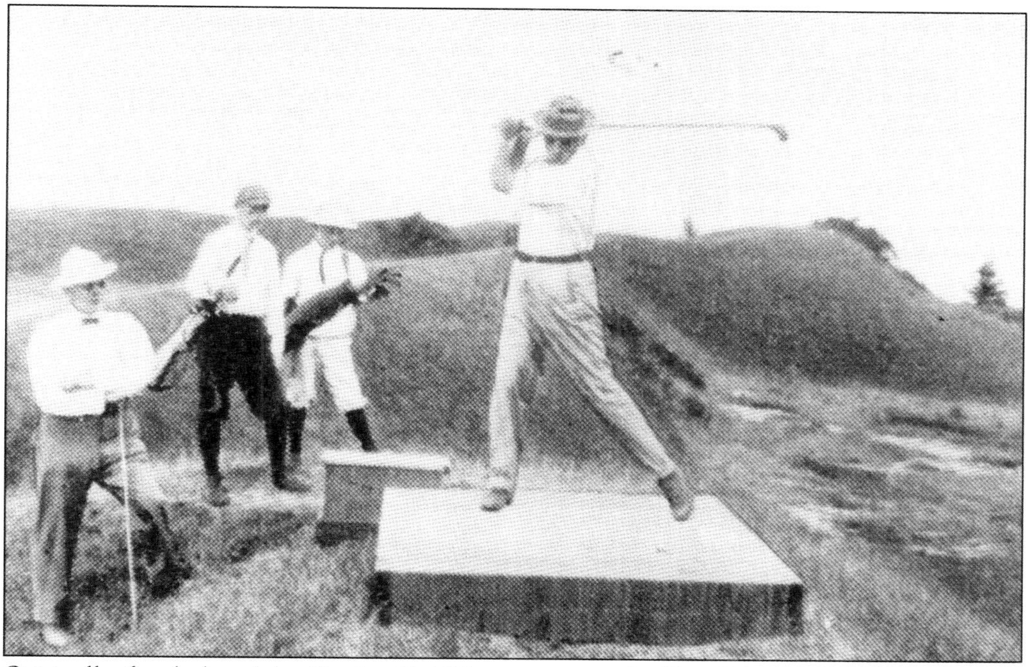

Originally, five holes of the Castine Golf Course were in the Fort George area. The tee for the first hole was on a rampart of Fort George. Golfers hit their first drive across Wadsworth Cove Road, past where the golf shop is now, and down the first fairway.

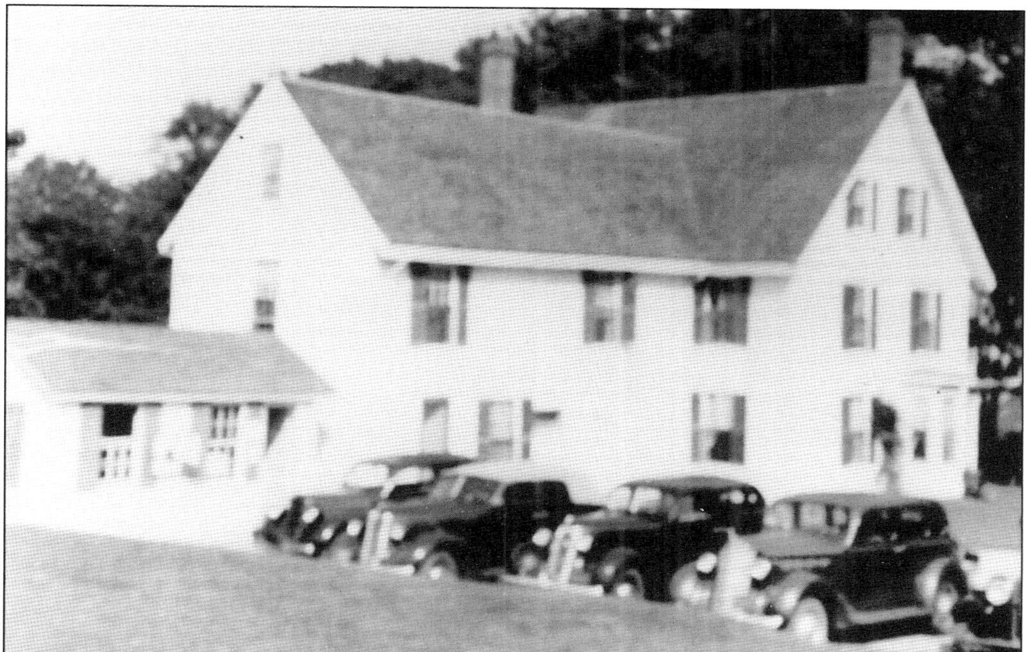

The Castine Golf Club was opened in 1897. The Stevens homestead became the clubhouse for the 9-hole course in 1918. W.E. Mikell, dean of the University of Pennsylvania Law School, was the club's first president.

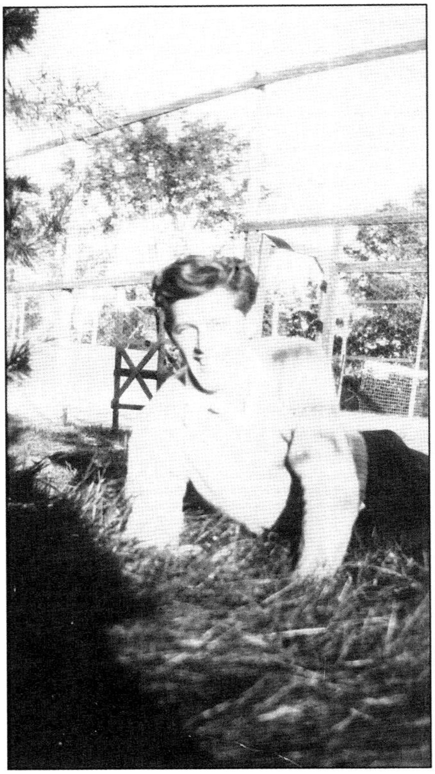

T.P. Perkins, who grew up in Castine, was one of the area's star tennis players in the 1930s.

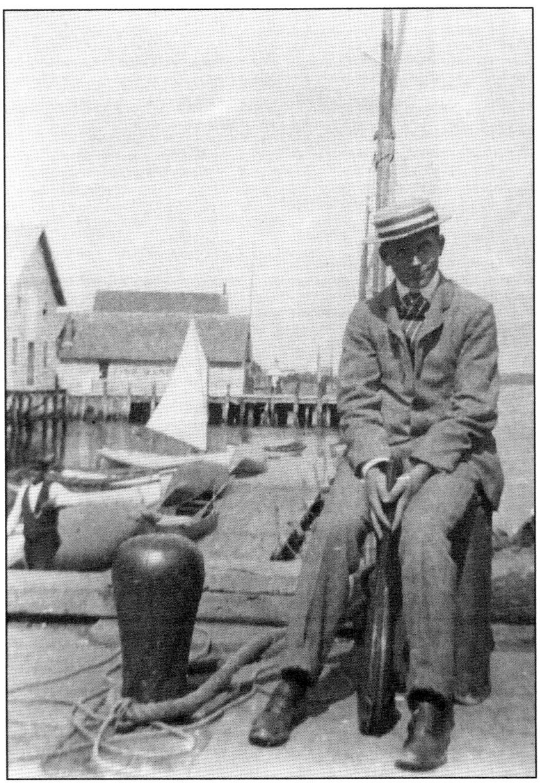

Sitting on Commercial Wharf with tennis racquet in hand, this young man waits patiently for a steamer in 1898.

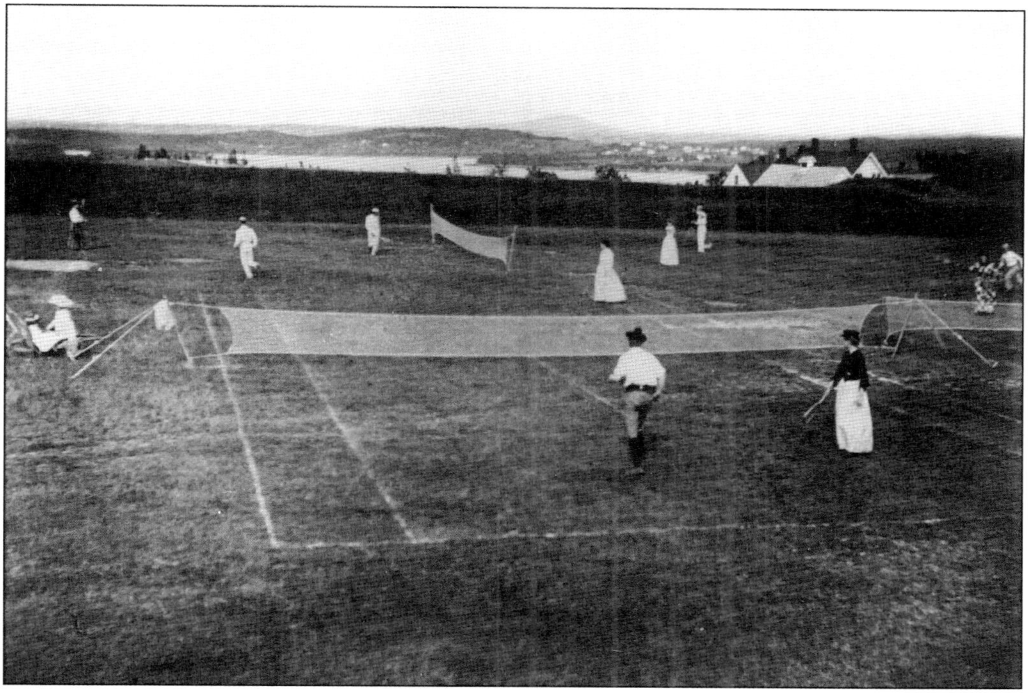

Sports attire at the end of the nineteenth century was very restrictive, as can be seen in this photograph of a tennis tournament in Fort George. Women wore full-length dresses with long sleeves, two full-length petticoats, and tightly-laced corsets. By the mid 1890s they were wearing shorter skirts so they wouldn't drag on the wet grass, sleeves were pinned out of the way, and hats were discarded. Men played in dress shirts and ties.

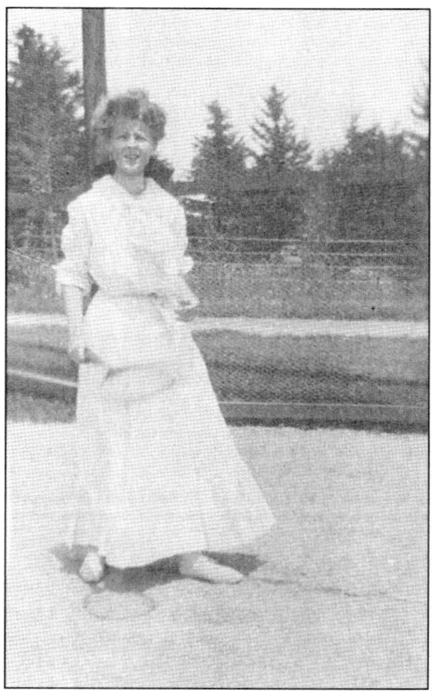

This tennis player is G.B. Rose, *c.* 1904.

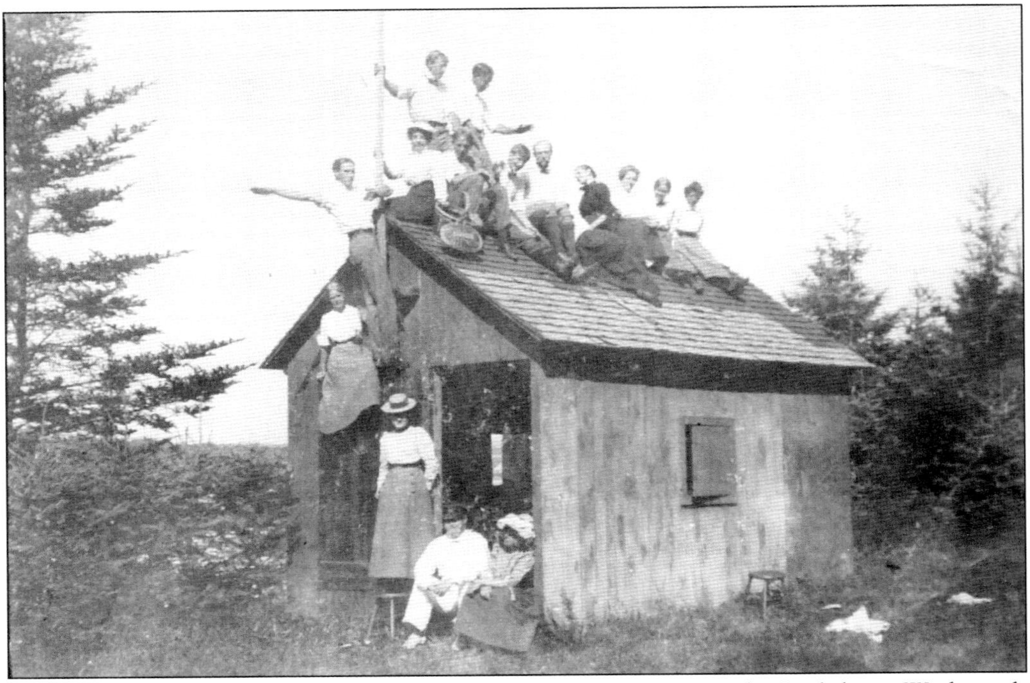

The Bates family and friends are shown here at the "girls' camp" on the Backshore, Wadsworth Cove, 1898.

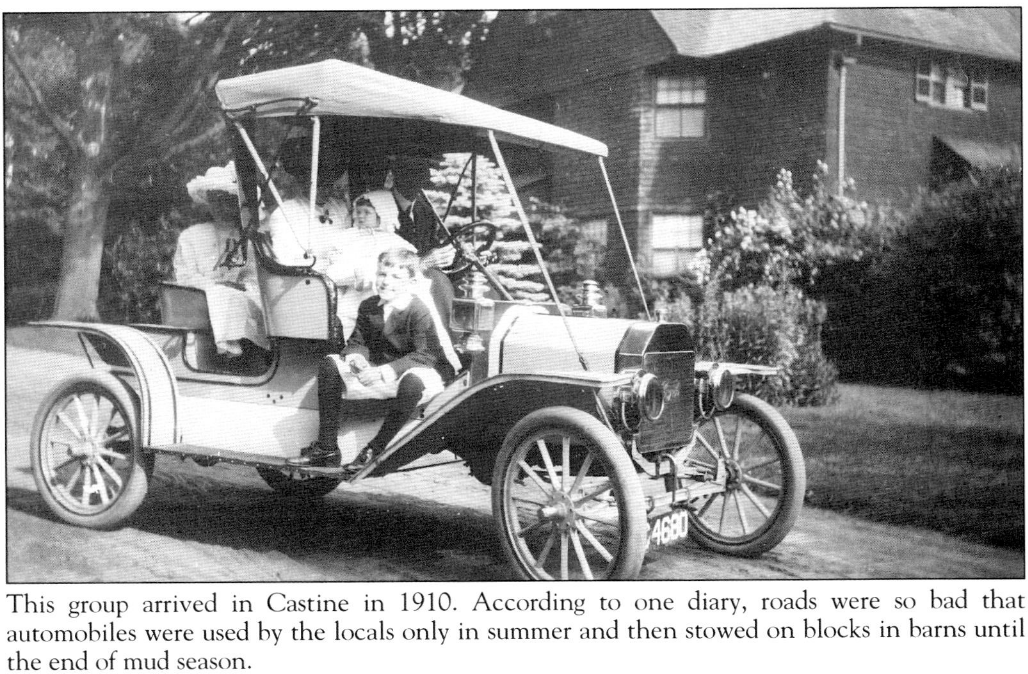

This group arrived in Castine in 1910. According to one diary, roads were so bad that automobiles were used by the locals only in summer and then stowed on blocks in barns until the end of mud season.

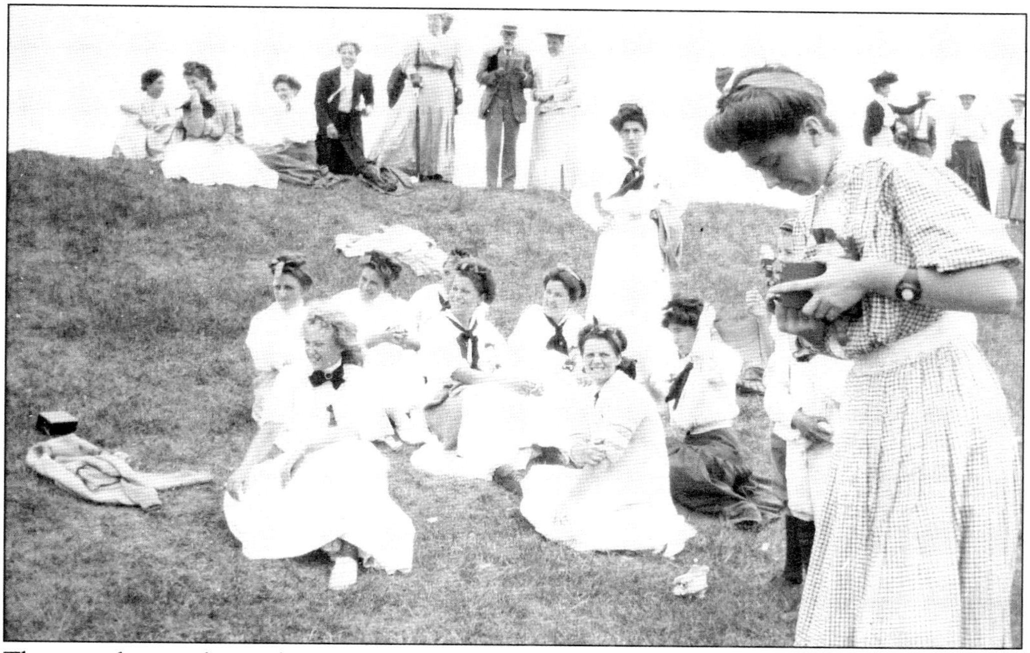

This crowd is watching a baseball game in Fort George, *c.* 1900.

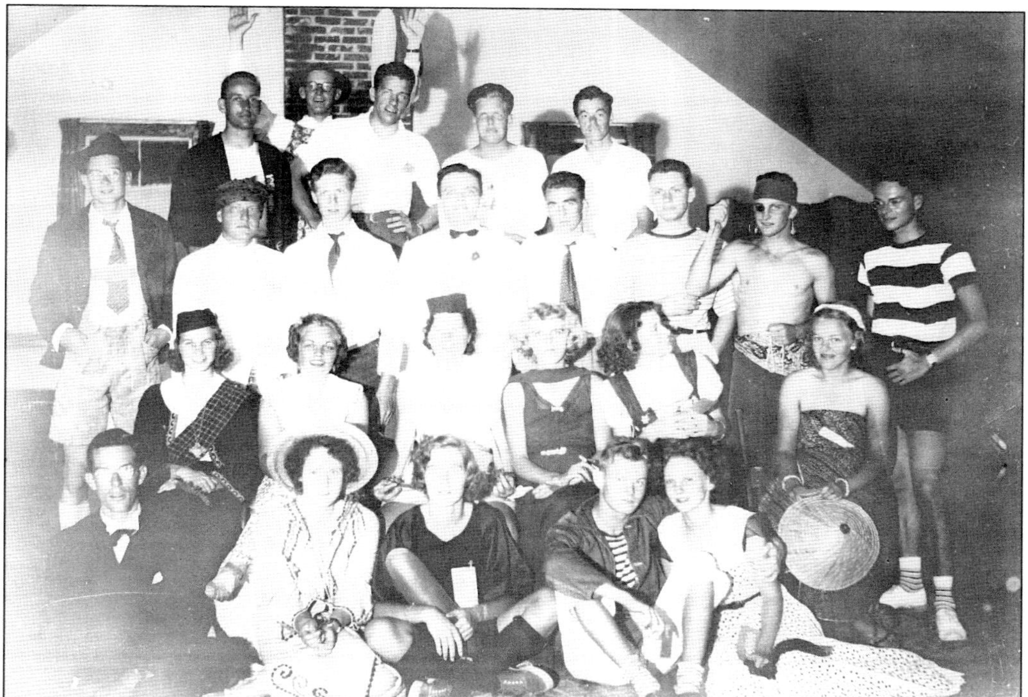

Teenagers in the 1930s who vacationed here had many opportunities for good times. This group put on plays and other entertainments in the Pierce barn on Perkins Street. "Wear what You Dare" was the theme of this party in 1937. Some of the families included were the Taylors, Wilsons, Nashes, Youngs, Pierces, Thomases, Nicholsons, and the Tenneys.

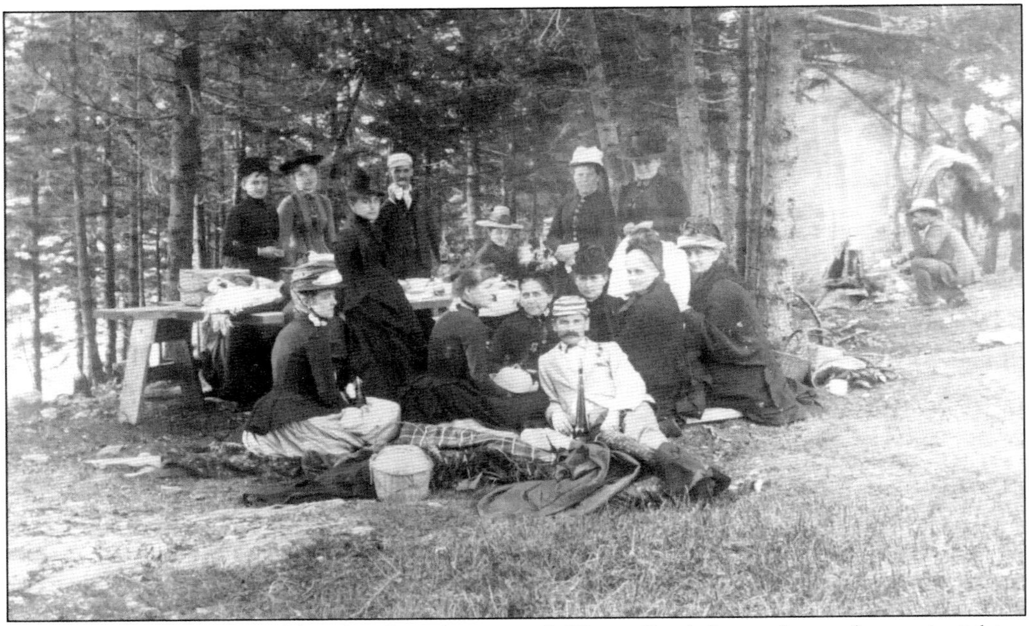

Members of the McLaughlin family, who owned "Otter Rock," are shown here picnicking in Witherle Park in the late 1800s. Vacationers also enjoyed rides in fringed buckboards on carriage trails in the beautiful woods, where they passed old forts, batteries, rifle pits, the site of the Blockhouse, and the Indian trail. The park is named after George M. Witherle, who opened the area to the public.

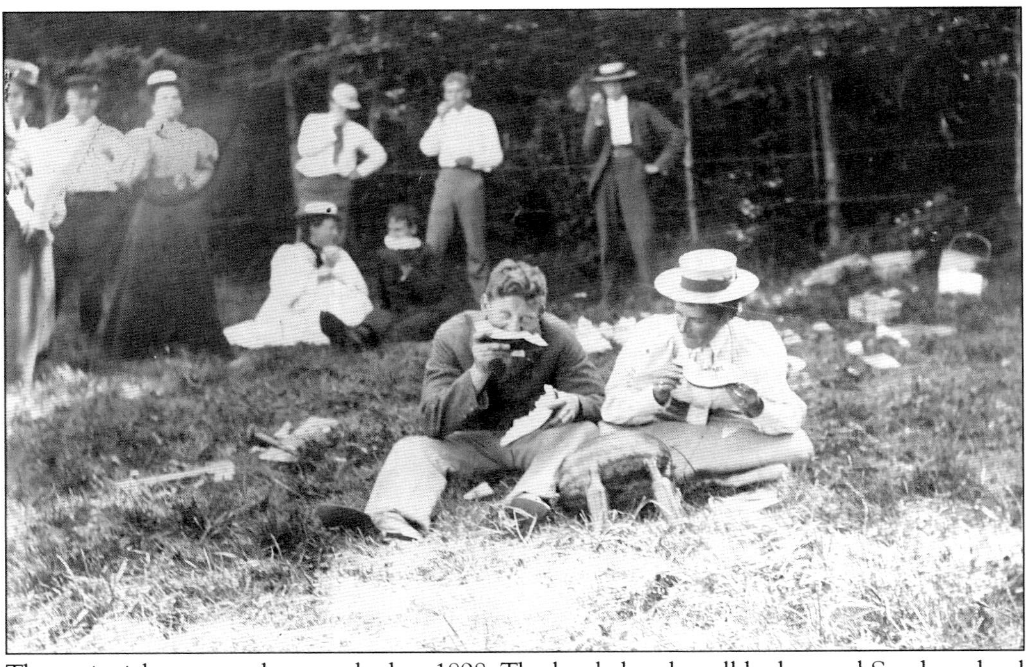

These picnickers were photographed, *c.* 1898. The local churches all had annual Sunday school picnics, traveling to Washington Grove in Witherle Park for a day of games and delicious food.

Seven

"Off-Neck"

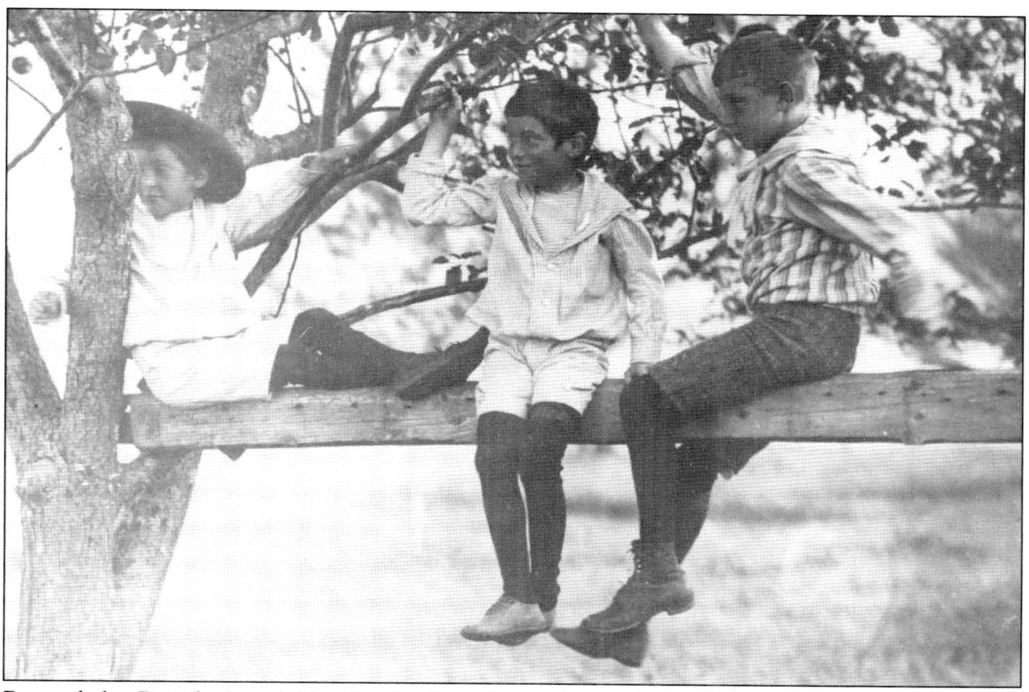

Beyond the British Canal (dug by the British in 1814 to keep the Redcoats from deserting), past Wadsworth Cove, Hatch's Cove, and over Neck Bridge, lies the rest of Castine known as "off-neck."

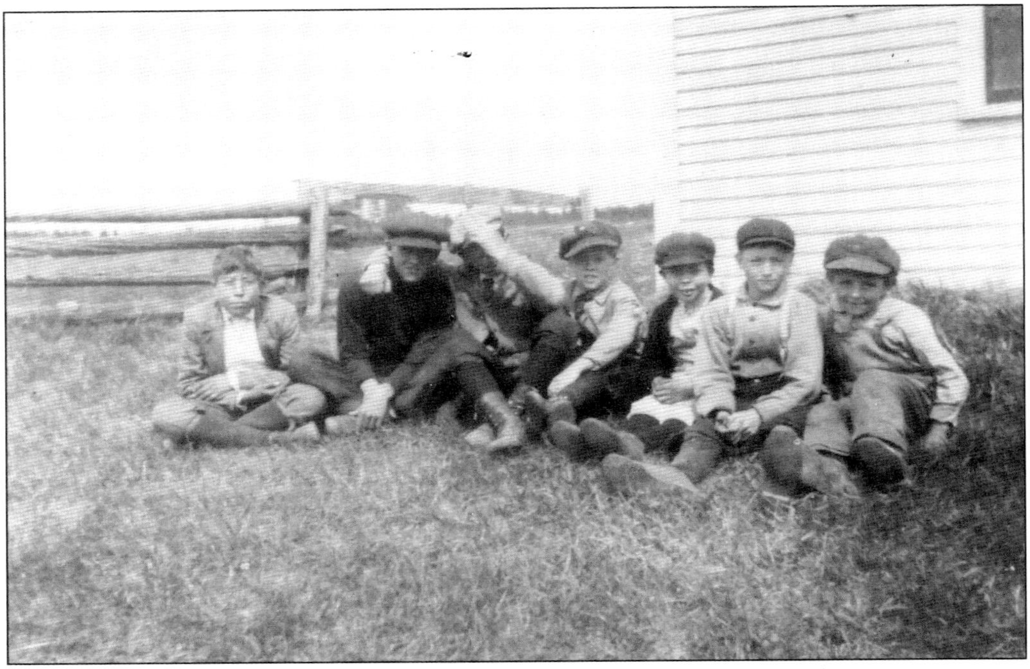

These children are in front of the Devereux School in Penobscot, one of the many one-room schools "off-neck." Until 1920, Castine's school system was divided into districts. Every 3 or 4 miles along Route 166 and 166A there was a school, usually named after the donating landowner. In the pre-bus era, children hiked to school, winter or summer.

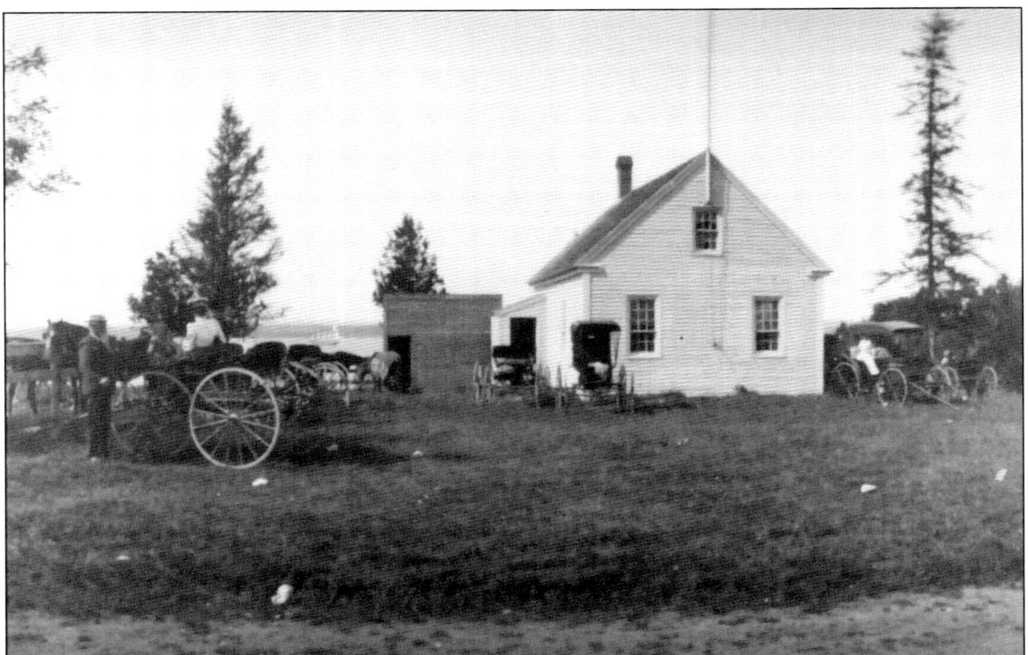

The Steele School was the site of a Grange fair in the late 1800s.

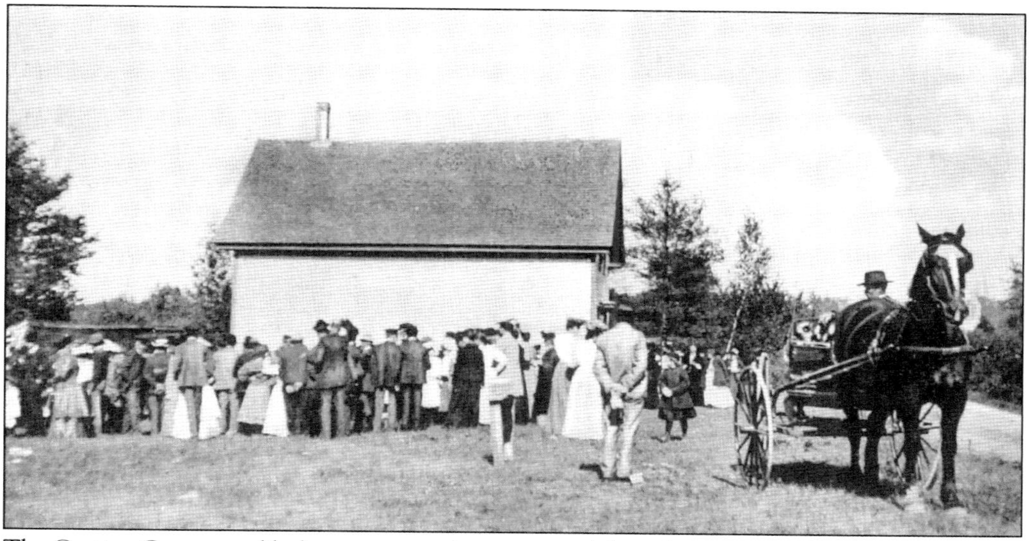

The Castine Grange and lodges were very important to life in Castine. Membership also brought such benefits as a burial fund or a retirement home. In 1883, there were five to six hundred members from Castine and the surrounding area enrolled in the Grange. Between 1870 and 1920 more than thirty clubs were formed in Castine, including a Shakespeare Club, a Minstrel Club, a Masonic Lodge, Eastern Star, YWCA, and many others. The Castine Grange remains active today.

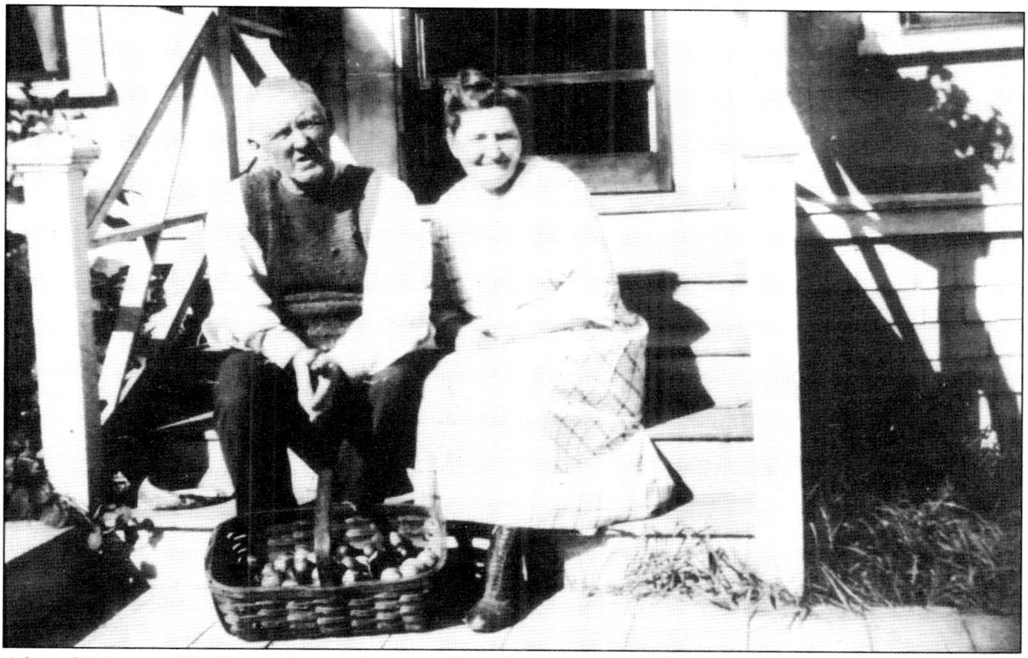

Al and Marion Clark are shown here in their later years, in front of their farm on Route 166, purchased in 1923. They built a large barn with a silo, and stocked it with sheep, hogs, and twenty-two cows. The barn stood in the Morgrage field, now the site of Castine Cottages, overlooking the Bagaduce. The farm provided produce for the Clark's hotels and general store (see pp. 21 and 59).

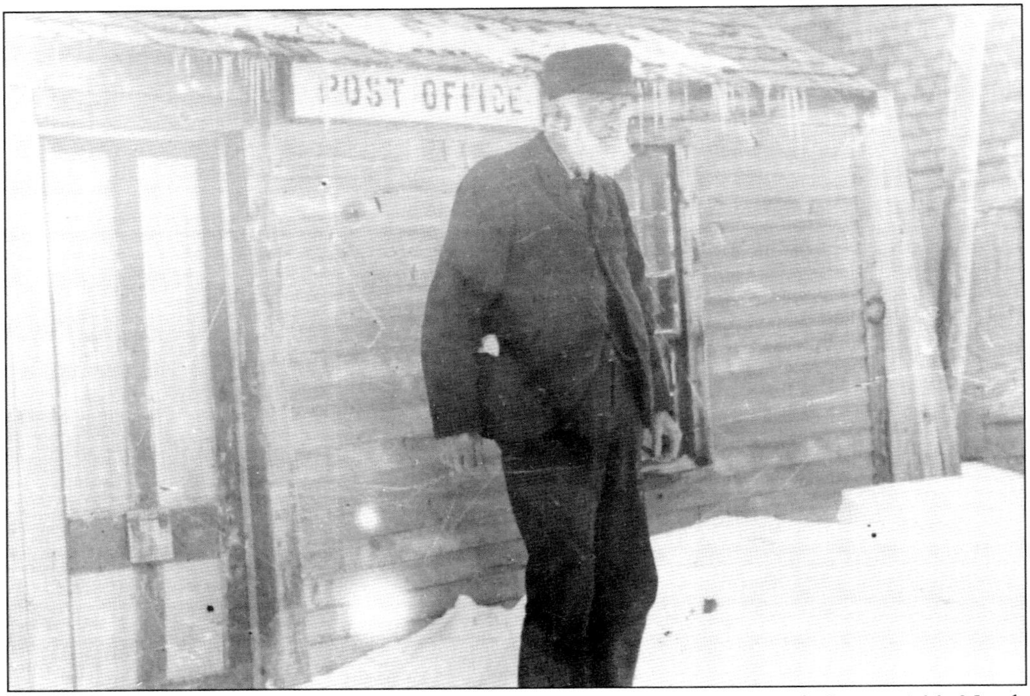

Postmaster Waters stands in front of his workplace on the Ferry Road, Route 166, North Castine, *c.* 1900.

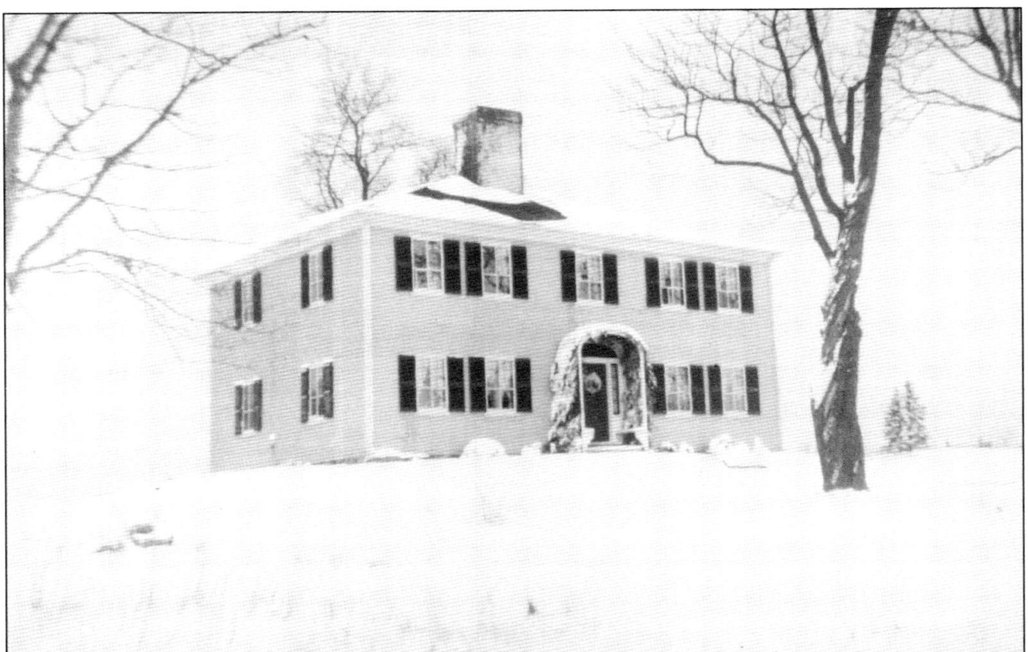

This center-chimney Federal house on the hill just "off-neck" overlooks the British Canal. The residence was built, *c.* 1795, for Jonathan Hatch.

Jeremiah and Phoebe Hatch, *c.* 1890, the grandparents of J. Merton Hatch and Frieda Hatch Matheson, lived on the Hatch farm. Four generations of the Hatch family lived there.

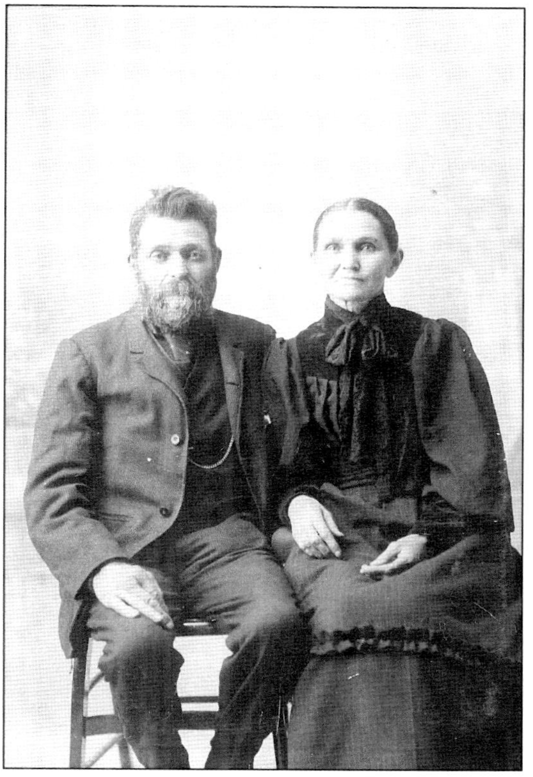

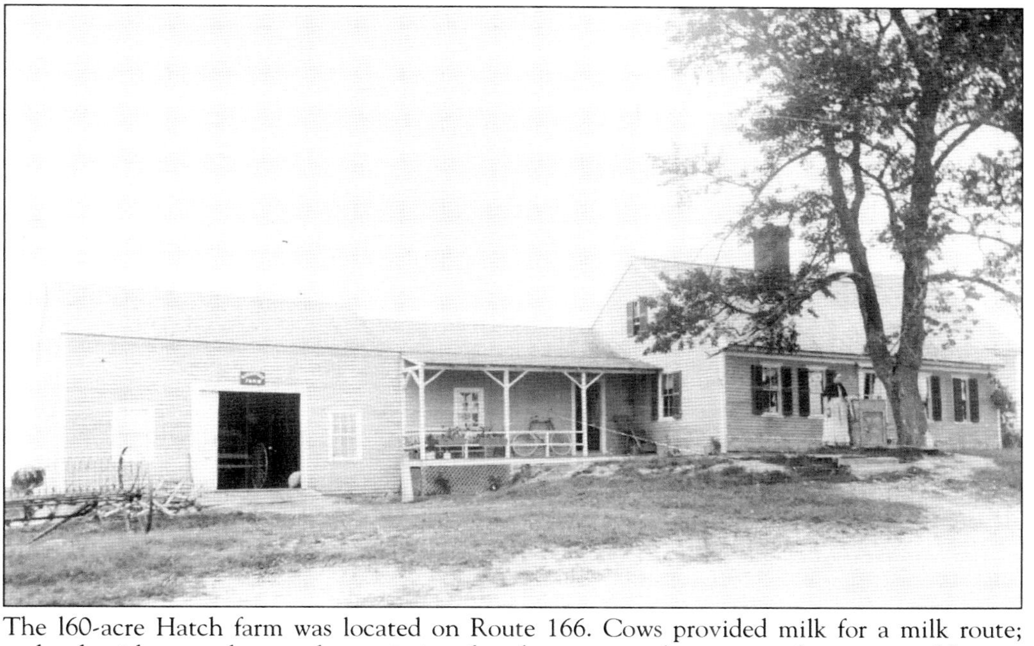

The 160-acre Hatch farm was located on Route 166. Cows provided milk for a milk route; orchards with more than twelve varieties of apples were another source of income, and haying was an important endeavor. All kinds of animals were raised on this farm as well. Today three houses sit on the land that was formerly called "Bagaduce Farm" by the Hatch family.

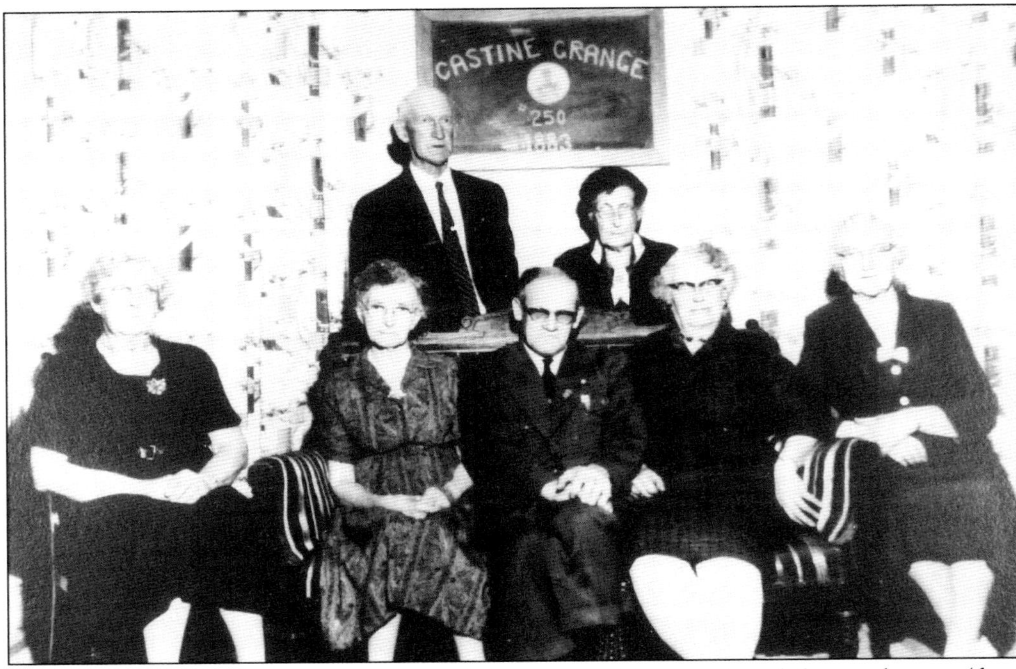

This 1940s photograph shows members of the Castine Grange. From left to right are: (front row) Florence Wardwell, Ethel Leach, Austin Heath, Mary Devereux, and Lawrence Devereux; (back row) Frank Devereux and Eva Bowden.

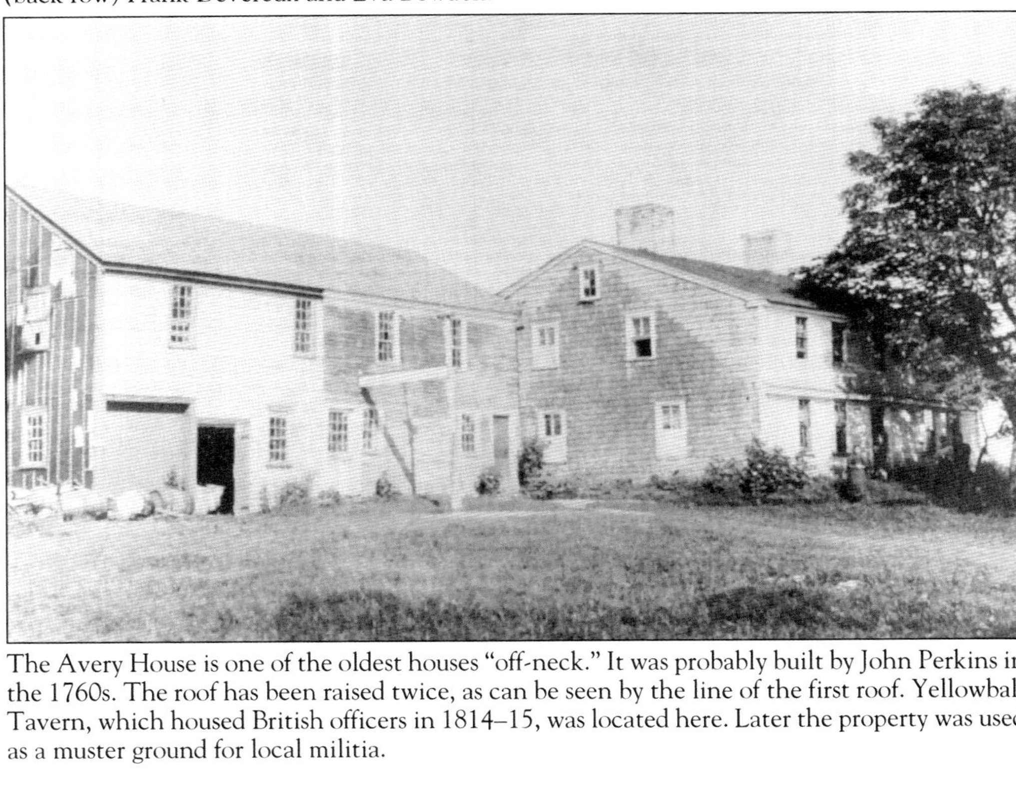

The Avery House is one of the oldest houses "off-neck." It was probably built by John Perkins in the 1760s. The roof has been raised twice, as can be seen by the line of the first roof. Yellowball Tavern, which housed British officers in 1814–15, was located here. Later the property was used as a muster ground for local militia.

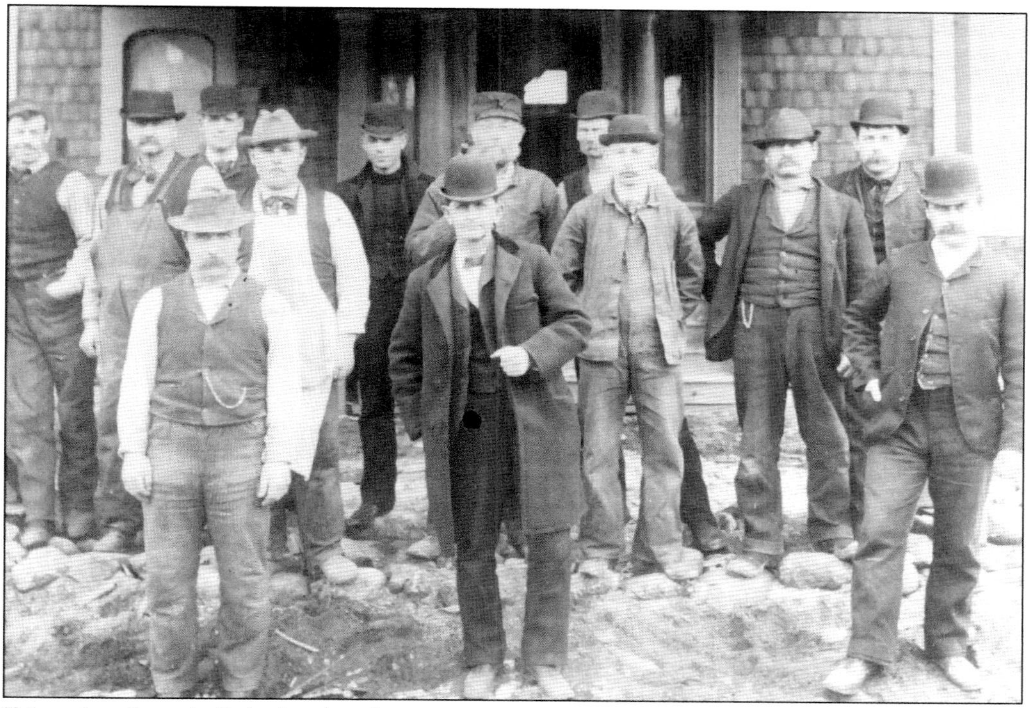

"Moss Acre" was built by local craftsmen.

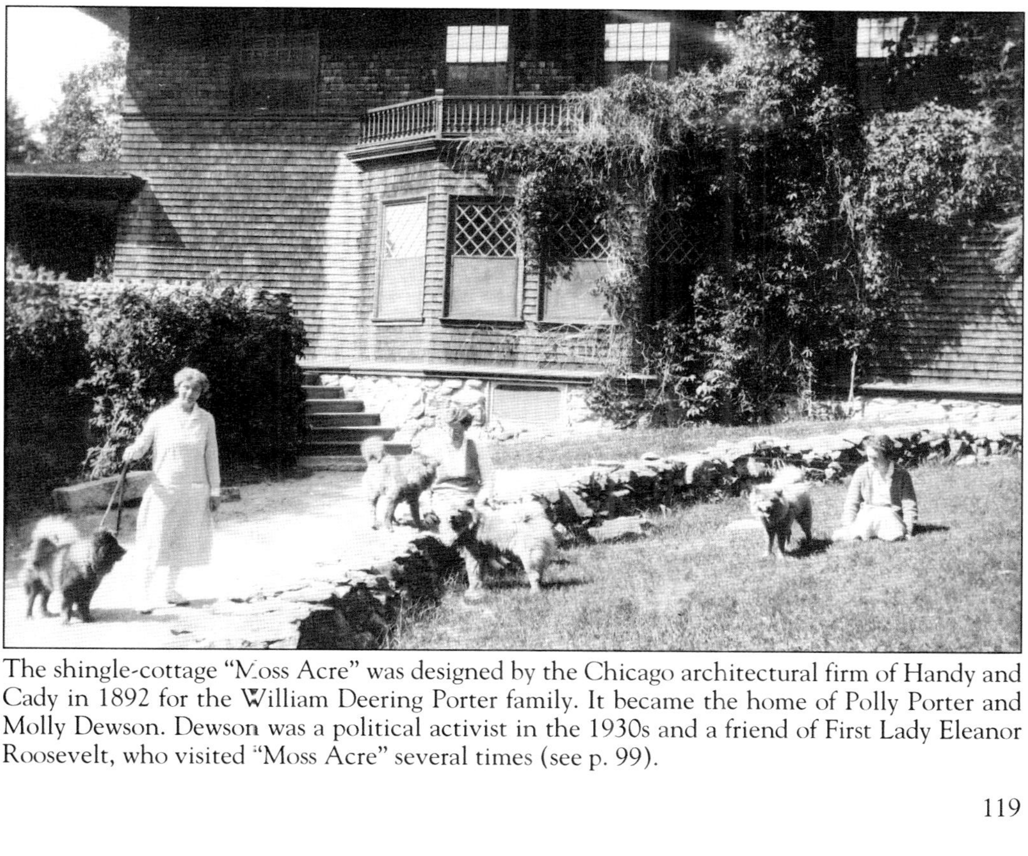

The shingle-cottage "Moss Acre" was designed by the Chicago architectural firm of Handy and Cady in 1892 for the William Deering Porter family. It became the home of Polly Porter and Molly Dewson. Dewson was a political activist in the 1930s and a friend of First Lady Eleanor Roosevelt, who visited "Moss Acre" several times (see p. 99).

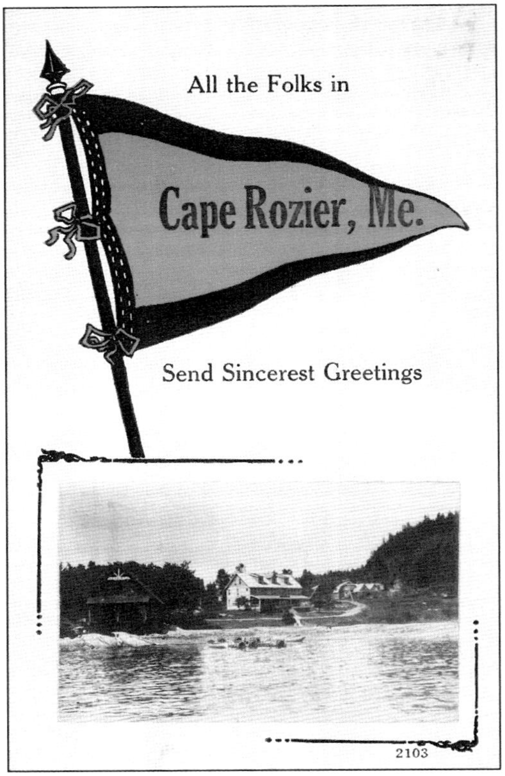

Cape Rosier, across Castine Harbor in Brooksville, was also a popular destination for "rusticators."

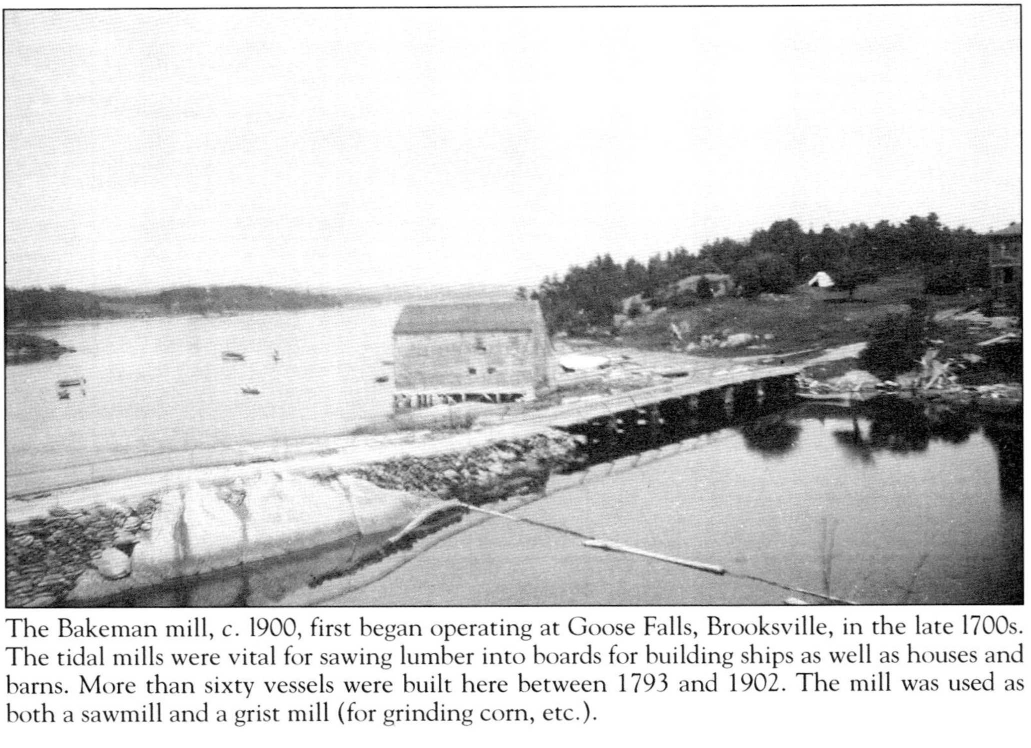

The Bakeman mill, *c.* 1900, first began operating at Goose Falls, Brooksville, in the late 1700s. The tidal mills were vital for sawing lumber into boards for building ships as well as houses and barns. More than sixty vessels were built here between 1793 and 1902. The mill was used as both a sawmill and a grist mill (for grinding corn, etc.).

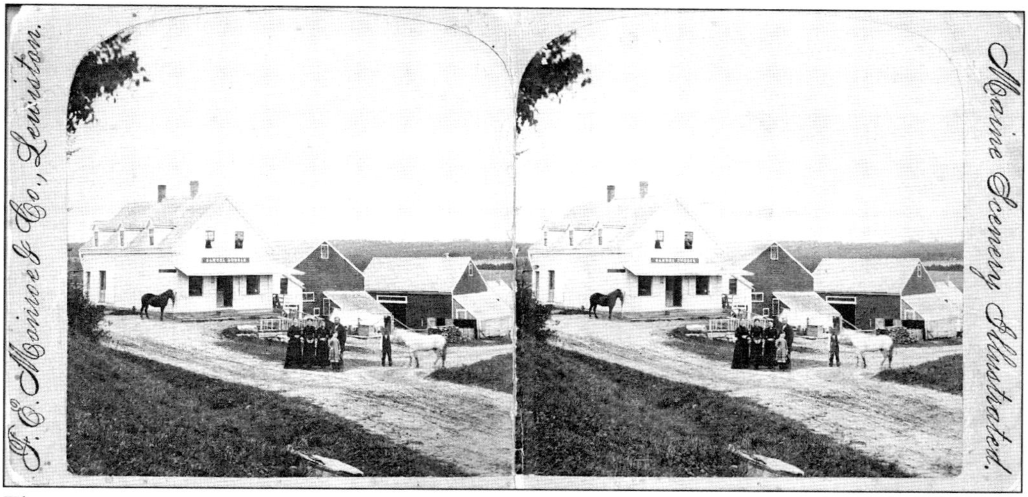

This is a stereoscopic view of the Dunbar Store, near the ferry landing. By the 1870s, almost every front parlor featured a stereopticon with dramatic slides of the pyramids or Niagara Falls, or even downtown Castine.

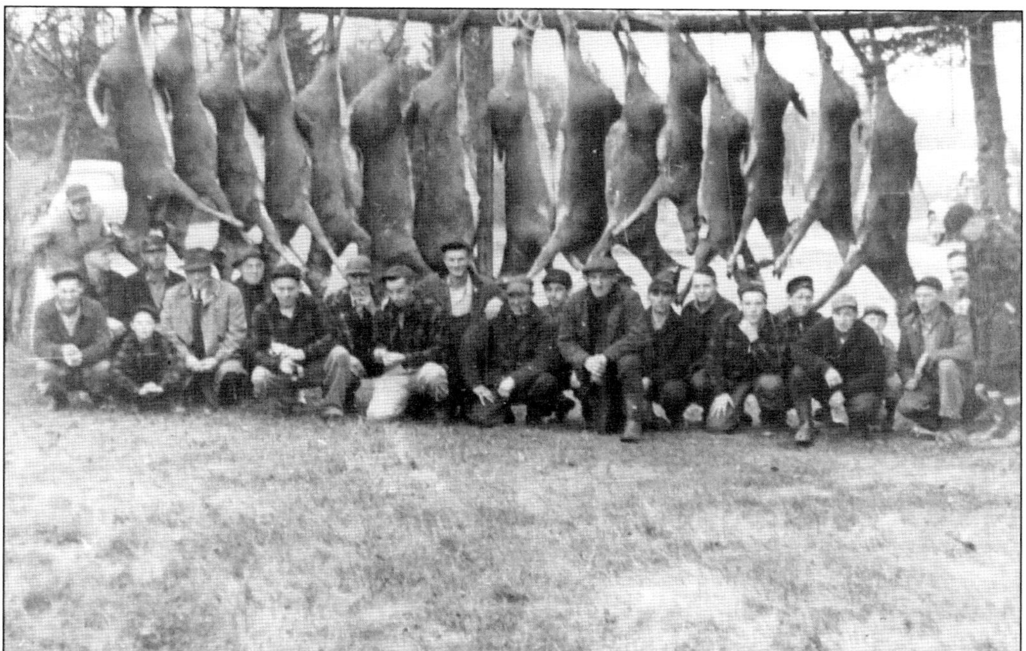

Some of the local Castiners who participated in this successful hunt were Dr. Harold Babcock, Phil Babcock, Fred Wardwell, Wallace (Bubbles) Wardwell, and Willis Leach.

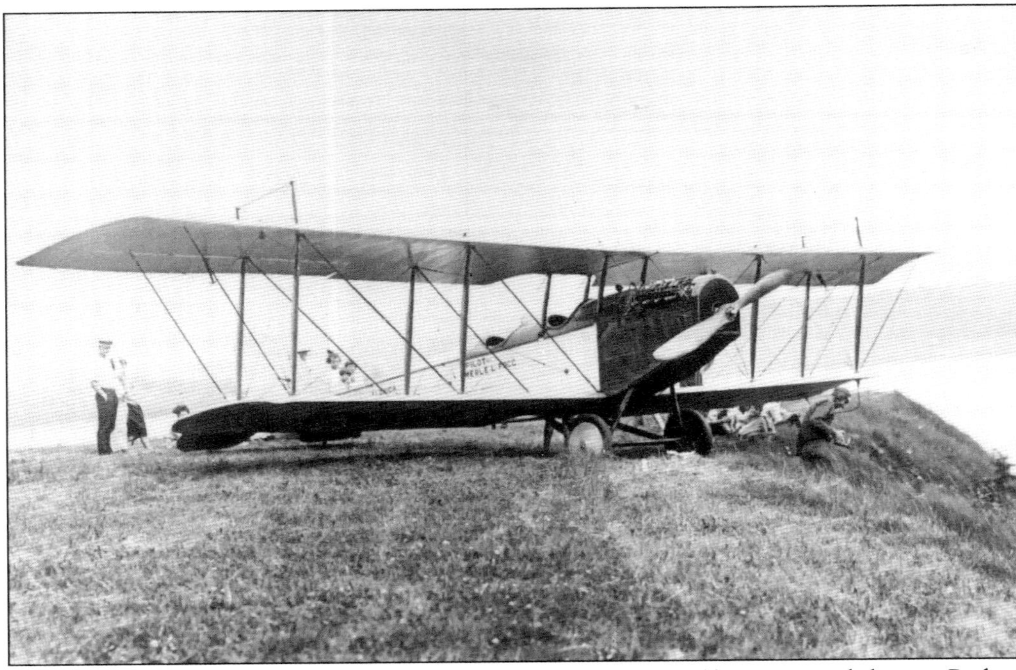

The first airplane to land in Castine, landed on the Castine Golf Course, and then at Perkins Point, North Castine, on July 17, 1923. Merle Fogg was the pilot of the World War I "Jenny," which took a few Castine residents for barnstorm rides.

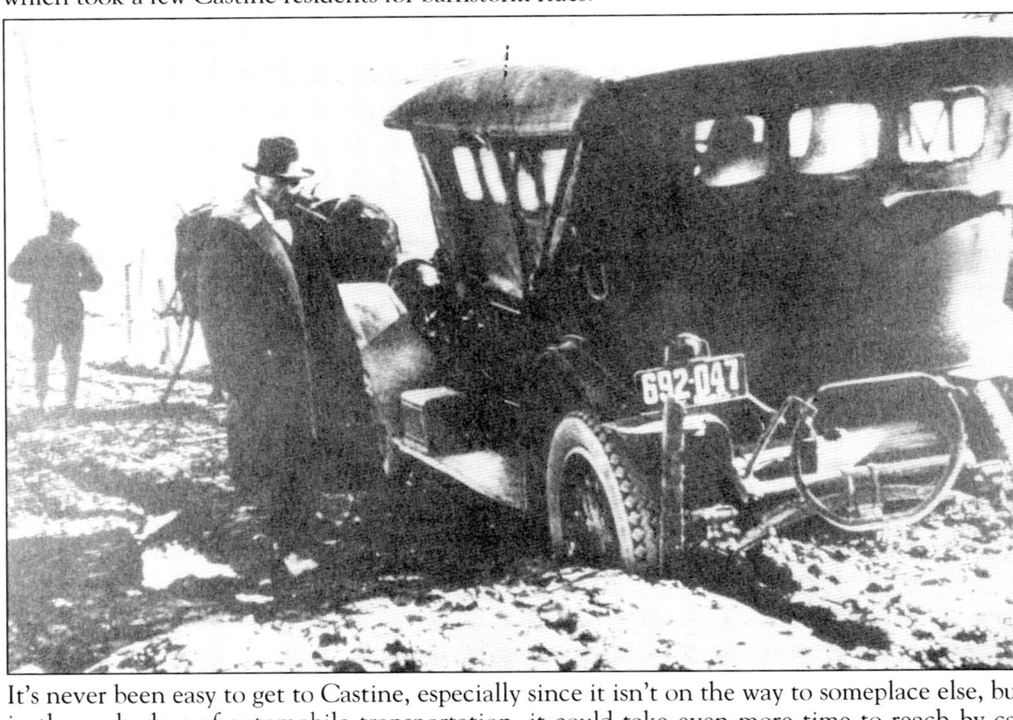

It's never been easy to get to Castine, especially since it isn't on the way to someplace else, but in the early days of automobile transportation, it could take even more time to reach by car than by boat!

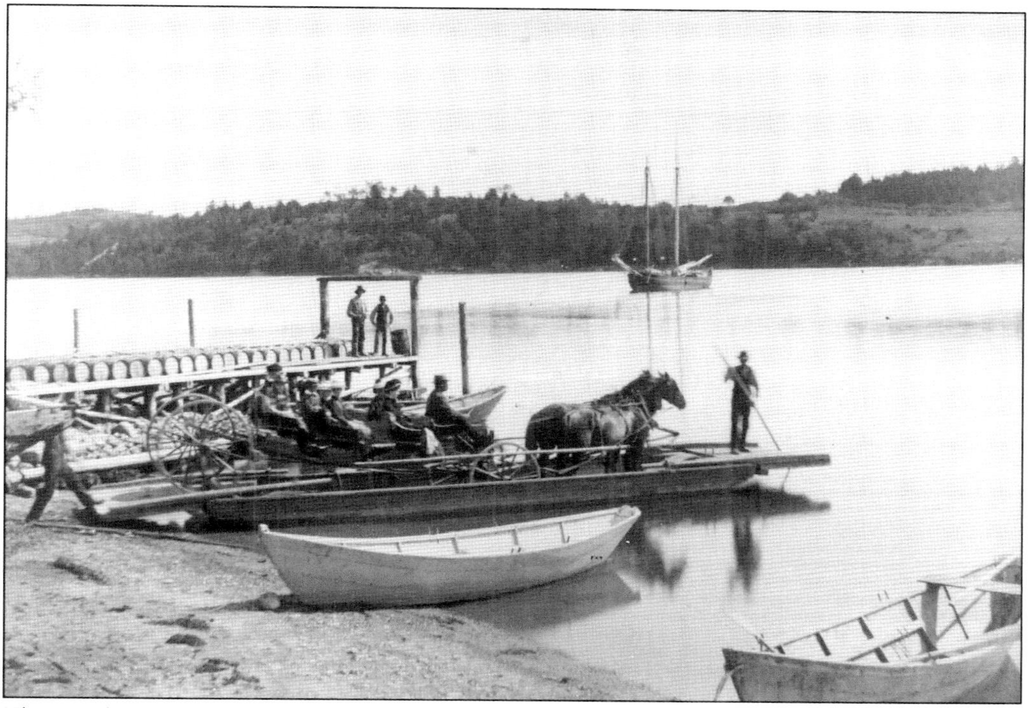

The North Castine-West Brooksville Ferry is shown here in a photograph taken from the North Castine dock. The ferry was powered by a man sculling, with a sail attached to the side of the boat. It operated from the 1790s to 1919, when the Ferry Road was abandoned.

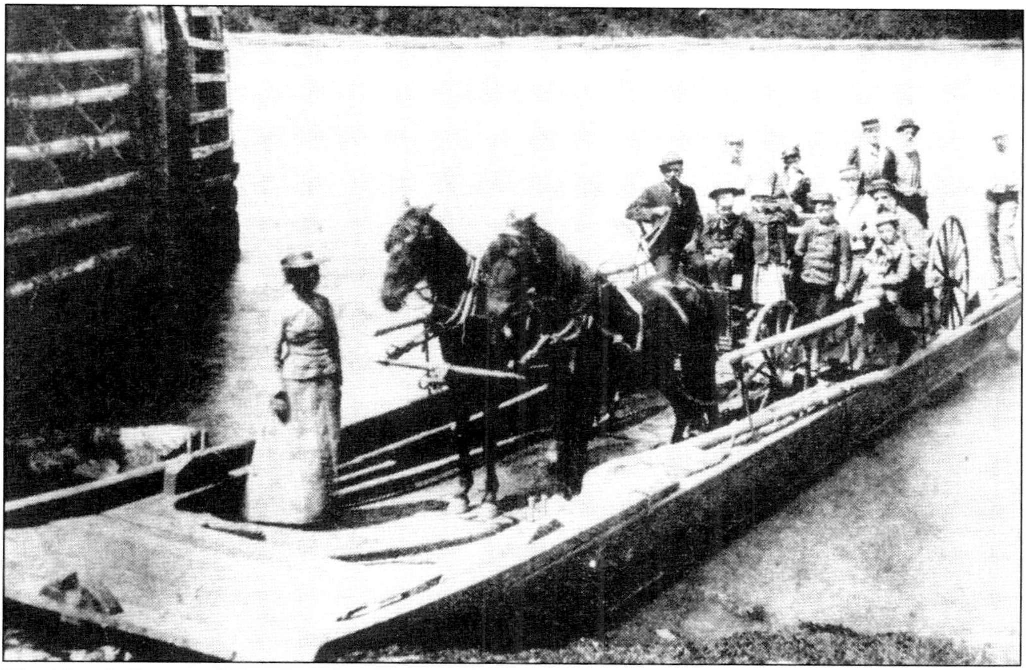

The North Castine-West Brooksville Ferry lands at Dodge's Wharf in West Brooksville.

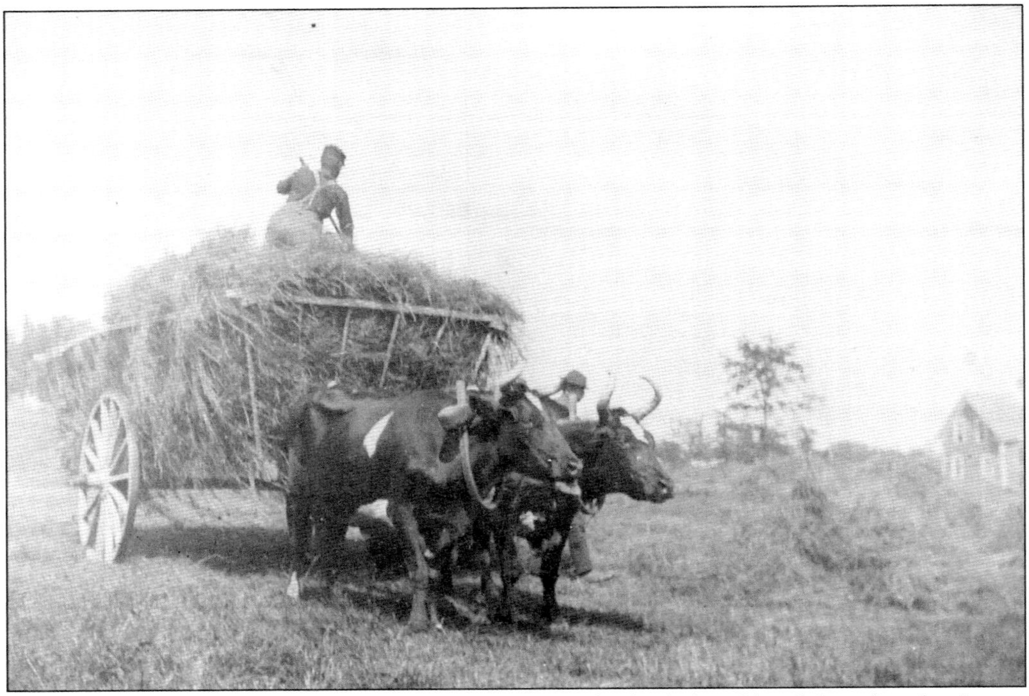

The Ames farm was operated during the summer with the help of local farm hands. Austin Bowden helped with the haying. Other chores included washing clothes (see below), which could be a pleasant task outdoors on a warm summer day.

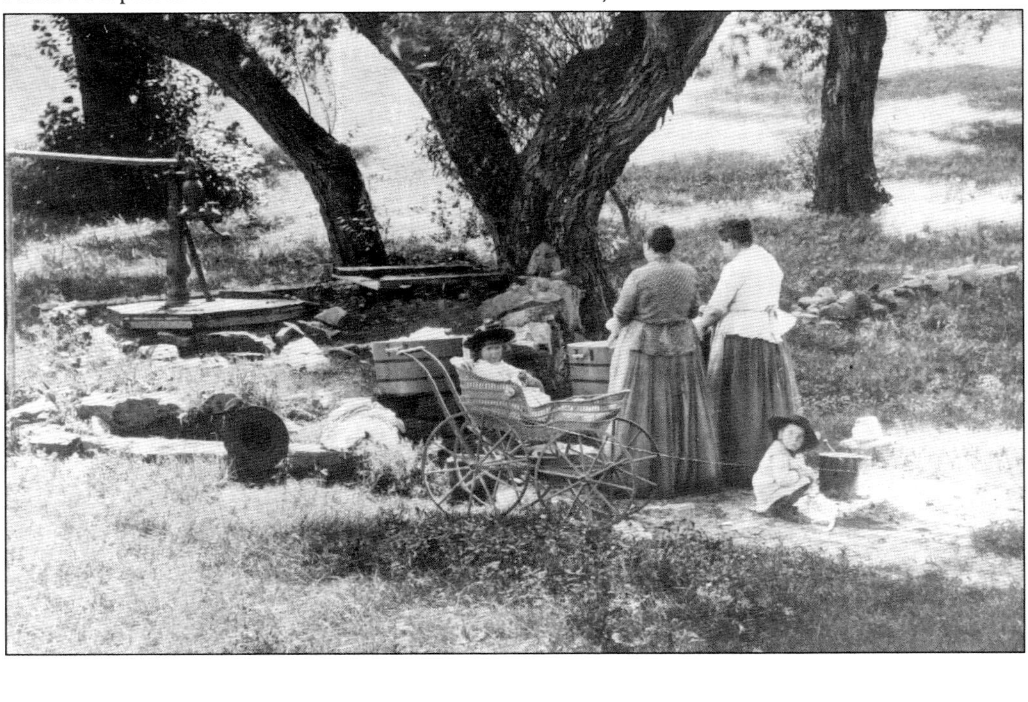

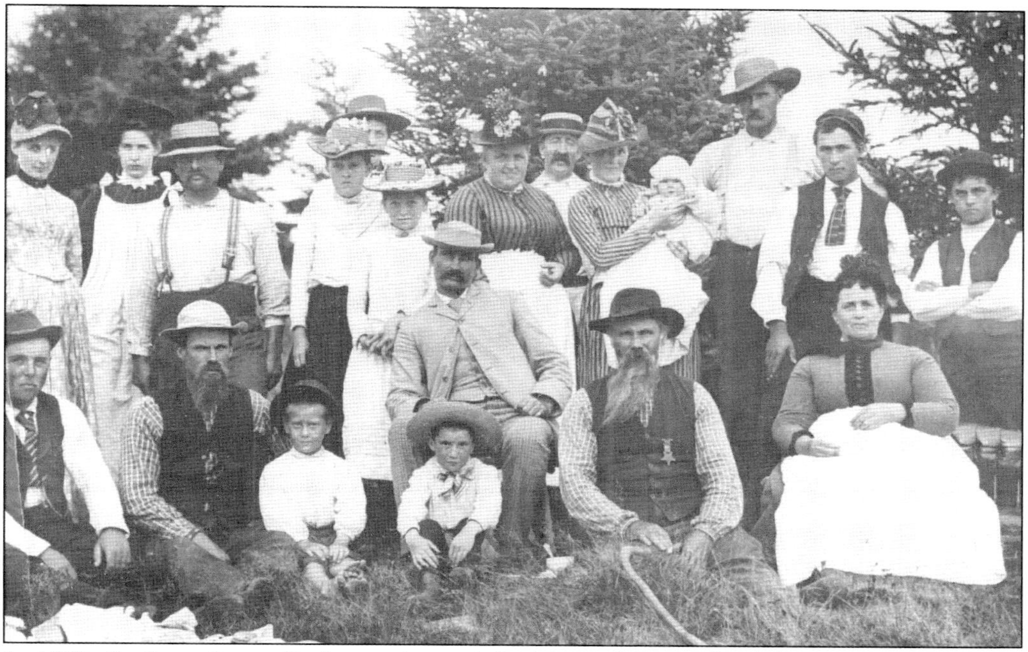

In 1889, Professor James B. Ames, dean of the Harvard Law School, bought the old Stover Perkins farm in North Castine at the end of Mill Lane. He and his wife summered here with their two young sons. Seated in the middle in this picture, he has his hand on his son Robert, who was to lose his life after being swept overboard during a transatlantic race to Norway in 1935 (see p. 98).

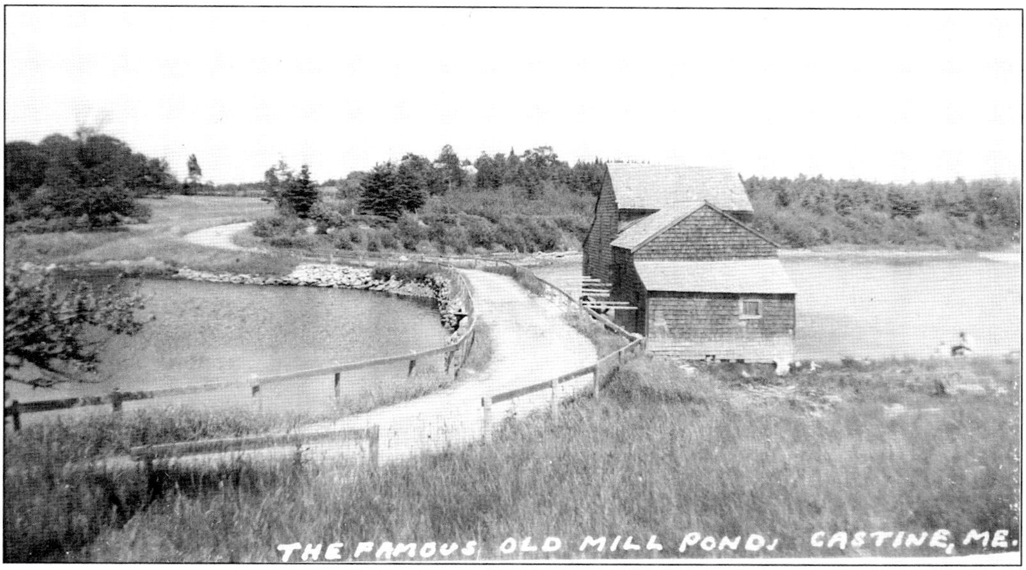

The Stover Perkins mill was built before the Revolution, and stood on the road to the Ames farm. It operated both as a sawmill and grist mill, and burned down within recent memory.

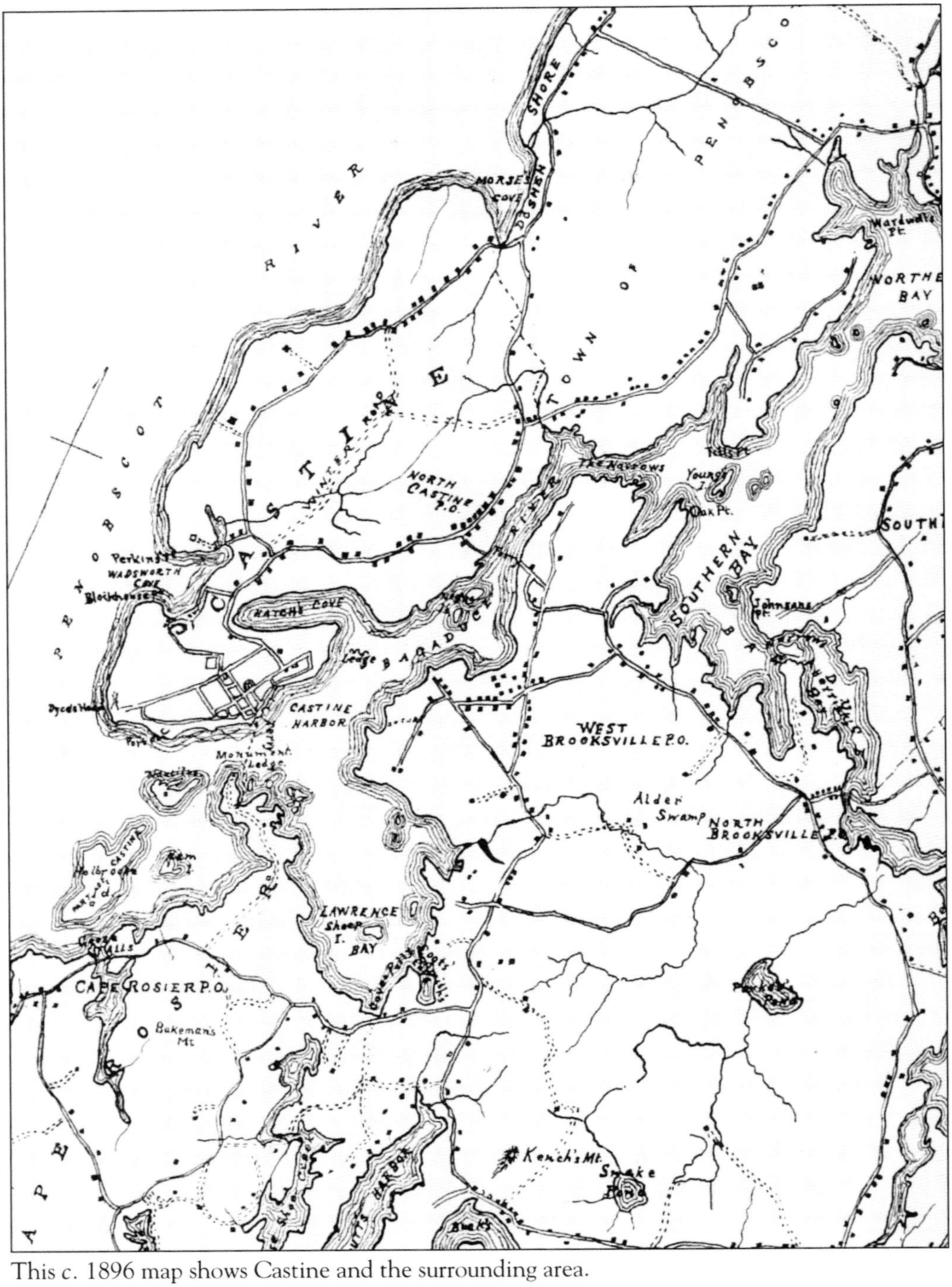

This *c.* 1896 map shows Castine and the surrounding area.

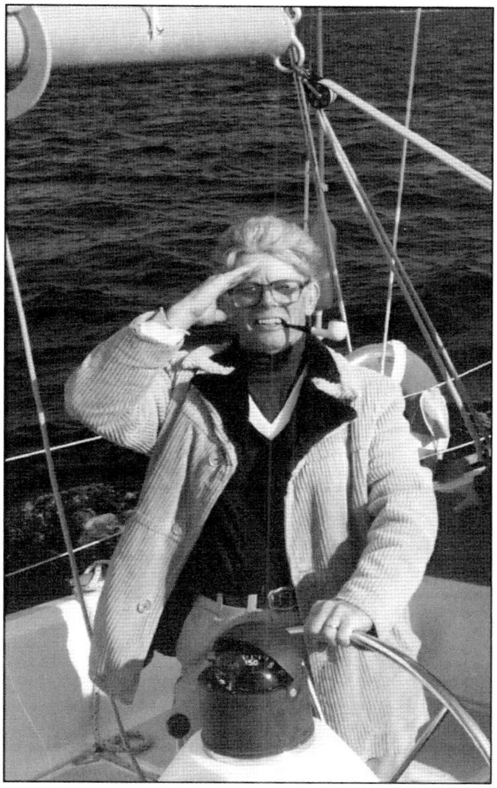

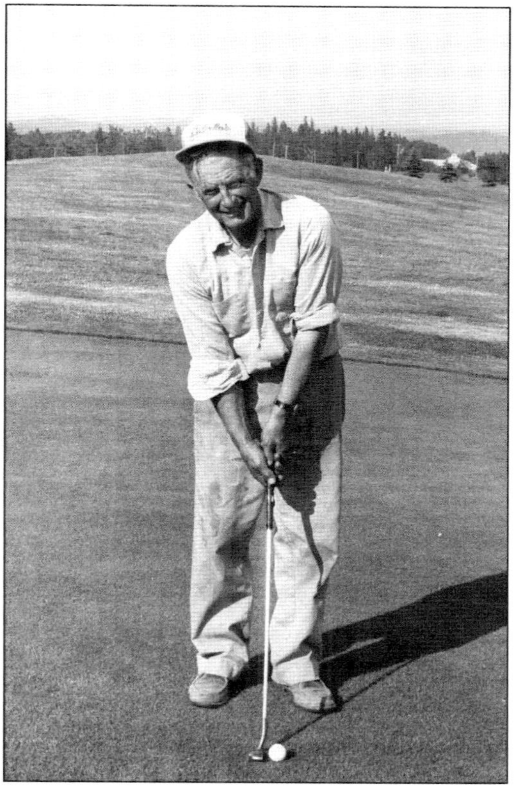

A Tribute

This book is dedicated to Gardiner Gregory, honorary archivist, and Philip Perkins, honorary historian, of The Castine Historical Society, for their interest in and reverence for Castine history.

Without Gardiner Gregory (left) this book would not have been possible. His vast collection of photographs and his documentation of the history of Castine will be of tremendous value to future generations. Philip Perkins (right) has kept alive the stories, legends, and spirit of the town. Most importantly, he's made history fun for many Castine residents and visitors.

Acknowledgments

The members of The Castine Historical Society who compiled this book emerged from this experience much enriched by the process of recording some of the photographs and history of Castine from the 1850s to 1945. The photographs and other resources which were made available to us were of outstanding quality and interest. Over 1,000 photographs were examined, and many excellent ones had to be eliminated because of space considerations. We have tried to show different aspects of life in Castine, from the fun-filled days of the summer people, to the lives of the industrious and hard-working town residents. Both groups recognized how special Castine is and did their best to preserve the town for future generations. In this bicentennial year of the incorporation of Castine, we are pleased to present this photographic history of our town.

Our thanks and gratitude for the use of their photographs and postcards go to the Bagaduce Music Lending Library, Robert Baker, Brian and Carole Barnard, "Bert and I," Philip Booth, Hope Brown, The Castine Historical Society, James and Leila Day, Kenneth Eaton, Frederick and Sally Foote, Gardiner and Anne Gregory, Margaret Wheeler Hall, Francis Hatch Jr., Laura Hatch, Kenneth Hooper, Maine Maritime Academy, Reverend Edward and Anne Miller, Jane Nichols, Our Lady of Holy Hope Church, Barbara Prindle, Lea Raymond, Barclay and Kate Robinson, Doris Russell, Barbara Tenney, Peter Tenney, Phyllis Tenney, Penny Tonry, and Louise Wheeler.

Carole Barnard
Leila Day
Sally Foote
Peter Tenney